97

54

2001

OUR GLORY AND OUR GRIEF:
TORONTONIANS AND THE GREAT WAR

IAN HUGH MACLEAN MILLER

OUR GLORY AND OUR GRIEF

Torontonians and the Great War

UNIVERSITY OF TORONTO PRESS
Toronto Buffalo London

© University of Toronto Press Incorporated 2002
Toronto Buffalo London
Printed in Canada

ISBN 0-8020-3592-2 (cloth)

Printed on acid-free paper

National Library of Canada Cataloguing in Publication Data

Miller, Ian Hugh Maclean
    Our glory and our grief : Torontonians and the Great War

    Includes bibliographical references and index.
    ISBN 0-8020-3592-2

    1. World War, 1914–1918 – Ontario – Toronto.   2. Toronto
    (Ont.) – History – 20th century.   I. Title.

    FC3097.4.M54 2002   940.3′713541   C2001-901998-X
    F1059.5.T6857M54 2002

University of Toronto Press acknowledges the financial assistance to its
publishing program of the Canada Council for the Arts and the Ontario Arts
Council.

This book has been published with the help of a grant from the Humanities
and Social Sciences Federation of Canada, using funds provided by the Social
Sciences and Humanities Research Council of Canada.

University of Toronto Press acknowledges the financial support for its
publishing activities of the Government of Canada through the Book
Publishing Industry Development Program (BPIDP).

For my parents

Contents

Acknowledgments

I have incurred many debts in the writing of this book. First and foremost, I must thank my adviser and friend, Terry Copp. Having developed the act of mentoring to a high art, he has given me enthusiastic guidance and direction, in addition to a thousand other kindnesses.

As a student in the Tri-University Doctoral Program in History, I was able to draw on the expertise of three fine history departments – at Wilfrid Laurier University, the University of Waterloo, and the University of Guelph. The faculty at these campuses have given generously of their time and energy. My thesis committee, composed of Terry Copp, John English, Wendy Mitchinson, and Eric Reiche, has encouraged my research from its inception.

Many other scholars at the three universities helped bring this book to fruition: Marc Kilgour, Joyce Lorimer, Gil Stelter, Keith Cassidy, Geoff Hayes, Michael Sibalis, Suzanne Zeller, George Urbaniak, Len Friesen, David Monod, and Richard Fuke.

None of the research could have been accomplished without the help of two Ontario Graduate Scholarships.

The first class of 'pioneers' who entered the program with me, Scott Sheffield, Tracy Penny Light, and Beatriz Bessa, have been a vital part of my life at Laurier. The sharing of ideas, perspectives, and not a few coffees over the years form the basis of many a happy memory. Deb and Michael Cohen provided a place to stay during my trips to Ottawa. Friends in the history department helped in numerous ways, but particular mention must be made of Michael Bechthold and Allan Thurrott. Members of my intramural soccer team have constantly reminded me of what really matters.

The process of turning the dissertation into a book presented new challenges, and introduced me to the dedicated team at the University of Toronto Press. Gerry Hallowell, Jill McConkey, Frances Mundy, Ward McBurney, and Siobhan McMenemy provided encouragement and direction.

My extended family, near and far, take pride in my accomplishments. My grandparents allow me to regale them with the intricacies of my latest findings. My brother, Bruce, has offered encouragement, his sense of humour, and a place to park in Toronto. Barley-dog makes sure I remember the finer things in life: a nap, a walk in the sun, and a day with friends. Liisa Peramaki joined me just in time to see me through the comprehensive exam. She has been my partner in this project, as in everything else, since then. Finally, my parents have given love, food, accommodation, and dogsitting in (seemingly) endless quantities.

I thank them all.

Royal Grenadiers marching through Toronto to entrain for Valcartier, 8 September 1914.

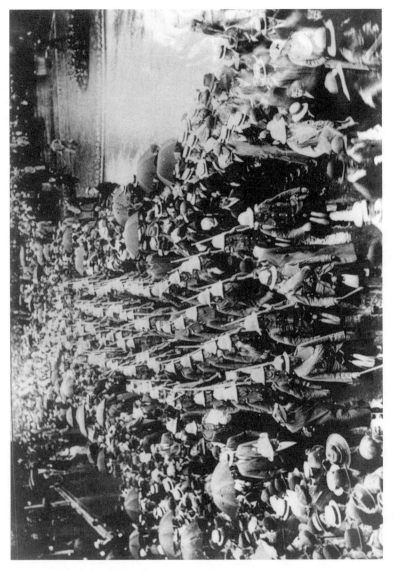

48th Highlanders leaving Toronto for overseas, September, 1914.

Recruiting scene at the Armouries, Toronto, 1 September 1915.

Recruiting soldiers in front of City Hall, Toronto, 13 March 1916.

Recruits line up for conscription at the Armouries, Toronto, 9 October 1917.

Recruiting meeting at City Hall, Toronto.

Overland float in Women's Day Parade, Canadian National Exhibition, 1918.

OUR GLORY AND OUR GRIEF:
TORONTONIANS AND THE GREAT WAR

Introduction

Armistice Day, 11 November 1919. At precisely 11:00 in the morning, Toronto stood still. Sirens shrieked. Bells rang out. Factory whistles wailed. Two minutes to remember. Everything stopped. Two minutes to remember sacrifice. To imagine his last smile before he boarded the train. To read the letters he sent from the front – until the telegram arrived that promised no further correspondence. To caress the personal belongings of dead heroes: a pen, a razor, a cherished picture. Sacred. At the corner of Yonge and Adelaide Streets, pedestrians and cyclists came to a halt; cars and trollies stopped their rumbling. The 13,809 workers at the T. Eaton Company stood silent. They honoured the 3,200 former employees who had enlisted, many now lying forever in France. Stores locked their doors. Factories stopped production. Warehouses ceased operations. Silence blanketed the downtown. Hats were removed. Heads lowered. Tears flowed.

After two minutes, citizens were showered in ticker tape, just as they had been in victory celebrations a year earlier. That night, a huge crowd replayed the carnival atmosphere of the original Armistice Night. People gathered downtown to dance, to sing, and to remember. Tanks rumbled among the revellers. Planes flew overhead. Military bands played. Firecrackers lit up the sky. The community celebrated sacrifice and victory.[1]

Two parts to a sacred day: remembering the dead, and celebrating their achievement. In the Toronto of 1919, these two aspects of the memory of the war could coexist. First, residents stopped to remember the past, to recall the sacrifices, and to honour the dead. This memorialization took two minutes. The celebration lasted for hours.

In the ensuing eighty years, the meanings of the words used to describe Remembrance Day have changed. Sacrifice is no longer equated with the giving of oneself for a nobler, higher purpose. The sacrifice of the Great War is now linked with senseless slaughter. This simple change makes celebrating sacrifice, for us, impossible. The construction of the *memory* of the Great War has resulted in accepting a vision of the conflict dramatically different from that possessed by those residents who took to the streets to celebrate victory in 1919.

Ten years after the 'war to end all wars' came to its bloody conclusion, veterans could plainly see that conflict would continue to mark the twentieth century. Italy had a fascist government, Russia had undergone a violent revolution and years of strife, and Germany nursed its wounds even as it adjusted to a new system of government. In this context, the sacrifices of the Great War appeared to have been in vain. It may have been this framework that influenced writers to dwell on the negative costs of the war, and to interpret its idealism as a superficial veneer that called the youth of the world to slaughter.

The veritable explosion of First World War literature began with the publication in 1928 of Erich Maria Remarque's *All Quiet on the Western Front*. This novel describing front-line service quickly became an international best-seller and was translated into the languages of the nations involved in the struggle. Although its main character was German, his experience was seen as typical of the infantrymen of all belligerent nations. Remarque helped establish what have become familiar themes in war literature: the contempt of soldiers for their officers, who stayed safely behind the lines; the ubiquitous mud and squalor; the inability of civilians to comprehend the nature of the fighting; the alienation of soldiers from the 'normal' world; and the futility of the attack. For the next ten years, best-seller lists were filled with war literature.[2]

Paul Fussell synthesized the trends and patterns of this type of postwar literature in his seminal work, *The Great War and Modern Memory* (1975), further entrenching the notion of the war as senseless slaughter. Although Fussell presented an analysis of the 'literary means by which [the Great War] has been remembered, conventionalized, and mythologized,' he also used his sources to comment on what he saw as the 'reality' of the war.[3] Fussell wrote in a time when the Western world was wrestling with the consequences and lessons of the Vietnam War, not the least of which was the idea that all war was meaningless. The memorial literature of the First World War provided a vehicle for similar discoveries about other conflicts.

The myth of the First World War as futile has become the single dominant construct used to remember it. The essential tenets of this myth are that 'a generation of innocent young men, their heads full of high abstractions like Honour, Glory, and England, went off to war to make the world safe for democracy. They were slaughtered in stupid battles planned by stupid generals. Those who survived were shocked, disillusioned, and embittered by their war experiences, and saw that their real enemies were not the Germans, but the old men at home who had lied to them. They rejected the values of the society that had sent them to war, and in doing so separated their own generation from the past and from their cultural inheritance.'[4] These themes continue to inform literary, cinematic, and popular notions about the conflict.

The futility myth persists despite several sustained attempts to debunk it. John Terraine's *The Smoke and the Fire: Myths and Anti-Myths of War, 1861–1945* (1980) attempted to move past the memory of the conflict, to uncover its reality, 'to blow away the smoke and get at the fire.'[5] Terraine and other historians have attacked the myth that the generals were buffoons who sent millions of hapless men to their deaths with reckless abandon.

By the end of the 1980s, historians were less prone simply to condemn the war, and instead attempted to understand it on its own terms. Modris Eksteins's *Rites of Spring: The Great War and the Birth of the Modern Age* (1989) presents the war as a cultural conflict between modernist Germany and traditionalist nations like Russia, France, and Great Britain. Samuel Hynes further developed this approach in *A War Imagined: The First World War and English Culture* (1991). He, too, used literary sources, but only those generated *during* the war, rather than those popular after its conclusion. He investigated the notion that the meaning of the war could change over time, arguing that initially Britain fought for the values of an old civilization. The tensions of the conflict and its costs killed those values, but no one could articulate replacements for them as the fight raged on. After a period of quiet, Hynes argues, a storm of writing appeared in the late 1920s, creating what we now see as the truth of the war.[6]

Recently, historians have attempted to evaluate how ordinary citizens perceived the event. Geoffrey Moorhouse's *Hell's Foundations: A Town, Its Myths and Gallipoli* (1992) analyses the reactions of the residents of the British town of Bury to the war's demands, recounting the impact in the decades that followed. The meaning of the war, as presented by Moorhouse, is contradictory. It was both brutal, involving the decimation of the locally raised unit in combat, and life affirming, promoting notions of noble sacrifice and a sense of community. Martin Stephen's *The Price of Pity: Poetry, History and Myth in the Great War* (1996) is a further plea for a more nuanced appreciation of the war. It celebrates the complexity of experience, arguing that no single understanding of the conflict is possible.[7]

Historians of the Great War now accept that the reality and the memory of the war are two distinct areas of study. This notion has been carefully developed by Jonathan Vance in his award-winning book, *Death So Noble: Memory, Meaning, and the First World War* (1997). In the first sustained analysis of the Canadian memory of the conflict, Vance examines the popular construction of memory through the writings of average people, memorial tablets, and civic ceremonies, concluding that the myth of the war gave Canadians a 'legacy, not of despair, aimlessness, and futility, but of promise, certainty, and goodness.'[8]

Comparatively little attention has been devoted to the impact of the war on the lives of citizens as it was happening. To remember an event, after all, requires having experienced it in the first place. Historians in other countries have published surveys of the French, British, and other combatant nations' experience, but the Canadian story has only begun to be explored.

Vance's study hints at a wealth of information to be found about Canada's total experience with war. And yet, the only published full-length monograph to examine the Canadian home front in detail is Jeffrey Keshen's *Propaganda and Censorship during Canada's Great War* (1996). Keshen maintains that there 'still exists no systematic examination of the naïvete, jingoism and nativism articulated through various means of mass communication, or how this affected society both during and after the conflagration.'[9] He assumes that Canadians could not have believed what they were being told, and concludes that they must have been duped. Largely based on the papers of chief censor, Ernest J. Chambers, Keshen's study leaves no room for the possibility that people were *willing* to fight for God, King, and Empire.

Contrary to Keshen's implications, however, the present study suggests that Torontonians, at least, *were* willing to fight, and contributes to the historical literature by examining the expressed values and behaviour of English Canadians living in Toronto during the First World War. Concentrating on one city allows previous assumptions about the war effort generalized from the national experience to be re-examined. What happened in Toronto? What did citizens know about the front? How were the enormous sacrifices of the war rationalized? If the war was futile, as historians have argued, why did Torontonians continue to support it, long after its cost became evident?

Toronto was a relatively new city in 1914. Established in 1793 as the Town of York, it was incorporated in 1834 as the City of Toronto with a population of 9,254. The site of the new Parliament Buildings at Front and Simcoe Streets was considered far removed from the city centre. Within two decades, Toronto was in position to challenge Montreal's hegemony as the leading city in British North America. It served as a commercial centre for south-western Ontario, building upon a vibrant and growing agricultural sector. By 1896, Toronto was well placed to reap the benefits of an economic boom which lasted until 1912. Manufacturing increased by over 600 per cent in the first two decades of the twentieth century, and almost two-thirds of Toronto's labour force consisted of blue-collar workers.

All this growth translated into increased influence. Toronto quickly established itself as a banking centre, and after the 1890s, the 'city's investment tentacles began to stretch.' It also became an obvious location for offices of all kinds of organizations and became 'headquarters for religious bodies, labour groups, professional organizations, and voluntary associations, not to mention legal, medical, and educational institutions.'[10]

The city had a long and close association with the military dating back to its early days as the garrisoned capital of Upper Canada, leading one observer to note that the city was founded by 'many soldiers and a few civilians.' The first battalion to be associated exclusively with the city was created in 1861, and named the Queen's Own Rifles in 1863. Several other companies of militia, which were drawn together on 14 March 1862, were known by 1880 as the Royal Grenadiers. Both units saw service in the Fenian Raids of 1866, and the Queen's Own took part in suppressing the Riel Rebellion in 1885. Another unit, the 48th Highlanders, was formed on 18 October 1891. All three regiments enthusiastically supplied volunteers for the Canadian force that fought in the Boer War (1899–1902), and continued to train in the years leading up to the First World War. They were an integral part of the city's early mobilization and subsequent recruiting campaigns.[11]

Toronto changed and grew rapidly in the years between 1900 and 1914. Fire ripped through the downtown commercial district in 1904, destroying fourteen acres and putting five thousand people temporarily out of work. The business community recovered rapidly, and city planners installed an improved water pressure system to fight future fires. In 1907, police handed out their first parking tickets. In 1908, the Toronto Street Railway finally placed doors to deep out the cold on the city's trolley cars, vacuum cleaners were introduced, and Torontonians had their first glance at the miracle of aeroplanes. In 1912, Ontario premier Sir James Whitney threw the switch that lit up the city's darkened streets, ushering in the age of hydro-electric power.

The city's population rose at an astonishing rate during the first decades of the twentieth century. Immigration, coupled with migration from rural areas, caused Toronto's population to explode from 208,040 in 1901 to 376,538 in 1911, and 521,893 in 1921: an increase of 251 per cent in just twenty years. There are no census figures for the war years; however, a survey by the military estimated that the population in August 1916 was 470,444.[12]

Toronto was a British city. Of the more than 150,000 immigrants who arrived between 1900 and 1914, three-quarters were from the United Kingdom. Many of the other immigrants were also British born, arriving from Australia, New Zealand, South Africa, and Newfoundland. Altogether, these 'British' groups accounted for 85 per cent of the total population of the city in the early decades of the twentieth century.[13]

Religion played a key role in the daily lives of Torontonians. Over 76 per cent of the population during the First World War claimed to be Protestant,[14] while approximately 13 per cent reported being Catholic. These percentages remained virtually unchanged throughout the first two decades of the twentieth century.

Irish Catholics constituted the most numerically significant ethnic group. Specific attention has been given to surveying the attitudes and opinions expressed in the *Catholic Register*, the leading Irish Catholic periodical in the city. Mark McGowan's carefully documented '"To Share in the Burdens of Empire": Toronto's Catholics and the Great War, 1914–1918,' (1990) argues that the war served to unify the Catholic and Protestant populations of Toronto. His evidence demonstrates that the city's Catholic population supported the war as strongly as did their Protestant neighbours, a finding reinforced by this study. McGowan writes that 'The Catholics of Toronto, both clerical and lay, did not imitate patterns established by Catholics in Quebec, Ireland, the United States, or Australia. In Toronto, Catholics enthusiastically endorsed the war effort and sustained their participation throughout the conscription crisis. The hierarchy and clergy justified the war in religious terms and took great pains to encourage recruitment, bond purchases, and national registration ... It is clear that the patriotic initiatives of Catholic leadership in Toronto were sustained and echoed ten-fold by the laity in the pews.'[15]

The other major ethnic group was the Jewish community, which grew from 1.4 per cent of the population in 1901 to 7 per cent by 1921. Stephen A. Speisman's authoritative *The Jews of Toronto: A History to 1937* (1979) gives only passing attention to the experience of Jewish Torontonians with the war. Judging from the voting patterns of the residents of Toronto Centre, where most Jews lived, there is every reason to suppose that they also supported a determined war effort.

The story of Toronto during the years 1914–18 is largely untold. Assessing the historiography on the city during the First World War, Eric Jarvis and Melvin Baker concluded in 1984 that the 'historical examination of the war and its aftermath has been meager.' This dearth of published material is partly the result of a scarcity of archival primary sources for the period. In his 1997 study of Toronto's Industrial Exhibition from 1879 to 1903, historian Keith Walden observed, 'Though ideally it would be otherwise, Toronto newspapers are the single detailed source of information about what happened on and off the fairground.'[16]

During the years between Confederation and the Great Depression, the press transformed itself from partisan political broadsheets for the Liberal and Conservative parties into the primary vehicle through which citizens learned about their world. It was the golden age of the press. The six Toronto dailies, the *Globe, Mail and Empire, Star, News, Telegram,* and *World* had a combined circulation of 433,023 by 1914. The numbers for each paper fluctuated throughout the war years as dailies competed for readership, but their combined circulation rose to 439,626 in 1917, meaning that on average more than one newspaper was received in each household per day. Waking up with a morning paper, or relaxing after work with the news, was part of the daily routine.[17]

Newspapers were a lively, integral part of the life of the city. By the beginning of the war, 'news ... had become the major kind of common knowledge, at least in urban Canada. News could set the tone and determine the objects of public concern. Not alone of course, but in conjunction with the perspectives and attitudes already present in the public mind.'[18] At the centre of each newspaper was the editorial page. The views expressed in its columns, however, reflected more than the opinions of its writers. Editorials shaped the public discourse by providing the information and the terminology to discuss current events. Thus, general patterns of opinion expressed in the Liberal and Conservative daily press provide an initial survey of the words and ideas citizens used in making sense of their world.

In addition, the papers reported on the activities of prominent citizens. The speeches reproduced, opinions expressed, and behaviour recorded provide a day-to-day database of the activities of the city's elite. The attitudes and behaviour of average citizens, however, are also discernible. Letters to the editor, and news stories that reported the actions of citizens, provide the researcher with an avenue into the hearts and minds of the people.

Most important for this study, the papers provide a daily record of life in the city, reporting the important activities and human interest stories which shaped Toronto's experience with the war. The newspaper offices served as gathering points for a public desperate for information, and citizens besieged these offices whenever a major military event took place. In addition, people routinely scanned the daily casualty lists posted in the windows of the daily papers. As a testament to the importance of the papers to daily life, when a coal shortage in the winter of 1918 caused the federal government to impose a mandatory shutdown of all industry, newspaper offices were allowed to remain open – even as munitions factories closed.

One of the most common mistakes historians make about 1914 is to assume that Torontonians were uninformed about the international community and blindly rallied behind Britain. In fact, Torontonians were long accustomed by August 1914 to reading about international affairs, and their behaviour that summer reflected years of interacting with the world around them. What they knew about the nature of diplomacy and war affected their behaviour. Citizens had learned that Germany was the primary threat to the Empire's security as early as 1909 when it was revealed that the Kaiser's navy had increased its ability to produce capital ships of the Dreadnought type, threatening Britain's long-standing tenure as the world's leading maritime power.[19]

Germany flexed its military muscle again in July 1911, demanding compensation following the French occupation of Morocco. To improve its bargaining position, the Germans dispatched the gunboat *Panther* to the Moroccan port of Agadir.[20] Even in the face of the ensuing international outrage, Germany maintained that the warship was required to protect German nationals: there were reputed to be two.

Torontonians read about the Agadir crisis in their daily papers. This aggressive diplomatic manoeuvre, however, did more than establish German militarism as the main threat to international peace. It also highlighted the critical role of diplomats in working to avoid war. Only days after Germany sent the *Panther* to Agadir, Britain declared that it would not recognize any decision in which it was not consulted. Daily papers were filled with accounts of British Foreign Secretary Sir Edward Grey's attempts to secure a peaceful settlement. Citizens trusted the diplomats to ensure peace.

Their faith proved well founded. Grey and his colleagues successfully negotiated a settlement. Newspaper coverage demonstrated to readers another key component in the early-twentieth-century security apparatus. Alliances and a general fear of a European conflagration *helped* diplomats find a peaceful solution since, the newspapers argued, 'it seems unlikely ... that France or any other nation, or coalition of nations, will go to war to prevent Germany getting a slice of the Sultan's territory.'[21] These assumptions about the nature of the international community appeared to have been vindicated with the signing of the Moroccan Treaty in November 1911.

By August 1914, Torontonians were also remarkably familiar with events in the Balkans. The First Balkan War in October 1912 shook the peace of Europe. Newspaper coverage informed the reading public that diplomats were working to localize the fighting. The costs of failure, journalists warned, were immense: 'the whole of Europe is likely to be plunged in war.'[22] Readers took comfort, however, in the belief that international diplomacy could exert its influence and restrict the scope and duration of the conflict.

Once again, their assumptions were vindicated. The fighting lasted less than three months. The diplomats of the world powers had successfully worked to ensure that the conflict remained localized. Newspaper headlines trumpeted Sir Edward Grey's successes: 'Declares Grey, Averted Crash; All Praise Him.'[23] Torontonians learned that settlement of the Eastern European question was not possible until the alliances clicked into place. Further, the fear of the general European war provided the impetus for concessions. No one, it was believed, was willing to risk Armageddon to secure local gains. Once the threat of aggression had escalated to such a point as to make negotiations mandatory, the peace of Europe would be secured. These 'lessons' about modern warfare and diplomacy were more deeply entrenched each time they were proven correct.

The outbreak of the Second Balkan War appalled Toronto readers. Citizens were contemptuous of the former allies who were now fighting among themselves over the spoils of the first conflict. Papers were filled with raw, jaded comments. The *Star* noted sarcastically that 'when all the best and bravest men of Bulgaria and Servia have slain each other, perhaps the Turk will reconquer what's left.' The Conservative press agreed, asking 'Who will the Bulgarians or the Servians wallop when they get through with each other?'[24]

The press recommended the pattern to limit the scale and destructiveness of the conflict followed during the First Balkan War. It had been restricted to that area of the world where 'civilization' had not yet completely taken hold, so editorials advocated the same policy, reaffirming the standard formula for solving Balkan crises: contain the conflict and let the diplomats find a solution. The Second Balkan War also reaffirmed the belief that a major European conflagration would be too costly, and entrenched contemptuous feelings towards the Balkan. There was a growing sense that the region would constantly erupt into short little wars over petty grievances. The accepted strategy was to limit the conflict to avoid drawing in the great powers.

These international crises and the lessons learned from them influenced the behaviour of Torontonians in the summer of 1914. The assassination of the heir to the Austro-Hungarian throne, Franz Ferdinand, on 28 June 1914 sparked press reaction, but the papers did not interpret the killing as a harbinger of a European war. In all likelihood, they reasoned, this incident was just the latest in a long series of Balkan flashpoints. Besides, their attention was focused elsewhere. The gravest issue in the summer of 1914 was not the tension with Germany, but the Irish Question and the prospect of a civil war in Ireland.

Once aware of the growing crisis in Europe, the papers demonstrated that editors and readers reacted as British Canadians, that is to say, important participants in the Empire. London was *the* metropolis for English-speaking Torontonians; their attitudes and preoccupations parallelled those of their British cousins. Waiting until the last moment to initiate hostilities was considered desirable as it allowed diplomats maximum latitude to solve the crisis. If all else failed, however, war was accepted as the last resort.

With regard to the Balkans, Torontonians took comfort in the lessons learned from previous conflicts. Readers must have hoped that the skills of Lord Grey combined with the prestige of the mighty British navy would again ensure that any belligerency would be short-lived. The reaction of the papers to the events of the summer of 1914 was likewise informed by experience. Editorialists trusted that Grey would be able to solve the crisis through diplomacy as he had in previous flare-ups. After all, Lord Grey had avoided war with Germany over the naval and Agadir issues, and helped orchestrate peace in the Balkans two times in as many years. The papers ignored the crisis until the last moment, not because they were naive regarding international events, but because of lessons learned from recent history. Sarcastic comments and reduced coverage indicated that the Balkans was now viewed as a backward region determined to destroy itself.

Ultimately, the assumptions that citizens used to interpret Europe's slide into total war proved to be incorrect. People living at the time had passed through a series of international crises that provided a particular set of lessons, formed through learning about, and drawing conclusions from, world events. That their assumptions were wrong proves only that the First World War was unlike any conflict which had preceded it. Torontonians continued, however, to learn about their environment, and to react to it in an informed way.

In time, the Great War's scale and scope pushed citizens to the limit. Examining what people knew about the war, and how they behaved as it happened, allows certain central questions to be asked: Is our memory of the war linked with the actual wartime experiences Torontonians had, or is it a construction that bears little resemblance to the way war was perceived at the time? Does our memory of the war take only pieces of the city's experience, or does it attempt to synthesize the entire process?

The influence of the conflict was too profound for its impact to be measured solely on the soldiers at the front. Citizens in Toronto could not understand the complete experience of their khaki-clad husbands, sons, and brothers. This does not mean, however, that they did not experience war's demands or sacrifices. Those living at home could not understand what it felt like to live under shellfire, but they did read and react to graphic accounts of it. They did endure something called 'war,' but differently. Confronting the steadily rising cost of living, dealing with inadequate coal supplies in the dead of winter, wrestling with the loss of loved ones, participating in local patriotic drives, and suffering through the influenza epidemic were also war experiences.

Throughout the years 1914–18, English-Canadian Torontonians reacted in a manner which was both informed and measured. Initially, they hoped that the fighting would be short-lived. When military events demonstrated that an ad hoc, voluntary approach would not meet the increasing demands of total war, however, they adapted. Voluntary organizations gradually gave way to popularly sanctioned government involvement in everything from financing to the supplying of men. Toronto was a community firmly committed to victory. Despite an enormous sacrifice, its citizens endured.

The impact of the Great War on Torontonians must be understood in its complexity. Who are we to pass peremptory judgement on their glory or their grief? It was not an uninformed, ignorant, disengaged populace who took to the streets in November 1919, but a people who had been deeply committed and engaged in a life and death struggle. They gathered to mark, simultaneously, joy and sadness: to dance gleefully with tears on their faces; to bear witness that dying for an ideal was not only cause for remembrance, but for celebration. The following pages explain the process that led to that victory party.

1

A Great Adventure:
Toronto Goes to War

News of the German invasion of France and the violation of Belgium's neutrality reached Canada on 2 August 1914. In Toronto, the editors of all six of the city's newspapers prepared editorials that reflected the broad consensus on the role that the British Empire should play in the crisis. Reaction in Toronto was similar to responses in other Imperial cities like Birmingham, Sydney, Glasgow, or Vancouver. Germany, which had repeatedly threatened the peace of Europe and challenged British naval power, was now waging war on France and ignoring the rights of the Belgian state. Britain would undoubtedly intervene and would enjoy the complete support of her Dominions.

Thousands of citizens gathered on Toronto's downtown streets to be a part of history as it happened. People recognized that great events were afoot, and they wanted to experience them for themselves. Crowds besieged newspaper offices looking for information all afternoon on 4 August. Their numbers increased in the early evening when warehouses and factories closed for the day. Soon Bay and Yonge Streets were 'black with people.' Policemen gave up directing traffic, which was at a standstill, and turned to crowd control. Newspaper boys did a brisk trade in Extras. Citizens knew that at 11:00 p.m. British time – 7:00 p.m. in Toronto – the British ultimatum to Germany would expire. If the Germans did not back down, then the Empire would be at war, alongside Russia and France. Torontonians watched and waited as the minutes ticked by.

When the bells of Toronto's Big Ben struck seven times, nothing else happened. The crowd waited. Thousands of miles away a telegraph operator in England cabled the news under the Atlantic Ocean. Fifteen minutes later, a newsboy's announcement, 'Get the War Cry,' disturbed the relative calm. Extras were purchased quickly. It was official: Britain was at war. Giant banners, unfurled from newspaper offices, read: 'Official Announcement That Great Britain Has Declared War against Germany.' At first the crowd met the news with silence. 'The news sank home. Then a cheer broke. It was not for war, but for the King, Britain, and – peace gone – victory.' Residents were singularly unconcerned with the reaction of the Canadian Parliament. No one wondered whether or not Canada would follow Britain to war. Constitutional distinctions between the two nations meant nothing to the average Torontonian. Britain was at war; Canada was at war.

Bulletin after bulletin, flashed in newspaper office windows, met with cheers. Men removed their hats and tilted back their heads in song. 'Rule Britannia' and 'God Save the King' filled the air. Arm in arm with their escorts, women joined in the singing. Young and old participated. Groups gathered at street corners: they talked of nothing but war. As the news spread, thousands more headed downtown to hear the latest. Union Jacks appeared in windows and storefronts. Impromptu parades, complete with marching bands, proceeded west along King Street before turning north on Yonge, then west again on Queen Street towards the Armouries on University Avenue. Militia regiment headquarters were assaulted by young men clamouring to enlist. The Armouries of the 48th Highlanders, Royal Grenadiers, Mississauga Horse, and Queen's Own Rifles were packed all evening. Outside, long lines waited for the chance to get in, even before word was received from Ottawa concerning the form of Canada's contribution. It was midnight before the crowds began to thin.[1]

Over the next two days, evening crowds actually increased in size as more and more Torontonians pressed to hear the latest. The dinner hour was poorly observed as citizens rushed directly downtown after work. Queen, King, Bay, and Yonge Streets were thronged with the patriotic and the curious alike until well after midnight. Crowds gathered on 6 August to hear the answer to the following questions: 'What means this sound of heavy firing borne on the wind? What means these hundreds of wounded and prisoners? What messages are flashing between the engaged fleet and London?'[2] The crowds grew each night as more and more people took an active part in the collective response to the war.

The most important manifestation of this early enthusiasm found expression in the numbers of men who flocked to the recruiting depots. Volumes of material have been written on the history of recruiting in

Canada during the First World War, most of it centred around evaluating whether or not the schemes used by the colourful Minister of the Militia, Sam Hughes, were a success or a failure.[3] What is missing from the literature is an assessment of the efforts required on the ground to secure troops throughout the war. There were many stages on the road that culminated in conscription, and these can best be uncovered by studying the recruiting *campaigns*, not just the *numbers*. Securing recruits in August 1914, however, was less a process of recruiting than it was of deciding who to enlist.

While awaiting orders from Ottawa, officials from local militia regiments met at 215 Simcoe Street to discuss the situation. In anticipation of having to supply men for a Canadian Expeditionary Force, units opened their doors to accept new members. Longtime Toronto resident and MP Lt.-Col. John A. Currie of the 48th Highlanders was one of the most active early recruiting officers. Born in Simcoe County in 1868, he had worked as a reporter for the *Mail and Empire* and the *News* for twelve years, and was elected to the House of Commons for Simcoe in 1908, and again in 1911. When war was finally declared, Currie offered himself as one of the first volunteers.[4] While waiting to go overseas, he contented himself getting the 48th Highlanders ready, announcing that the regiment would welcome three hundred new men.

There was no difficulty in securing volunteers. Currie and his counterparts in other local militia regiments were awash with recruits as thousands of young, male Torontonians offered themselves. The number would have been much higher but for the measures taken by militia regiments to stem the tide. The Queen's Own Rifles, for example, announced that it would consider enrolling only men who had served previously with the unit. All others had to wait. This announcement sent many from the crowd of around four thousand men from the Armouries at Queen and University to swell the throng already gathered in front of the headquarters of the 48th Highlanders. There, recruiting officers sifted through the flock, taking only the best physical specimens into the building for examination. Hundreds were turned away. The Royal Grenadiers were similarly overwhelmed. All over the city, the galleries of local armouries were filled with onlookers who watched newly enrolled soldiers 'form up' and begin to drill.

Recruiting officers selected men with previous military experience. This requirement was born out of the desire to form as competent a force as possible and out of the need to impose a filter to help sort out the thousands who came forward. The result was that many men were passed over in favour of others with experience. This fact was recognized at the time, papers reporting as early as 10 August that 'several of the regiments are now limiting their recruits to former members and ex-service men, as they are anxious to have as many experienced men as possible ready for the first contingent from Canada.'[5] These reports would have been reinforced by the stories of hundreds of local men who did not have the experience or the physical stature to even enter an armouries, let alone pass the strenuous medical exam and join the ranks. Recent immigrants of British birth were more likely to have had military training, and it was primarily for this reason that relatively few Canadian-born men were chosen initially. Had the criteria for service included being born in Canada, the ranks would still have been filled.

Against the backdrop of this enthusiasm, the Canadian war effort took shape. On 6 August 1914 His Majesty's Government cabled from London that it would gladly accept the offer of a Canadian Expeditionary Force and asked that it be 'despatched as soon as possible.' Minister of Militia Sam Hughes sent secret night telegrams directly to the 226 unit commanders of the Canadian Militia, ordering the preparation of descriptive lists of men between eighteen and forty-five years of age who would serve overseas. On 10 August an Order in Council set the strength of the contingent at twenty-five thousand men. Once it was determined how many members from each militia regiment would be allowed to serve, those selected would proceed to Valcartier, Quebec, on the north shore of the St Lawrence River, for training before embarkation to Britain.

Events in Toronto quickened their pace as militia commanders struggled to create the 'descriptive rolls' demanded by Hughes. At the beginning of the war, the most commonly used word to refer to volunteering for overseas service was 'privilege.' 'Inspiring scenes' were played out at various armouries as hundreds of young men clamoured for the 'privilege' to fight. Report after report in daily newspapers proclaimed the recruiting drive a complete success. Rumours flew around town as citizens hoped that local militia regiments would be able to serve as distinct units in France. On 10 August it was announced that the 48th Highlanders and the Queen's Own Rifles would go to the front as separate units. Thousands gathered just to see the Highlanders train. While no doubt encouraging to the men, at times the crowds posed an impediment, as 'people surged round the principal entrance [to the Armouries] in hundreds and constables had all they could do to keep them in check.'[6] Men paraded in civilian clothes and made their best efforts to appear soldier-like as officers scrambled to secure enough khaki uniforms.

Arrangements were made to create a military camp at nearby Long Branch, at the site of the rifle ranges. A tent city was constructed overnight to house between two to three thousand new soldiers after 17 August 1914. Lieutenant-Colonel Currie organized the training and waited for the order from Ottawa to proceed to Valcartier. His recruits mastered the rudiments of rifle and bayonet practice, drilled, marched, and 'stormed every position in the neighbourhood of the camp.'[7] Since participation was a privilege, men were asked to obey the highest standards of behaviour: the camp was dry.

It was not long, however, before troops began leaving for Valcartier. Large crowds gathered in driving rain on 20 August 1914 to see the first of Toronto's soldiers off to war. The people were thrilled to be part of the great adventure; they were also concerned for the welfare of their sons. Cherry Street Station was the scene of the final parade of one thousand volunteers before they left the city. Military bands played martial music from the platform, with soldiers and civilians alike joining their voices in song. Just over two weeks ago, these men had been office clerks and factory workers. Now they were leaving loved ones to face the might of the German army. The people gathered at the station did not for one moment miss the portentousness of this fact. Those being left behind passed trinkets and good luck charms to arms outstretched from railcar windows. The final goodbye was a sober one. In their wake, the departed trains left only silence. After a final wave, a last glance, loved ones turned in the mud, and began making their way home.[8]

During the next ten days, wave after wave of volunteers were ushered to Cherry Street by large, cheering crowds. The day after the first large contingent left, another 1,522 soldiers, many from the Queen's Own Rifles, entrained for 'points East.' Well-wishers stood twenty deep, filling the entire platform. Others jammed the overpass for one last look at the departing heroes. On the afternoon of 29 August, another seventeen hundred recruits entrained. Finally, on 31 August, the last major draft of volunteers left town. 'The tens of thousands who cheered the Kilties [the 48th Highlanders] on their way to Valcartier camp, and the war, saw the most workmanlike regiment that ever marched through Toronto streets ... The training at Long Branch has bronzed the faces of the men, and their whole appearance was most impressive.' Toronto Mayor Horatio Clarence Hocken[9] spoke to the soldiers: 'You will have the proud privilege of fighting not only for the British Empire but for the cause of civilization.' Toronto had sent just over four thousand of its men to war.[10]

The mood of the period was captured in a series of letters from a young university graduate who returned home to Toronto shortly after the outbreak of hostilities. Writing to his sister in Halifax, Ian Sinclair reported, 'I've left Pembroke for good & am going back to Toronto to get some training as I think I'm going to join the 48th [Highlanders]. However, I do'nt [sic] think I'll get in in time to go to England with the first lot. Gib [a friend] is'nt [sic] likely to go with the first contingent either ... It must be rather exciting in Halifax as I suppose a lot of warships are in & out all the time.' Sinclair's early enthusiasm for the war and the scope of events continued after he enlisted with the 48th Highlanders, along with most of his friends from university. A week later, he assured his mother that 'practically every friend I have in Toronto has volunteered to go and I'm mighty glad I took some step towards helping a little.' [11]

Sinclair also began to keep a diary that records his impressions of the public response to the war. On 23 August he noted that all recruits had to turn out for church parade: 'The beautiful hot Summer day had brought crowds of civilians out to see the parade, which started off with great playing of bands and much eclat generally. However, it didn't take the sun long to effect the lately inoculated troops and before the service ended, half the battalion had either fainted or sought refuge in their tents.' Despite the mishap, crowds continued to number in the thousands. Late in August, Sinclair paraded with his colleagues one last time before leaving for Valcartier Camp. He recorded his impressions of the attendant throng in his diary: 'The whole [parade] route was a solid mass of cheering humanity, who gave us a great roar of cheers all the way to the station, where we were all soon stowed away and started off on the first leg of our journey to Europe.' [12]

This was a collective enterprise. The training of these men was conducted in full view of the local population. Route marches wound their way through city streets, citizens watched new recruits struggle with drill, and thousands participated in the process of taking their leave of soldiers when they departed for Valcartier. As the city surrendered thousands of its young men to the military, both civilian and soldier alike were united in a common cause. The enthusiasm for the war effort, however, was not uninformed. Even as citizens were excited by the notion of a great adventure, they worried about the safety of loved ones at the front. Poignant scenes of leave-taking, even amidst the cheers and patriotic songs, became a regular feature in this first month of the war.

While a great deal of attention focused on enlistment and seeing young men off to Valcartier, the women of Toronto were also engaged in helping the war effort. Despite a growing and rich literature on Canadian women's history, there is a paucity of information on what women did during the years 1914–18, but the available sources leave no doubt that most women living in Toronto eagerly joined the war effort in any way they could. Over two hundred women volunteered for active service as nurses on the evening war was declared. The Armouries at Queen and University were crowded with over three hundred women wanting to take the St John's Ambulance Corps course. Officials stated that twice that number had to be turned away due to lack of space. Reports emphasized that the majority of potential nurses appeared to be from 'good homes'; most were quite young. The women agreed to gather on Tuesday and Thursday evenings to learn the rudiments of first aid so that they might be accorded the privilege of proceeding overseas.[13]

Most early women's efforts, however, were dedicated to raising enough money to equip a hospital ship. The Imperial Order Daughters of the Empire (IODE) met on the evening of 5 August 1914 at their headquarters at Bloor and Sherbourne Streets to begin fund-raising. After declaring that the 'privilege of sharing in the work will be [every Canadian woman's], whether she belong to the organization or not,' the IODE agreed on a national campaign to raise $100,000 by 20 August. The money would be entrusted to the Canadian government, to be transferred to the British Admiralty. At an organizational meeting to discuss the issue, local chapter president Mrs A.E. Gooderham read the following resolution: 'I would like to remind every member of the privilege and obligation enjoined upon them at this time of Imperial crisis. The call has come to us to do our duty as urgently as to the soldiers and sailors of the Empire. The Daughters of the Empire ask the co-operation of the women of Canada to give this tangible expression of their sentiment in the service of King and country in providing a hospital ship to be placed at the disposal of the British Admiralty.'[14]

This initial enthusiasm translated quickly into action through a mass meeting called to develop the idea. Chaired by Mayor Hocken, women packed into the Young Men's Christian Association building on College Street. Another meeting of over a thousand women took place two days later, this one chaired by Mrs A.M. Huestis, president of the Local Council of Women. Once again the meeting was so well attended that it was hard to gain admission, with hundreds turned away or forced to listen from nearby hallways or windows. A leading suffragist, Mrs L.A. Hamilton, announced that 'the fight for the franchise is to be laid aside and forgotten by the suffragists of Toronto in the face of the present fight for national freedom.' Mrs Hector Prenter of the Political Equality League made a similar vow. Every other activity was to take a back seat to the campaign to build and equip a hospital ship. At the close of the meeting a group of Boy Scouts proceeded through the crowd, soliciting donations to the campaign: $230.35 was raised.[15]

Many women took to the streets on 14 August to seek out donations. Local newspapers spread news of the campaign. While all Toronto daily papers were involved, the *Globe*'s response was typical: 'An army bent on war – war on the pocketbook – will invade Toronto, North, South, East and West, at 8 o'clock to-day. The city has been divided into fifty districts with a captain over each. The captain will be a woman, her rank and file, girls, who will patrol the district allotted, enter shops and offices and ask the inmates to put as much as they can into one of the 3,500 boxes the Kilgour Company made specially for the collection of the Canadian Women's Hospital Ship Fund.' The evening papers told a story of far-reaching success: 'It was ladies' day all over the city to-day. They owned the place, and the people, and before noon almost every man, woman and child was tagged with a British flag, which told how thoroughly they were doing their work of getting contributions for the Hospital Ship Fund.'[16]

The hospital ship campaign, organized and executed by women, was a resounding success. While the immediate goal for Toronto had been $15,000, initial counts of the returns indicated that donations had exceeded twice this amount. In less than a week, women had covered the whole city, involved over 650 volunteers and made use of 150 automobiles. Newspapers interpreted their great success as a demonstration of how well women could work together, as well as an indication of the generosity of the population. Due to local donations exceeding initial estimates, the national sum of $100,000 was secured before the deadline.[17]

While the hospital ship fund was the most visible campaign by Toronto women in the early days of the war, their efforts did not stop there. By the middle of August, other women were working to raise funds and gather clothing to donate to families whose breadwinners had departed as soldiers. On 18 August 1914, all women, but especially those representing women's societies, were invited to an organizational meeting. Despite a heavy downpour, hundreds turned up to 'prepare for any service that women could do.' This gathering gave birth to the Women's Patriotic League, with Mrs Willoughby Cummings as temporary chair. The league's mission was to see to the needs of soldiers' relatives. It arranged events to raise money for poor relief, including a

benefit concert at Massey Hall. Still other women dedicated their spare time to knitting socks and scarves to see to the comfort of the soldiers. Local nurses sponsored a mass meeting where several hundred women sewed en masse. All classes were welcome; if the poor could not supply their own wool, provision was made to secure material for their use.[18]

Sporadically, individual women opposed the war. When they did, however, the response by others was swift and decisive. On 21 August, the *Star* published a letter to the editor that supported the position taken by the Canadian Women's Business Club (CWBC) in not donating to the Hospital Ship Fund. Other women wrote in to express their consternation that any woman would fail to support the war: 'Heaven grant that they [the CWBC] are the only body of women in Canada or elsewhere who are chary of abetting the murderous perpetrators of war. Have they no imagination? Supposing Britain and the Empire had not taken the stand they have, what then? And where, then, does the honour of our Empire rest? We all deplore the circumstances that has made it necessary, but if the powers that be had neglected to fulfil their obligations, I, as a unit, a wife and mother, would be ashamed of the proud claim I hold of being a true Daughter of the Empire.' Another woman, calling herself 'One More Patriotic Soul,' also wrote to the *Star* to express her support, maintaining that the war had 'become a question of national honour, and as such it is the duty of every citizen to stand shoulder to shoulder and help alleviate the suffering when they see that nothing else can be done.' The Canadian Women's Business Club changed its mind and became a strong supporter of the ship fund.[19]

This exchange illustrates why women supported the war. The conflict was perceived as something to be abhorred, but endured. They believed Germany had brought the war on the world and Britain was drawn into the conflict reluctantly. Once committed, however, the Empire would fight with every ounce of strength. As was the case with recruits, the opportunity to serve was often equated with the word 'privilege,' demonstrating that women also wanted to help, and did so willingly. Those lucky enough to be selected as nurses were envied, even as those at home set to the task of provisioning against the new reality of war. There was no formal structure available for these activities so new organizations were formed, channelling the already existing enthusiasm. Despite these innovations, the focus on raising money for a hospital ship reflected pre-war beliefs about women's place in society. It was their duty to succour and to provide the comforts necessary to keep the

Empire's men fighting. The long-standing fight for an equal franchise was given second priority to the demands of the war effort, demonstrating the degree to which activists in the women's movement came together with all women to fight for a common cause.

The religious press, reflecting the attitudes and values of their constituent groups, supported the Empire's stand against German autocracy and aggression. Editorialists informed readers of the necessity of the conflict and prayed for victory. The language used in the Anglican *Canadian Churchman* reflected the dedication of the populace to the upcoming trial by fire: 'O Lord of hosts, the God of our fathers, who sittest on the throne of righteousness, judge now between us and our enemies; stir up Thy strength, O Lord, and come and fight for us, for in Thee alone do we put our trust.' Trusting in God, citizens girded themselves for war, and pledged 'to make whatever sacrifice may be necessary for British honour and British freedom.'[20]

Editorial endorsements were supplemented by a variety of others. The pages of the religious papers were filled with reports of the actions and words of prominent religious figures in and around Toronto. The *Christian Guardian* published a message from the Rev. Dr Samuel Dwight Chown, who had recently moved to Toronto to direct the Methodist Church. Chown's association with the military, however, was lengthy. Born in Kingston in 1853, he had served with the Princess of Wales' Own Rifles during the Fenian Raids. He remained a persistent and vocal supporter of the war effort throughout, accepting the honorary rank of Lieutenant-Colonel.[21] In these early days, Chown appealed to readers to pray for God's support, and to 'unite as ministers and congregations in humble supplications to the God of the nations to aid our arms in the present awful conflict on land and sea.'[22]

The *Catholic Register* was also quick to support the war. On 13 August, the journal published 'German Peril,' an article which reviled Germany and supported the struggle. A week later, the same paper reproduced a circular written by Archbishop Neil McNeil to the priests of the archdiocese of Toronto: 'You do not need to be reminded of the duty of patriotism. You are as ready as any to defend your country and to share the burdens of Empire. But those of us who are remote from the scene of conflict, and cannot leave Canada, may be tempted to think that our part is simply that of interested spectators. It is not. We can all help, and therefore should all help, by taking care to stop all unnecessary expenses in our homes and in our daily lives. It is no time for luxuries or festivities when millions of men are in mortal combat, and the poor

everywhere are likely to need all we can spare next winter.' Archbishop McNeil played a large role in Toronto's war effort. From its very early stages, he appeared at rallies arguing that there was no difference between Catholics and Protestants in their support of the war.[23]

The major churches (Anglican, Baptist, Methodist, Presbyterian, Roman Catholic) were all active participants in campaigns and rallies across the city. In a combined effort, religious leaders asked that the daily newspapers publish the following passage:

> We urge on all occupying the pulpits on Sabbath, 23rd [August]:
>
> 1st. To announce a public patriotic meeting for Monday evening, August 24th, in Massey Hall under the auspices of the above association [Toronto and York County Patriotic Association].
>
> 2nd. Also to announce that following the meeting there will be a campaign started to raise $500,000 for the aforementioned purpose. We commend most heartily this campaign to the generous support of the people.
>
> Whilst we greatly deplore war, and are unalterably opposed to it, yet, believing that our empire is facing a crisis which leaves no other course clear for lovers of liberty, honour and right, we feel justified in making this appeal.[24]

Duly instructed, priests and ministers devoted their 23 August sermons to the subject of the war and its necessity.

Local political leaders were also committed to the cause. Beginning with the speech made by Ontario premier J.P. Whitney on 4 August, politicians endorsed the war effort. Whitney proclaimed that the 'momentous crisis we now face makes plain what Canada's course must be. That course is to exert her whole strength and power at once in behalf of our Empire.' At the municipal level, shortly after the outbreak of war, Toronto City Council recommended that all employees of the City be paid their full wages during the time they were on active service. City Hall's generosity did not end there. It also promised that it would insure the life of each citizen who served in the Canadian contingent. It even contributed one hundred horses from the Civic and Police Departments.[25]

The cornerstone of the effort at the municipal level was the creation of the Toronto and York County Patriotic Fund, which quickly became a part of the Canadian Patriotic Fund. Initial meetings on 10 August involved leading figures in local and national life: Chief Justice Sir William Mulock (who became Chair of the fund committee); Edward R. Wood, president of the Central Canada Loan and Savings Company (who became treasurer of the fund); Joseph E. Atkinson, editor of

the *Star*; Stewart Lyon, journalist; and W.K. George, Governor of the University of Toronto. Also present were many prominent members of the local business, legal, and banking communities, including Elias T. Malone, Herbert C. Cox, D.R. Wilkie, Gabriel T. Somers, Aemilius Jarvis, and William J. McWhinney.[26] The Patriotic Fund was formally brought into existence with the passage of a resolution by the City Council on 14 August. Its object was to raise money to benefit the wives, children, and other dependants of men of the military and naval forces being organized and recruited in the City of Toronto. Organizers were certain that the people of Toronto and York County would come forward and donate money to see that no family member of a departed hero would go wanting.

The announcement of the creation of the fund and its initial campaign for donations were greeted enthusiastically by the press. In a manner typical of the dailies, the *Star* claimed editorially that it was 'not a burden, but a privilege' to support the fund, and that each person should give 'not what costs us little, or even what costs us something substantial, but, each in his degree, what costs us much.'[27] Accordingly, the first campaign sought $500,000 in donations just over three days, 24–6 August 1914. The press supported the effort ardently and informed residents of the upcoming 'whirlwind' drive. Local clergy devoted their Sunday sermons to emphasizing that the need was genuine and the cause was good. The campaign's focal point was a giant rally at Massey Hall to 'proclaim the city's realization of its duty. It will be an inspiring affair significant of a city's gratitude to the brave citizens who go out against the foe.' At the forefront would be the 'greatest combination of public men who have ever been associated for a public purpose in Ontario.' Buoyed by the coverage in the newspapers, citizens awaited · the opportunity to demonstrate their commitment also.[28]

Half an hour before the meeting was scheduled to begin, Massey Hall was filled to capacity and several hundred disappointed citizens had to be turned away. Thirty-five hundred gained entry. While they waited for the meeting to begin, the crowd inside was entertained by the bands of the 48th Highlanders, the Salvation Army, and the Queen's Own Rifles. Sir William Mulock presided. At 8:15 p.m. he rose to lead the singing of the national anthem, 'God Save the King.' Voices joined together in song, followed by a stirring rendition of 'Oh God, Our Help in Ages Past.' Patriotic speeches were given by leading citizens, prompting cheers and applause. Those lucky enough to find a seat spent the evening 'wildly applied in patriotic sentiments and patriotic airs, and

cheering the names of Lord Kitchener, Sir Edward Grey and other personages now in the public eye.' It was a night like no other in the history of the city: 'Never before has the great heart of Toronto throbbed and pulsated with more patriotic enthusiasm or been thrilled with a greater loyalty to the mother country.'[29]

The next morning, the front pages proclaimed that in the first three hours, over a quarter of a million dollars was subscribed. The city's population, however, did not rest on these early successes. During the entire campaign, energy levels were kept up and the drive to secure as much money as possible was maintained. City wide, over $700,000 was pledged in the first three days. Encouraged by these results, the Patriotic Fund increased both the length of the campaign and its target total – the latter to $800,000. When the drive finally came to a close after five days, $882,000 had been raised, the city council itself having contributed $50,000.[30]

City Council was not the only body to offer a lump sum to the Patriotic Fund. Business leaders and corporations were also solid supporters, irrespective of the turmoil international markets experienced with the outbreak of war. A spokesperson for Massey-Harris Limited, a major farm equipment producer, announced that in Toronto twenty-five hundred workers would be laid off owing to the 'very large numbers of orders for the European markets [which] were cancelled at the first sign of war.' Despite such disorders, business leaders sought public avenues to demonstrate their support. From its offices at 21–23 Wellington Street, the Kilgour Company donated the boxes used by women to collect money to equip the hospital ship. The most generous patron, however, was the owner of the T. Eaton Company, John C. Eaton, prominent local businessman and son of the famous Eaton's founder, Timothy Eaton:[31] 'Mr. Eaton has tendered ... to the Minister of Militia [Sam Hughes], first, the sum of $100,000 to purchase, fit up and equip a battery of Vickers quick-firing machine guns, mounted upon armoured trucks, for the use of the Canadian contingent; secondly, he offered his palatial steamer, *the Florence*, the largest and fastest boat of its kind on the Great Lakes; thirdly, the free use of his wireless station at Toronto, the most powerful north of Long Island.' Even children were not sheltered from the reality of war. The Girl Guides were 'up and ready to do their part for the Empire and the flag they are taught to love.' They made red cross armbands for one hundred Boy Scouts who were forming a first aid ambulance corps to confront 'any emergency that might arise.'[32]

While much of the Patriotic Fund's campaign depended upon corporate donations, it would not have been successful without the participation of individual workers. All across the city, the employees of major firms announced that they would each be donating a full day's wages. The diminutive president of the Newsboys' Union, Harry Roher, brought forward a copper box filled to the brim with cash. Thousands more dollars, a day's wages for each employee, were pledged by workers at the 190–218 Yonge Street T. Eaton Company and the 160–78 Yonge Street Robert Simpson Company. Employees of the Rice Lewis Company at 25–33 Victoria Street took up a collection, along with a large number of other firms. Local policemen donated one day's pay each, further swelling the total.[33]

From the foregoing, we can see that supporting the fund was a community undertaking. Business leaders, political leaders, church leaders, women, workers, campaign officials, the press, and even children all worked together to aid the families of the men departing for the front. The enthusiasm of the general population was so great that the boundaries of the fund had to be expanded – and *still* the people of Toronto oversubscribed. They recognized the sacrifice of the men who left to serve the Empire and pledged their financial resources to ensure that the families of these new citizen-soldiers would not be left wanting.

What sustained the population in this great adventure? The behaviour of Torontonians sprang from their confidence in a complex series of beliefs about why Canada and the Empire were at war. Most blamed Germany for starting the conflict, but war was joined to do more than defeat Germany. Liberal and Conservative papers, along with the religious press, responded editorially to the crisis and reproduced speeches made by local elites, thereby helping to define the public discourse used to justify the fight. This collective mindset is fundamentally important since it was these beliefs and assumptions that shaped the nature of the early war effort. Different ideas were presented, but there was no discussion of which was the most critical. Each was added into the mix, allowing citizens to choose their own and do their part.

Premier Whitney was one of the first public personages to offer a detailed justification of why Canada was at war. He maintained that Canadians must give as much as possible to the cause since they were a part of the Empire 'in the fullest sense and we share in its obligations as well as its privileges. We have enjoyed under British rule the blessings of peace, liberty and protection, and now that we have an opportunity of repaying in some measure the heavy debt we owe the Mother Country, we will do so with cheerfulness and courage.'[34]

Not all justifications, however, were of a high and noble character. Some writers argued simply that the Empire was 'determined to give the bully of Europe [i.e., the German Kaiser] a trouncing.' Most reporters detailed more traditional arguments, contending that 'in simple fidelity to her pledges and alliances, she [Britain] has joined with Servia and Russia and France and Belgium to end a perpetual menace, to establish her own security, and to restore settled conditions in Europe.'[35]

The reasons underpinning the war effort, however, were not static. Over time other justifications were added as events from the front were reported and debated. In light of advances by the German army through neutral Belgium, the press generalized their notion of what the fight was about. The reaction of the *News* was typical: 'Great Britain, France and Canada are not striving for dominion ... The Allies have engaged in this world struggle in order that mediaeval barbarism may be checked and those free institutions for which our fathers bled established more securely upon the face of the earth.'[36] As the scale of the fighting increased, the justifications expanded. Not only were the Allies fighting a noble struggle against a barbarous foe, but in doing so they were supported by the notion that they could not break faith with their ancestors who had provided the freedoms they now enjoyed.

Participation in the war, however, was not only the result of factors outside the British Empire. The *Globe*'s description of the situation on 5 August stressed both internal and external elements: 'Had the obligations of honour, as regards France and Belgium and Holland, been less binding than they are, Britain's high duty remains: duty to herself, duty to all British democracies, duty to the ideals of freedom and self-government in all the world. Were German autocracy to win, Holland and Belgium, and perhaps Scandinavia too, might become German States with a vast shore line to menace Britain on the North Sea.'

There was no hiding of the eventual cost, nor the currency in which it would be counted. Casualties were to be borne with heads held high, since the very foundation of British society was at stake: 'The price is beyond all reckoning. The cost of it is not in fabulous money, but in rivers of blood. The pain of it will run through the months to a million mouths. But that price for the word of "a scrap of paper" [referring to Germany's promise to respect Belgian neutrality] Britain will pay to the uttermost farthing. That word was the pledge of Britain's honour.' Honour committed, the secular press was willing to bear any cost to achieve victory.[37]

The religious press, too, offered a host of justifications. An editorial in the *Canadian Churchman* was typical of the impassioned commitment of the churches to the war. It argued that church and laity were one on the issue of war's necessity: 'It is no use to cry Peace! Peace! when there is no Peace. And there has been no Peace in the past years. There has been pause, but no peace ... War is a hateful thing, but since the appeal has been carried to that court it must be answered in the language of that court. We sought no fight. We tried to pacify our enemies. Now we may ask God's blessing on our arms. *Blessed be the Lord my God who teaches my hand to war and my fingers to fight* [emphasis in the original].' The churches believed that the war was of Germany's making and that it challenged the honour and integrity of the British Empire. Printing patriotic poetry in its pages, the *Churchman* presented an image of Britain as mediator forced to fight, arguing 'Thou, peacemaker, fight! Stand England for honour.'[38] Faced with the reality of German affronts to international peace and honour, Britain had been forced to draw the sword. As time went on, the religious papers added weight to the reasons for waging war. They hoped that God would give them the strength to defeat 'tyrannical and autocratic governments.'[39]

Torontonians understood why the Empire was at war. They were sustained by interlocking beliefs which allowed them to justify the expenditure of men and resources. They understood that the costs would be enormous. However, they believed that fighting was necessary to keep faith with those who had stood in the line in the past, to quell a potential threat to the Empire, to satisfy the demands of national pride, to make a stand against tyranny and autocracy, and to punish Germany for its crime of invading neutral Belgium.

There were, however, more than 'push' factors demanding that the Empire go to war. There was also a series of 'pull' factors: contemporaries believed that the war would provide a variety of benefits, which was all the easier because in the first month of hostilities Toronto had not yet been forced to justify the deaths of any of its sons. Training was conducted in a jovial atmosphere. Citizens jostled with one another to get a better view of the soldiers on parade. Small children marched along with the troops down main streets. Residents approached the war as a necessary adventure.

In the days after war was declared, papers extolled its unifying benefits. The drawing together of the Empire was emphasized as a 'silver lining to the vast cloud of terrific blackness.' British and Irish stood together, as did French and English Canadians, in the face of the common enemy. The war had put everything in its proper perspective. No longer would people be concerned with trifling matters when the future of their civilization was at stake. Neighbours would be brought closer together, and people would no longer suffer from the 'narrowness of vision' that existed before the war.[40]

The Torontonians of 1914 were living at the end of almost a century of peace and progress since the Battle of Waterloo had ended the Napoleonic threat in 1815. People believed in Empire. They believed that God would gradually improve their lot. Members of a deeply religious society, they never questioned His means. They interpreted the causes and consequences of war from this religious perspective. God and the Empire would, they believed, emerge stronger as a result of the great test.

The transition from peace to war, however, was not accomplished without some intellectual gymnastics. Germany, after all, was also a nation of believers. Citizen and newspaper editor alike had to construct an image of the enemy which would not undermine their pre-war faith in scientific progress and the advancement of Christian civilization. Germany had occupied a central position in mainstream thought that believed in the steady progress of humankind towards a better world. Germany's educational standards, its commitment to scientific endeavour, and its rapid rise to international prominence had been held up as examples for other nations to follow in the secular press. It now fell to that same press to construct a vision of Germany that would allow them to fight the German army without discarding pre-war beliefs in the merits of education, science, and faith. At the beginning of the conflict, this difficulty was overcome by blaming the war directly on Kaiser Wilhelm II. The German people, the press argued, were innocent dupes of a madman who was using them to advance his own ambitions. By extension, Torontonians fought as much *for* the German people as against them. When the Kaiser's armies were defeated, his deluded citizenry would be permitted by a benevolent coalition to construct their own government and regain their rightful place with other Christian nations.

There were some factions in Toronto, however, who were less inclined to be tolerant. Shortly after the war began, the papers reported on isolated incidents of crowds venting their patriotic fervour on visible German targets. On 5 August 1914, a mob of five hundred citizens surrounded the Liederkranz Club, the 'premier German institution in Toronto.' The stage had been set by the refusal of the club's management to lower the German flag and raise the British Ensign. The mob demanded that the situation be rectified immediately, and were it not for the intervention of about twenty police officers, 'the building might have been raided.' The crowd was successful, however, in its bid to tear down the German flag.[41]

On 7 August, the directors of the Liederkranz Club met to decide whether or not to raise the British flag. Speaking through the press, the club's director argued that had he been approached in a friendly manner, he would not have objected to replacing the German flag. He would not, however, be 'ruled by a mob of rowdies.'[42] Cooler heads prevailed, and after tempers lowered, the British flag was raised. Editorialists chastised those who attacked either those of German descent or their organizations, reminding readers that the object of malice was not the German people, but their leader.

Throughout August 1914, the blame for the chaos of war remained squarely on the shoulders of the Kaiser and his advisors. Their 'vaulting ambition,' editorialists argued, caused them to ignore international treaties, to violate the neutrality of small Belgium, to plunge the world into economic turmoil, and to unleash upon the international community 'the prospect of starvation, pestilence and death in a ferocious and devastating war.' Even as events proceeded and the German army began its sweep into Belgium, the enemy remained Wilhelm II. Constructing the German enemy in this way allowed the secular papers to maintain their pre-war idealistic portrait of the Germans as 'an industrial and commercial people, with a fondness for their homes, churches, and schools.' When the war was over, Germany would be 'free to manage her affairs for the benefit of her inhabitants instead of for the entertainment of one who is substantially a lunatic.'[43]

The religious press followed similar lines. The remarks in the Methodist *Christian Guardian* were typical, blaming the Kaiser and his minions for keeping alive the spirit of militarism against which the world was fighting. A week later, an editorial drew parallels between Englishman and German: 'The Englishman is of the same race and the same religion as his German brother, and, while rivals in trade, the Englishman is ready to acknowledge the many excellences of his German competitor. There is no feud between Briton and German, and yet at the will of one man, these hundreds of thousands of men who cherish not the slightest enmity the one to the other are arrayed against each other, and are seeking determinedly to kill each other.'[44] That Torontonians conceived of the enemy in this manner suggests that they believed the German army was fighting for the wrong reasons. The enemy soldiers would be unable to sustain their attacks when they realized that they were fighting for a corrupt system of government. This assumption was based as much upon the perceived weakness of the German system as it was upon the strength of British and French forces. This image of the enemy also indicates that secular and religious beliefs could be changed to adjust to events at the front.

The boundless enthusiasm of the first few days was not sustainable. The massive crowds that took to the streets to hear the early news began to dwindle in size as it became obvious that the war would not end in one decisive battle. Gradually, more and more people were willing to wait for newspapers to reach their homes to learn the latest. As the month drew to a close, the initial wave of support had produced incredible results. As September dawned, it became clear that enthusiasm alone was not enough to continue the war, which in turn changed Torontonians' experience of it. As the way they understood the war changed, the nature of the war effort itself underwent a gradual transformation.

2

A Great Crusade:
Keeping Faith with Those Who Died

Public opinion – or at least public opinion leaders – in Toronto were virtually unanimous in their support for an active Canadian role in the war, but what kind of war did they envisage? Most expected it to be over quickly, perhaps before Christmas. They had been taught to believe that European wars involved great and decisive battles on land and at sea. They were confident that the British and French armies, in combination with the 'brave Belgians' and the 'Russian steamroller,' would bring the war to a speedy and victorious conclusion. The triumph of the Royal Navy was considered a foregone conclusion.

The belief that the war would end quickly helps to explain Sam Hughes's decision to ignore existing mobilization plans and despatch a force of the keenest volunteers to England as soon as possible. It also explains public support for the ad hoc and chaotic response of governments and voluntary organizations in 1914. The belief in the certainty of an early Allied victory persisted despite the news from the front.

The first four divisions of the British Expeditionary Force (BEF) arrived in France in mid-August 1914 and were deployed near the Belgian city of Mons. Facing a numerically superior enemy, British commander Sir John French fought a defensive battle before beginning a hasty withdrawal to avoid encirclement. The retreat from Mons began on 24 August 1914 and ended in the early days of September with a French counterattack that became known as the First Battle of the Marne. The following weeks were marked by a German retreat to favourable defensive ground and the 'Race to the Sea.' This attempt by each side to outflank the other ended in stalemate and the construction of a line of trenches on French and Belgian territory from Switzerland to the English Channel.

Belgium suffered terribly from the German army, which burned its cities, smashed its army, and brutalized its citizenry. Confronted with this horror, secular and religious publications in Toronto advocated a variety of measures to comfort victims. The performance of the outnumbered Belgian army in slowing the advance of the Germans, so that Britain and France had time to organize their forces, epitomized the heroic vision of war. The sacrifices of the Belgian people, therefore, demanded the utmost attention and energy.

It seemed that everyone in Toronto had a suggestion on how best to aid the Belgians. Newspapers, both secular and religious, emphasized the virtues of the Belgian nation, and the need to support it: 'no call can count upon a more willing response than that made upon the behalf of the destitute people of Belgium.' Letters to the editor were consistent with the spirit of giving, one citizen suggesting that Canada offer fifty acres of farmland to Belgian refugees able to come to Canada. An unnamed woman proposed the transportation of Belgian orphans to Canada, arguing that the cause was worthy, and the costs to Canada a 'mere bagatelle.' The religious press paralleled this attitude, suggesting that Belgians be placed on Canadian farms.[1]

This climate of sympathy translated into a variety of efforts to lessen Belgium's burden. The City of Toronto donated a rail carload of foodstuffs and clothing to Belgian relief, at a total cost of approximately $10,000. Toronto Mayor Hocken sent a cablegram 'to King Albert of Belgium [which expressed] to him the admiration of this City for the valor and bravery of the Belgian army and people in their magnificent struggle against the German invasion.' In October, the Toronto Board of Control recommended City Council grant $25,000 to the Belgian Repatriation Fund, as a recognition of 'the heroic and valiant conduct of the Belgian troops in resisting the invasion of their country by the German enemy in superior numbers.'[2] Even without a formal organization, Ontario's farmers donated twenty-five rail carloads of produce from the fall harvest. The Women's Patriotic League collected clothing donations at their Sherbourne Street headquarters, counting their totals by the ton.

Individuals, too, took it upon themselves to provide aid. Through a letter to the editor, one resident offered 'to take care of an entire Belgian family.' Others organized aid projects for the Belgians out of existing structures. The Board of Trade, for instance, donated $20,000 and 'a hundred dozen heavy men's sweaters.' Individual churches promoted the participation of their brethren in the relief effort. The Rev. W.T.

Herridge, moderator of the Presbyterian Church, hoped that members of his denomination 'will persevere in their efforts to assuage the sorrows of that brave little people whose splendid stand against oppression is the most heroic event of modern history.' A special collection was taken at the next Sunday service.[3]

The plight of the Belgians, added onto the casualties suffered by their heroic army, struck a chord with Torontonians. They knew that hundreds of thousands of civilians had been forced from their homes by the advancing German army into the overcrowded parts of unoccupied Belgium. They could imagine the streams of refugees abandoning everything during their escape. Torontonian support, however, galvanized around Belgium's strategic predicament. Long before stories of German atrocities were reported in the papers, citizens talked about the need to defend the rights of a small nation against an overwhelming foe. Britain and the Empire had promised to defend France and restore Belgium's national boundaries.

These activities to aid the Belgians were part of a deepening commitment by city residents to the war effort. Secular and religious newspapers reiterated the reasons for fighting they had articulated in August 1914 and built upon them. Understanding these reasons is essential to understanding the nature of the war effort since Torontonians' willingness to sacrifice depended upon the breadth and depth of their commitment to it. Reports that thousands of British soldiers had been killed did not undercut support for the war: they reinforced it. A Rudyard Kipling poem, published in the papers, encapsulated the spirit of the fall of 1914: 'for all we have and are, / for all our children's fate, / stand up and meet the war.'[4]

Everything that the Empire stood for, and everything that it might become, was wrapped up in the verdict being determined on the battlefield. Citizens permitted no compromise, since they believed their democratic way of life was threatened. Even in December, when it was obvious that the war would *not* be over by Christmas, support did not ebb. Liberal papers, including the farmers' *Weekly Sun*, echoed these sentiments. The *Globe* argued that the war was about ideas: 'Mere money, or mere war equipment, or mere battleships, or even mere men – these the nations are pouring out with the lavish hands of spendthrifts. And why? For the sake of Ideas: the idea of Honour, the idea of Truth, the idea of Freedom. Ideas alone are worth fighting for. Things may be counted, weighed, measured, paid for. But Ideas – the things that are unseen – are eternal.'[5]

Anglican, Methodist, Baptist, Presbyterian, and Catholic church leaders were all consistent supporters of a war waged for ever-expanding ideals. The principal difference between the secular and religious press was that while the former placed the debate in the context of right and wrong, the latter viewed it as a struggle between good and evil. The *Canadian Churchman*, for instance, maintained that Britain was justified in 'taking up arms for the prevention of any great evil threatening to overwhelm the social and political system of which the nation is a member.' The Anglican paper rejected the notion of an early peace to reduce casualties, arguing that the war was one of survival for the British Empire and that it must be fought to a successful conclusion.[6]

Secular and religious papers believed in the Empire's cause, but as part of a society accustomed to progress, they also believed that good things would arise even from the slaughter itself. The *World* stated that as a result of Britain's willingness to fight 'for a scrap of paper,' the war was ushering in new and higher standards of 'national and international morality.' In that common struggle, Britain and the Empire would also benefit from a breaking down of class divisions. The fact that casualty lists included both officers and enlisted men was seen as one of the hallmarks of the 'new social order that will come with the close of the war.' Canada was sacrificing, temporarily, some of its prosperity, but would be the better for it in the long term.[7]

The religious press was similarly convinced that as part of God's higher purpose, the war would ultimately benefit humankind. This position was articulated in the knowledge that the scale of the destruction was going to be immense. The *Christian Guardian* stressed the heroism and glory of laying down a life for the cause, while praising the opportunity to rid the world of 'King Alcohol.' It also welcomed the solidarity of the Empire, the common purpose of the churches, the development of the patriotic spirit, and the breaking down of national prejudices. The *Canadian Baptist* also dwelled on the positives of the conflict, publishing stories which recounted the 'wonderful qualities of sympathy and kind and respectful consideration for others in many persons who never desire to live in the light of public admiration.' One such story told how, in 1914 in England, a wounded soldier waiting for a bus was put into a taxi paid for by a patriotic gentleman. The emphasis was placed on the positive influence of the war and how it had prompted this gentlemen to sacrifice for someone else. No mention was made, however, of the horrors the soldier went through in sustaining his wound, or the fact that the war demanded a much higher price from some than from others.[8]

As the war expanded in scope and cost, so did the commitment of local citizens. By the beginning of 1915, there was no longer any debate about whether or not a man who picked up the sword to fight was acting as a good Christian; the debate now turned on whether the man who *failed* to pick up the sword was worthy. Torontonians were committed, body and soul, to defeating Germany. They believed that everything the Empire stood for was being tested in the great conflict. Citizens understood that they were fighting for more than territorial or political gain. They were fighting for the very future of the civilization they had created. It was these ideas which would sustain them through the dark days ahead, and moreover, citizens were convinced that their sacrifice would pay dividends. Giving of themselves and their families, they believed, would ultimately result in a better society. Their willingness to sacrifice ran deep, and they would need all of that resolve in the coming months as Canada's soldiers finally closed with the enemy.

In late April 1915, the war hit home for Torontonians. After months of training in Britain, the Canadian Expeditionary Force made the voyage to France – and the front. On the morning of 22 April 1915 the Canadian 1st Division held a portion of the front line near the town of Ypres with a British division on their right and a French Algerian division on their left. Troops could feel a slight breeze blowing into their faces. At 5:00 p.m., observers reported greenish clouds of poisonous chlorine gas moving towards the Allied trenches, causing the Algerians to flee, opening a large gap in the line. That night parts of the Canadian 1st Division attempted to retake the lost ground, at incredible cost. The fighting continued for several days as the Canadians struggled to close the gap before withdrawing on 27 April. This battle, called Second Ypres, cost over two hundred officers and almost six thousand other ranks killed, wounded, or missing – almost one-third of the total Canadian force then overseas.[9]

In the context of a war for adventure and glory, Toronto newspapers greeted the first news from Second Ypres with tremendous enthusiasm, trumpeting the official word from the British War Office: 'Their [the Canadians'] gallantry and determination undoubtedly saved the situation. Their conduct was magnificent throughout.' In a commentary typical of the daily newspapers, the *Star* interpreted the fact that Canadians were outnumbered as a further measure of their achievement: 'This contingent, out-numbered and forced to give way, covered themselves with glory and apparently saved the day, preventing the on-rushing

Germans penetrating the main Anglo-French-Belgian line. They lost heavily, the War Office admits, but their conduct is praised in the warmest terms.' Torontonians were thrilled to learn that the actions of the Canadians at the front were recognized worldwide and 'every single evening newspaper [in London] contains the word "Canada."'[10]

It was not until two days after the initial news of the Canadian stand, while the battle continued, that concern was expressed about the human cost. Along with articles which focused on the glory of Second Ypres, Toronto was filled with 'feverish anxiety and dread' waiting for casualty lists. Learning of casualties was a public phenomenon and crowds gathered outside newspaper offices to scan the lists. Sunday was 'one of the most anxious days' ever experienced in Toronto. When the long list of officer casualties arrived, it only heightened feelings of foreboding: a longer list of other ranks was inevitable.[11]

The outcome of Second Ypres prompted Sam Hughes to announce that a third and fourth contingent would be mobilized for service overseas. While Hughes pledged more of Canada's sons, citizens' individual struggles to find information continued in the midst of the accolades. Newspaper offices were inundated with queries made in person and by telephone by Torontonians wanting to learn the fate of loved ones. For several heart-wrenching days, their attempts failed. It was in this context that Mayor Tommy Church, elected on 1 January 1915, began to assert himself as a populist civic leader. Church was a life-long resident of the city and trained as a lawyer before entering municipal politics. He served as an alderman from 1905 to 1909, then as the City Controller in 1910.[12] Church announced plans for a memorial service at Massey Hall, providing that militia and municipal authorities were in agreement, but that was scant comfort to waiting relatives.

As news trickled into Toronto, the terrible price paid by local soldiers became clearer. On 28 April 1915, it was reported that fully 15 per cent of the officer casualties were men from Toronto, and that the total list would not be known for some time. By the next day, some citizens had received news of the fate of other ranks, but most were still waiting. Local militia units passed on the information they had received, the 10th Royal Grenadiers reporting having lost, in one casualty list, two officers killed, five wounded, and six missing. The Queen's Own Rifles were similarly devastated, the unit reporting that of the original twenty-eight officers assigned to the Third Battalion, only five remained. Other reports reflected growing awareness of the battle's cost, noting that it 'becomes daily more evident that the battle in which the Canadians saved the day was one of the bloodiest of the war ... Reports to hand last evening show that nearly 50 per cent. of the officers of the 3rd (Toronto) Battalion fell on the field of Langemarck.'[13] Reports like this only worsened the anxiety of those still waiting for news of enlisted men, and papers cautioned readers about the inevitable lists of dead and wounded.

The fate of the 15th Battalion of the Canadian Expeditionary Force, consisting almost entirely of men from Toronto's 48th Highlanders, remained uncertain as late as 1 May 1915. Only ten officers of the original twenty-eight survived the battle unscathed. The *World* assumed that the scope of the Highlanders' casualties meant the battalion was simply missing, and hoped that more officers would be located in the coming days. The *World* argued that since the unit's casualties were so high, the entire regiment must have been captured by the Germans – any other explanation was too horrible to contemplate. Almost a week after the first officer casualties were reported, however, there was nothing to do 'but wait for the lists.'[14]

After two more days of uncertainty, the cost of Second Ypres to other ranks was announced in front page headlines: 'Canadian Casualties Are 5,400.' If anyone failed to recognize the scale of the sacrifice, the *Mail and Empire* put it in perspective: 'This means that half of the infantry at the front have been put out of action.' It was now clear that former members of 48th Highlanders serving in the 15th Battalion were not prisoners, as had been hoped. Citizens understood the nature and cost of the fighting through early telegrams from wounded soldiers who had been in the battle. One unnamed, wounded Highlander cabled back to reassure his family: 'The British troops came in time to take up supporting trenches, three-quarters of a mile back, but we [48th Highlanders] saved the day. Other Canadian regiments who were in action did equally well. We saved the line and the guns. We hope some officers and men who held the forward trenches, which were a series of redoubts, may have been taken prisoner, but they fought too hard and were likely killed almost to a man. The same is true at St. Julien Village. Only one who was there when the Germans entered came back.'[15]

The extent of the losses, however, was interpreted by all daily newspapers as a further sign of the glory Canadians had won. The *Star*'s reaction was typical, noting that the tale of the battle 'is a straightforward story of a stand in the face of terrible odds, as inspiring as any in history, and indicates that there was not a single of the now-terribly-decimated battalions and their officers who did not cover themselves with glory.'

The *World* defined for its readers the nature of the glory won at Lange-marck: 'The price of glory is a heavy one, and we may be thankful that our soldiers have not been asked to pay the price of glory as the soldiers of the Kaiser have. We have asked them to pay the price of freedom, the glorious heritage of British citizenship. They have paid the price, and they have taught us the value of that treasure of liberty for which unsparingly they laid down their lives. That is their glory.'[16]

A mother of one of the men, Mrs H.D. Warren, learned that she had lost her son and a 'loved companion.' She told reporters that her 'great comfort is that we, the mothers, fathers, sisters, and brothers, at home in this dreadful time, are fighting with those who are fighting at the front. The greatest solace is work [at the Women's Patriotic League].' Mrs Angus Sinclair wrote to her son, Ian, who was serving as an officer at the front with the 13th Battalion: 'You have been through terrible times the past few days and we have been feeling the strain here dear. We thank God not hearing of harm to you, and feel for the ones who have lost their dear ones.' Despite the cost, Mrs Sinclair was elated at the victory, and praised the 'wonders the Canadians did. The British say you saved the day – so with all the sorrow and anxiety there is tremendous feeling of pride in ours, who have done so nobly.' A week later, after news of the casualties had arrived, Ian Sinclair's brother wrote from Toronto: 'We are all so proud of our boys who have shown they can live nobly and die nobly for all our Empire stands for – I am no good at the expressing of these things old man but you know how we all feel in our heart of hearts.'[17]

Many ministers read the names of Canadian casualties from the city's pulpits to recognize their sacrifice and to comfort those left behind. The Rev. Dr W.H. Hincks of Trinity Methodist Church advised his parishioners not to despair, but to take comfort in the knowledge that 'there are still thousands of boys ready and willing to step into the vacant places of those who have given their all for their country.' Mayor Church extended the sympathies of the City of Toronto: 'To those of our bereaved citizens we tender our deepest sympathy in their hour of trouble and trial. We may well be proud of our beloved boys and heroes who have fallen in the greatest engagement around Langemarck.'[18]

While headlines, editorials, and poems celebrated the glorious aspects of the battle, there was a need to mark the passing of so many young men. Each militia regiment held a service for its fallen soldiers, however, communal grief crystallized around the funeral for a young captain of the 48th Highlanders, Robert Clifton Darling, whose body was brought home by his wife for burial in Toronto. Mrs R.C. Darling arrived in Toronto on 5 May 1915, two days after the headlines announced six thousand Canadians had become casualties at Second Ypres. His body lay in state at his family's home at 2 Dale Avenue until the funeral.

Robert Darling had figured prominently in early days of the war as city officers attempted to turn heady enthusiasm into an organized effort. He was among the first to volunteer for service, and proceeded overseas with the newly formed 15th Battalion as an adjutant. His war ended on 23 March when he was wounded in the shoulder by a German sniper bullet while cutting across the open behind the front line. He died later in hospital in London. His obituaries carry no information about his background, but there is no doubt that he was from a prominent family. His uncle, Henry W. Darling, was a wealthy local businessman who sold his Toronto interest in a dry goods company for over $1 million and moved to New York just before the war. Robert's wife was also from an upper-class family. Her father, Isidore Frederick Hellmuth, was a distinguished Toronto lawyer, and one of the 'leaders of the bar.'[19]

The particulars of Captain Darling's background mattered little to the people of Toronto. What mattered was that he, like so many from the city, had served his country and died in the line of duty. The whole city was in mourning on 6 May. The flags in front of the Parliament Buildings and City Hall, as well as all other public and private buildings, flew at half mast for Captain Darling and the men killed at Ypres. The funeral service was conducted in a crowded St. James' Presbyterian Church on Gerrard Street. Along the sidewalks and boulevards of Gerrard a silent crowd participated in the ceremony going on within. Men, women, and children stood stoically even as tears formed in the eyes of many imagining their own men still on the battlefields of Europe. Densely packed, the crowd extended west to Yonge Street and east to Church Street, a distance of two blocks in both directions. The church was filled with Darling's comrades from the 48th Highlanders. The rostrum and organ were draped in black while the flags of the Allies were centred around the royal flag of Scotland at the lectern. The coffin was piped into the church to the strains of 'The Flowers of the Forest,' and, upon its arrival at the front, the congregation sang, 'O God, Our Help in Ages Past.'

The Reverend Dr Robertson presided, taking as his text, 'Greater love hath no man than this, that he lay down his life for his friends.' 'We are gathered to commemorate more than death,' he said. 'We are here to commemorate sacrifice. Gallant soldier, winsome comrade, constant friend, man of stainless honour; he laid down his life when life was opening for him, holding everything he hoped for or could desire. I am not sure any of us would have it otherwise. It is good to die so. Death is not the worst thing that can happen to a man.'[20] It was not death, the Reverend Robertson argued, which had brought them together on that day. It was the *sacrifice* of the dead, and it was that sacrifice which was commemorated.

At the end of the service, Captain Darling's oak coffin was taken out to a gun carriage to be drawn by six horses to Mount Pleasant Cemetery. At the front of the procession marched the 48th Highlander Piper, playing 'Lochaber No More.' On the carriage, alongside the Union Jack–draped coffin, were Darling's sword and bonnet. Tethered to the carriage was the captain's charger which, with empty saddle and stirrups, followed its departed master. The coffin was accompanied by Captain Darling's 48th Highlander colleagues, who marched with rifles reversed. Thousands lined the route of the funeral procession up Yonge Street to the cemetery. Lieutenant-Governor John S. Hendrie, Mayor Tommy Church, Leader of the Ontario Opposition Newton W. Rowell, and President Robert A. Falconer, University of Toronto, were among the dignitaries. So many floral arrangements had been received that it took two additional carriages to transport them to the cemetery. As the funeral cortège neared the burial place, it resumed a slow pace until it arrived at the family plot, where three volleys were fired. Bayonets were fixed and arms presented in the last salute, a piper again played 'Lochaber No More,' and then the bugles sounded the 'Last Post.' Toronto's symbolic, lost son was laid to rest under a marker in the shape of a cross. The inscription reads: 'Captain Robert Clifton Darling, Adjutant 48th Highlanders, 15th Battalion, 3rd Brigade, 1st Canadian Division. Wounded in Action 23rd March Near Neuve Chapelle France, Died London, England, 19th April 1915.' He was twenty-seven years old.[21]

The casualties from the Second Battle of Ypres transformed the war from a great adventure to a great crusade. Prior to the battle, citizens equated warfare with adventure. In the wake of the devastating casualty lists, such a conception of the war was impossible. In its place, Torontonians began a great crusade. They continued to be sustained by the ideals articulated in the early months of the war, but they were further supported by the need to make good the sacrifice of so many men. The war effort continued to be a collective enterprise but with a new impetus born of loss. Crowds formed to learn the fate of loved ones, and they mourned their dead together by participating in the funeral for Capt. Robert Darling. The thousands who gathered to mark his passing were no doubt thinking of their own loved ones buried in France, in the hospital or still in the trenches.

The pace of the war did not allow Torontonians an adequate period of mourning. One day after Captain Darling's funeral, headlines focused on the loss of the giant passenger ship *Lusitania*, pushing the news of Second Ypres from the front page. On 7 May 1915 it was reported that the *Lusitania* had been torpedoed by a German submarine during the seventh day of its voyage from New York to Ireland. Many local residents were known to be on board. Once again, newspaper offices were besieged by concerned relatives searching for information. Crowds also converged on the ticket distributor, the Robert Reford Company, at 50 King Street East. Around ten o'clock in the evening on 7 May, a company spokesperson announced that all passengers were safe. Shortly thereafter, however, it was confirmed that the *Lusitania* had been sunk off Kinsale, Ireland, by a German submarine with large loss of life. There was no more information available that night. Concerned relatives left their vigils at newspaper offices and headed for home, hoping for the best, but preparing for the worst. It was not until the following day that more details became available. One report claimed that there were seventy-five Torontonians on the passenger liner, and all were assumed dead. Later, the good news was that there were 703 known survivors; unfortunately, at least 1,364 passengers were lost at sea.[22] Toronto waited to find out how many of its citizens fell into each category.

While they waited, a renewed debate about the nature of the enemy erupted. The German introduction of poison gas at Second Ypres, and the accompanying attacks, had cost over six thousand Canadian casualties, and now the enemy had fired on an unarmed passenger ship carrying women and children. Editorials were filled with condemnations of Germany's war effort and its people. While the sinking of the *Lusitania* was the first atrocity which affected the lives of civilian Torontonians directly, it was just the latest in a series of highly publicized, barbarous acts by the German military. No longer was the Kaiser perceived as the sole enemy. The German people were no longer portrayed as his innocent dupes, but his willing pawns. Germany's officer class had joined the Kaiser in a toast 'To the Day,' referring to the moment when German armies would be unleashed on the world. German academics endorsed German activities. Average German soldiers participated in the raping

and pillaging of Belgium. German citizens took to the streets to celebrate German victories. All this evidence was digested in the papers,
reinforcing the notion that the Empire was involved in a fight for its way
of life against a particularly barbarous enemy.

Toronto continued its *Lusitania* vigil. Some citizens were relieved
when relatives, once safely ashore at Kinsale, sent telegrams home. On 8
May, John Eaton's sister Mrs Burnside and her daughter were reported
safe. Many others were not, however, and the papers carried stories of
the scale of the losses, including the toll of more than 150 babies who
died in the water: 'One mother lost all her three young children, one six
years old, one aged four, and the third a babe in arms, six months old.
She herself lives, and held up the three of them in the water, all the time
shrieking for help. When rescued by a boat party the two oldest were
dead. Their room was required in the boat, and the mother was brave
enough to realize it ... With her hair streaming down her back and her
form shaking with sorrow, she took each of the little ones from the res-
cuers and reverently placed it in the water again, and the people in the
boat wept with her as she murmured a little sobbing prayer to the great
God above. But her cup of sorrow was not yet completed, for just as they
were landing her third and only child died in her arms.'[23]

By 10 May the cost of the tragedy to Toronto was clearer, with reports
claiming sixty-three from the city safe and ninety-six still missing.
Churches condemned the German atrocity even as they provided solace
and comfort for bereaved families. In an address typical of the major
denominations, Archdeacon Henry John Cody of St Paul's Anglican
Church told his congregation, 'This policy of frightfulness is designed
to inspire terror, but it will only deepen the grim determination of every
Briton to fight through until this hideous, war-god of militarism and
brute-force is shattered forever.'[24]

Citizens continued to travel to newspaper offices seeking information,
more often than not without success. Gradually, stories of local survivors
reached home. One young passenger, eleven-year-old Frank Hook, had
been returning to England with his father and sister. When the torpedo
struck, he was thrown overboard and broke his leg on a piece of floating
wreckage. The boy came up again beside an upturned boat. His father,
who at first did not know that his son had survived, was reunited with
him in a hospital in Queenstown.[25]

Col. George Sterling Ryerson, president of the Canadian Red Cross,
had been told that his wife and daughter had both survived. Many
Toronto citizens had included the Ryerson family in their prayers. His

wife had been on her way to London to visit her son who was recuperating in hospital after being wounded at Second Ypres while vainly trying to save his brother. However, once ashore, Miss Ryerson confirmed that her mother had drowned.[26] Tales of families being torn apart were commonplace, and funeral services were conducted all over the city. It was not until 11 May that the final tally was complete: Toronto had lost eighty-six citizens.

Ministers set aside 16 May as a day of public mourning. A service at the Sherbourne Street Methodist Church was typical. It was conducted in memory of the late Mr and Mrs Frank A. Rogers and Franklin A. Peardon, employees of the Robert Simpson Company, travelling to Britain as part of 'the Dominion's war-time promise of "business as usual."'[27] It brought together a large crowd of mourners, seeking some outlet for their emotions.

The sinking of the *Lusitania* and Second Ypres changed Torontonians' experience of the war. These calamities also changed their notion of who they were fighting. This transformation in turn profoundly altered the nature of Toronto's war effort. Now that they were pitted against an enemy who would stop at nothing to win, the Allies would have to use the very tools they abhorred to ensure victory. The fight was now against the German people, and this translated into much rougher treatment for local enemy aliens. In the wake of the German attack on the *Lusitania*, Mayor Church announced that he would ask the local German community to close their clubs. They closed voluntarily two days later. The City Council unanimously passed a resolution requiring the heads of civic departments to dismiss from service 'all persons of German, Austrian or Turkish birth, who are aliens or not naturalized subjects of His Majesty the King.'[28]

While citizens were coping with the news of Second Ypres, letters written by soldiers who survived the battle began to arrive in Toronto and, forwarded by their addressees, became a regular feature in the papers. The most striking aspect of these private letters is the details they contained about the nature and cost of trench warfare. One of the first letters to arrive was written by Capt. C.E.H. Morton of the 10th Royal Grenadiers, serving with the 3rd Battalion, to Maj. J. Cooper Mason, DSO, of the Toronto Infantry Brigade. It was published in the *World*.

It was a veritable inferno; shell after shell broke around us continuously, half-a-dozen at a time, from 7 a.m. till 1 p.m., all sorts of conditions of shells – 'Johnsons,' 'Whistlers,' shrapnel, and God knows what not. I had been attending to wounded men in the open with the help of two chaps of the 2nd Battalion, who were mortally wounded on the job; they fell by my side and gave me an unpleasant twenty minutes until they were beyond help. I crawled away, and a few minutes later was hit myself in the right thigh by shrapnel. I tried to carry on, but could not stand, so I crawled about 75 yards to a tree trunk which had been felled, and hugged the leeside of it until 9 p.m., when I was picked up by the stretchers. You may believe me, it was not pleasant to lie there helpless, expecting every minute to be landed by one of the shells that were incessantly bursting around me.'[29]

Another letter from Pte. E.G.B. Relt, Toronto Battery, described the gas attack at Ypres. 'It is deadly poison, and causes the victims to suffer terrible agony first. It burns their eyes terribly. It causes suffocation also, and altogether is the deadliest, or one of the deadliest, war machines used in the war. I was near enough, as was the battery, to experience the effect it had on the eyes, and, believe me, it burns some.' Transport officer Lieut. R.W.E. Jones wrote to his father, describing his experience and impression of the battle's cost to the infantry: 'What they went thru in that terrible battle no one engaged in it can possibly realize. Just fancy, the dead are piled in heaps and the groans of the wounded and dying will never leave me. Every night we have to clear the roads of dead in order to get our wagons thru. On our way back to our base we pick up loads of wounded soldiers and bring them back to the dressing stations.'[30] Torontonians learned through these letters of the general conditions of the front, which included the indignity of being strewn like cordwood at the side of the road with other corpses to await burial, or, if one was lucky enough to be merely wounded, lying alone for hours before receiving medical attention.

Other letters told of the infantrymen's experience at first hand. Pte. E.A. Foy, serving with the 4th Battalion, wrote to his sister:

We had about 1,500 yards to go over absolutely open ground, no cover whatsoever, and their trench was on a beautiful slope. Believe me, if hell is anything like Friday, I'm for reforming. They simply raked us with machine gun and rifle fire, and our fellows began dropping before we got properly started. How I lasted as long as I did I hardly know, as at every rush the fellow next to me copped it, and once when we were lying down the man next to me got it square through the head. Only one sergeant and four men including myself out of our platoon got within 200 yards of the trench when the fellow next to me was hit in the arm. I sat up beside him to get out his bandage to tie him up, when I got it myself through the back, and the next fellow got it in the shoulder. So that just left two. Suppose they got theirs later.[31]

Thus Canadians had ample opportunity to learn the grizzly details of front-line combat. The public opinion leaders used editorials, church sermons, and other means of communication to make the case for the necessity of the war and to argue that sacrifices were not in vain, but the horrors of the conflict were never hidden from the people. Rather, these gruesome descriptions were given a high profile by the newspapers in their desire to provide a demanding reading public with as much information as possible. Eight months after Second Ypres, the *Star* ran a series of articles by poet and storyteller Robert Service, who was serving as an ambulance driver at the front. His reflections were just as disturbing as the initial reports:

Beyond the crosses there are many open graves. They will not wait for long. Already I can hear the guns that are making for each mouth its morsel. They will soon be filled – those gaping graves. Then in years to come, when the names on the crosses are blurred and worn, mothers and children will come here to weep. And perhaps it is well so. Peace so precious must be bought with blood and tears. These are the men who pay the price. Come, let us honour and bless them, aye, and envy them the manner of their dying, for not all the jewelled orders on the breasts of the living can vie in glory with the little wooden crosses the humblest of these has won.[32]

Detailed accounts of front-line life were readily available to the Toronto public. Captain Morton's letter describing a bombardment demonstrates that soldiers portrayed war neither as heroic nor as glorious. The publication of his letter dispels the notion that everyone at home was told only of quick victories, nobly won. Soldiers were not killed in a heroic dash by a single bullet to the heart, but often died a slow and painful death even as they attended to wounded comrades. Fear was a constant companion. Death and wounds descended upon defenceless soldiers from hidden guns, often miles away. Private Relt's letter describes the gas attacks in grizzly detail, allowing civilians at home to construct an image of one of the front's hazards. Private Foy's gritty description recounts how the Germans, in possession of the high ground, were able to make effective use of superior weaponry to halt the attack. The cost to Canadian infantry is also clearly outlined, as he notes that fully 86 per cent of the members of this platoon became casualties in a single attack. Our task then is not to explain the reaction of a public which was denied the opportunity to learn of the reality of war, but to try to understand why a population that was well informed about what awaited its young men in the trenches of Europe continued to mobilize its resources, including manpower, to achieve victory.

Defensive warfare of the type conducted by the Canadians at Second Ypres continued for more than another year. Allied forces were too weak to conduct a sustained attack and devoted their attention to building up resources for a summer 1916 offensive. The Germans were largely content to fortify their positions in the west and hold their ground, concentrating on dealing a knock-out blow to the Russians in the east. Canadian troops participated in largely diversionary attacks at Festubert in late May 1915, at Givenchy in mid-June, and St Eloi and Mount Sorrel in March and June 1916, respectively.

The first major British offensive of the war began on 1 July 1916 by the Somme River. The new British commander, Sir Douglas Haig, hoped that a massive artillery bombardment followed by waves of infantry would overwhelm German defenders, allowing cavalry to break the trench deadlock. The offensive was designed to relieve the French armies at Verdun, to engage the German armies in an attritional battle, and to prevent the transfer of German troops to the Eastern Front. While Haig's attempt was a reasonable way to try to break the stalemate, it failed. On 1 July alone, the British Expeditionary Force sustained over 60,000 casualties, including almost 20,000 dead, the costliest day ever for British arms. Despite the losses, Haig hoped that sustained attacks would break the German defences; the offensive ground on into November.[33]

In Toronto, the public discourse recognized the Somme offensive for what it was: a starting point. Even though Canadian troops were not involved until September 1916, Torontonians were keenly interested in the Somme battle. Saturday July 1st was Dominion Day, celebrated with parades and patriotic enthusiasm. In the midst of these celebrations, preliminary news filtered in about a huge British offensive. The morning papers went to press too soon to cover the story, but the evening *News* carried a bold headline: 'BRITISH CARRY GERMAN LINE; TWENTY MILE FRONT IS TAKEN IN ASSAULT.'[34] It was not until Monday, 3 July 1916, that the papers were able to give fuller details of the offensive. The dailies all trumpeted that something momentous was under way. They were careful, however, to place recent events in context and advised residents not to expect instant results. A *Star* editorialist commented that the Germans had spent hundreds of thousands of lives in recent attacks at Verdun, cautioned readers that the upcoming British offensive would not be easy, and advised that 'the best that can be hoped is that it will be possible.'[35] Papers warned readers against the kind of enthusiasm characteristic of the early days of August 1914.

There is no mistaking, however, the general mood of optimism. Even with warnings to keep things in perspective, the public discourse reflected a hope that a turning point had been reached. Each of the daily papers, as well as the weekly religious periodicals, believed that the war had entered a new stage. Newspapers commented that Dominion Day, 1916, would long be remembered as a turning point since the first news of the offensive reached Toronto as her citizens were preparing to enjoy themselves in the bright sunshine of the first summer holiday. As the news spread, it added 'zest' to the day. Following the usual pattern, residents swamped newspaper offices with inquiries and Extra after Extra was printed and posted in office windows.[36]

A small sample of the type of news available to local readers demonstrates that citizens had access to important information about the strategic direction of the war. The reporting in the *Globe* on 12 July was typical of the daily papers. After eleven days of fighting, headlines trumpeted that the whole *first* German line had been taken. This 'success' was illustrated with the advance of the British into Mametz Wood after 'six costly assaults.'[37] If this information had been received by a readership which did not understand the nature of trench warfare, it could not possibly have been presented as a success. After all, it had taken almost two weeks to take the first of several German trenches immediately before the British positions. Readers, however, had been consistently well informed about the progress of trench warfare for almost two years. They had been told that trench systems were organized in depth, and they could clearly see from the daily maps provided in the papers that the trench lines moved very little as the months passed. The meagre progress of the first days of the Somme offensive was not presented to a populace which expected grand strategic movements and sweeping arrows across maps of Europe. Local residents were aware of the nature of attritional warfare.

While Torontonians absorbed the available news, Haig reinforced areas at the front where the Allies had gained ground. He poured in troops and munitions, trusting in God that a breakthrough was only days away. The Canadian Corps moved into the front lines on 30 August with British General Julian Byng as their commander. It was the first time the Canadians, now three divisions strong, had made a strategic move as a corps. They were allotted a quiet sector to allow continued training for offensive work as part of the general Somme battle. While their posting was not without incident, the Canadians were kept out of the news, awaiting their turn in the 'big push.'

Sir Douglas Haig has been the target of some of the most virulent personal attacks in the years following the end of the First World War. He is held up by writers such as Frederick Manning in his post-war memoir *Her Privates We* as the epitome of the selfish general who sent tens of thousands of men to their deaths in the vain hope of a cavalry breakthrough. For the most part, historians have reinforced this portrait. Recently, Martin Stephen's *The Price of Pity: Poetry, History and Myth in the Great War* (1996) has attempted to resurrect Haig's shattered reputation. The cornerstone of Stephen's view is the necessity of understanding the strategic situation as it existed in 1915 and 1916; he argues that Haig made the best of an awful situation. For their part, Torontonians took the trouble to inform themselves of the dilemma facing Haig, and accepted the necessity of sacrificing large numbers of men for the greater good.

Torontonians spent the first two weeks of September 1916 in familiar activities. The degree to which they saw the war through the experiences of Canada's and especially Toronto's troops is evident in the newspaper coverage of the Somme offensive. Front page stories conveyed the main events but the press and community leaders were not fully emotionally enjoined until Canadian soldiers went into action in the second week of September.

By this point in the war, casualties from normal front line duty did not elicit a massive response on the part of the press; the major preoccupation in the late summer of 1916 was the price of coal. The war had put great demands on the coal supply, but the problem was further compounded by the lack of planning on the part of coal companies in the United States. Ontario depended entirely on its southern neighbour for its supply of anthracite coal, but American companies had expected a short war when it erupted in 1914 and had not expanded their distribution networks to handle the prolonged and enlarged demand. The resulting backlog of orders drove up the price.[38] The rise was so pronounced that many papers favoured creating a civic coal yard. All dailies recognized the problem, but differed in their assessment of the proper way to cope, some advocating a coal yard, others favouring more direct regulation of the coal industry.

By mid-month the Canadian Corps finally took to the offensive, resulting in a costly final two weeks of September. All three divisions advanced
for the first time in the battle of Courcelette, 15–22 September. The
Canadians acquitted themselves well, but in a week's fighting sustained
7,230 casualties, while all along the line final objectives had not been
secured. Poor weather and a shortage of ammunition brought a temporary halt to offensive operations. On 26–30 September the Canadians
renewed the attack, focused at Regina trench, but they were unable to
secure it and took heavy casualties.[39]

The news about the Canadian operations at Courcelette was received
in Toronto by a population increasingly stressed by the demands of the
war. The papers, prominent citizens, and local organizations were
becoming vocal about the need for conscription. In addition, the high
cost of living was a source of concern as workers struggled to provide for
their families. The City of Toronto came under criticism from its
employees for failing to increase salaries commensurate with inflation.
Representing the men of the sewer department, A. Bellchambers called
upon the Board of Control to increase wages to compensate for the rising cost of bread. Aware of the demands of the war, workers were not
threatening to strike, but were only expressing their concerns: 'All we
ask is that you give us consideration.'[40] The Board of Control initiated
an investigation into the ever-increasing cost of bread.

While Torontonians faced calls for conscription and rising costs, their
continuing concern was the men at the front. The fighting at Courcelette
first broke the news 16 September and even initial reports, while stressing
the offensive character of operations, revealed that casualties were heavy.
Despite extensive preparations, when the artillery stopped firing and the
infantry went forward, 'it was certain there were many of the enemy still
living and waiting with machine guns to give the Canadian assailants a
fierce reception ... I may perhaps be allowed to state that included among
them were certain battalions who suffered pretty severely in heavy
encounters.'[41]

While the Canadians were still in action, there was little information
about casualties; the papers, however, prepared to receive more bad
news. An ominously worded report from the *Globe* noted that information was still forthcoming and that 'casualties are not as heavy as might
have been expected, considering the ground gained, and the impetuous
character of the Canadians' attack.' Despite the censorship of immediate reports from the front, Torontonians were informed, '*It was the
Canadians' first offensive on any big scale* [emphasis in the original].'[42]

The toll from the battle was indeed a heavy one. Daily newspaper reports gave some indication of the scale of the human cost. On 23 September alone, lists told of 104 local dead or wounded. Reports of this type continued until the end of September, reaching 804 by 27 September. And still the casualties came in, 125 reported on 29 September, another 101 listed on 30 September. More than one thousand local men had been killed or wounded within a week.[43]

The Canadian Corps continued its gruelling work at the Somme front for two more months. Regina trench appeared for a while to be an unreachable goal. The Canadians could fight their way into it, but it was impossible to hold. Again and again, troops were forced to abandon their attack on the infamous trench. Concerted attempts were made on 1 and 8 October, but to no avail. The main line did not come under Canadian control until 11 November, with its supporting trenches not consolidated until 18 November. Canadian troops remained in the front lines until 28 November when they withdrew to train and re-equip.[44]

Gruesome attritional warfare had a profound impact on Toronto, but the cost of living also did not let up. Confronted with rising prices, dwindling supplies, and another harsh winter, organizations lobbied the federal government to increase its involvement in the economy, and papers reported receiving countless letters from people expressing anger about the high cost of foods and other necessities. Lobbying continued throughout October, with editorials pointing out measures other countries had taken to deal with the stresses of wartime, arguing that Canada do something similar. While pressure grew, so did the price of goods. Front page reports at the end of October warned of another increase in the cost of bread, this time rising 12.5 per cent to eighteen cents for a large loaf.[45]

In addition to coping with scarcity, Torontonians continued to be inundated with casualty reports. Throughout October and November, each day brought a new list of killed and wounded. In the early part of October, as a result of two separate attempts to take Regina trench, over 589 casualties were sustained by local soldiers. Throughout October, the casualty lists continued to arrive, recording the killing or maiming of 2,872 Toronto men since the beginning of the Somme offensive.[46]

Despite the stream of casualties and the knowledge that the Canadian offensive had stalled, the secular and religious press maintained that the sacrifice was justified. The *Christian Guardian* was pleased that the Allies had been able to continue smashing the German lines yard by yard, arguing that such a strategy would eventually win the war. After outlining the likely price for this victory as a generation of young men, the *Canadian Churchman* asked if it was worth the cost: 'We believe it is, and it is this belief that reconciles us to the loss. It should, however do much more than that. It should make us put forth every effort in our power to preserve that for which they are giving their lives.'[47] Similar examples of patriotic dedication appeared in both Liberal and Conservative papers. All articles recognized that the real fighting had only just begun.

Soldiers serving at the Somme wrote home to friends and family, thereby helping to shape the public discourse. They also wrote to prominent Torontonians whose speeches and appearances were instrumental in shaping the local war effort. One unnamed military chaplain wrote to Archdeacon Cody, who himself served as the chaplain for the Queen's Own Rifles, about his experiences at Regina trench: 'Unconsciously the men throw light on what it all means to them. The other day, one chap about 40 yrs. old, nearly smashed to pieces and yet wonderfully strong and cheerful – told me how a group of them, and among them a boy, were hit by a shell. It killed two, wounded others, and tore off the poor boy's hand. In his agony and terror the poor lad started to run up and down the trench crying, "Mother, Mother" – the men fled. They couldn't stand it. The thing absolutely broke their nerve and they fled. My friend was wounded – and to get out of reach of that pitiful cry – he ran away – down a trench and fainted – and when he came to – he was back in a dressing station. Isn't it terrible?'

Soldiers or their relatives sent personal letters to the papers to be published for the community to read. First-hand accounts from the Somme left little to the reader's imagination. Pte. George Rice from the 74th Battalion wrote to his wife in a letter later published in the *Telegram*:

I have just been through the battle of the Somme, and I pray God I shall not have to go through another one; the sights I have seen at the front have been pretty hard to stand. My battalion was in the front line of trenches; the boys stood it pretty well as Fritzy put over his three bombardments on us. Just as we were going in a shell hit my platoon, killing one and wounding several. I was thrown about fifteen feet in the air, landing in a shell hole, not a very pleasant sensation for me I can assure you. Really, I thought my end had come, but thanks to God I was not harmed at all, only a bad shaking up. Well, dear, I must say that your prayers have been answered; how one could come through such a battle without a scratch is a mystery. Only about 41 men, counting NCOs are left of my company [usual strength 250]. Capt. Kendall was killed, and a brave man he was. What my thoughts were you can well imagine. I was expecting to go down at any minute. We should have been relieved 24 hours sooner than we were, but owing to the heavy firing that was on, they could not get up that night, so it was up to us to stick it out another day.

Both the chaplain and Private Rice emphasized the arbitrary nature of the killing and wounding of men. The latter is just one example of a stream of soldiers' letters published in the papers. Neither letter tells of anything remotely resembling a victory, both writers electing instead to comment on the cost in human life.[48] Individuals often bore witness to being overwhelmed by the technology of war.

Torontonians knew what was going on at the front, understood that soldiers were dying by the thousand, and yet they did not falter in their support for the war. Citizens demonstrated their steadfastness by donating to patriotic drives, including the British Red Cross campaign, 17–19 October 1916. This campaign was far more organized than the ad hoc arrangements common in the early part of the conflict. In the weeks leading up to its opening, ads ran in all the dailies, appealing to average Torontonians to contribute money: 'The British Red Cross Society urgently needs, FROM YOU, who read this appeal, HELP in carrying on its beneficent activities. It may be that at this moment your son, or the son of someone near and dear to you, is being borne to safety from a shell-torn battlefield in a Red Cross ambulance, or is receiving the ministrations of a Red Cross surgeon, whose skill will TURN THE EBBING TIDE OF LIFE when a longer wait for aid would have brought death.' The whole city was involved in the drive to raise $250,000 in three days. Ministers preached from the pulpit, public theatres offered free advertisements, and workers donated one day's wages. Women, labour groups, employers, schools, churches, and influential public figures all participated. At the front of Nordheimer Building on King Street East, the hands of an enormous clock tracked the campaign's progress. Papers, too, offered extensive editorial comment in support. A giant rally at Massey Hall the night before the drive opened was the final pre-campaign booster, and residents filled the hall, singing and cheering the Empire's cause.[49]

The morning of 17 October, Torontonians opened their morning papers to be confronted by full-page ads about the Red Cross drive. The *Globe* carried a standard advertisement which showed a soldier being blown up by an exploding shell and, in another picture, the same soldier recuperating in a Red Cross hospital, with a nurse at his bedside.

The cost of the war was not hidden from the people; it was used to help raise funds to continue the fighting. Editorialists stressed the merits of the Red Cross, and the City of Toronto gave a large boost with the donation of $75,000, a threefold increase over the previous year. The first day raised $104,000, a good beginning to reach the quarter-million desired, but not sufficient to outpace the 1915 total of $538,000. Ads continued to stress the need for donations. One picture showed a mother saying goodbye to her soldier son, and another portrayed him later, wounded, being carried by a Red Cross officer and nurse. Despite the organization, the deadline was extended on 19 October for another day to allow canvassers to cover the entire city. With a total of $273,000 after two days, workers redoubled their efforts.

They were helped by the arrival of a film unlike any other. Citizens besieged the Regent Theatre on Adelaide Street to see the first moving pictures from the Battle of the Somme. Showings began at 10:00 a.m., continuing until 11:00 p.m. Each screening brought the war home to another 1,680 people. Advertisements lauded the film as the 'first official moving pictures of a British battle ever shown, and a living illustration of the biggest news event to British eyes since Waterloo.' All week, the film played to packed audiences, reaching over fourteen thousand spectators a day. It showed men rising out of the trenches, only to be cut down by artillery and machine gun fire, often as they struggled with enemy barbed wire. Echoing sentiments of writers of the other papers, a *Globe* editorialist described what he saw: 'The whole panorama is one nerve-straining spectacle. The spectators watch men moving along communication trenches with fixed bayonets, alive and healthy and next moment see them emerge on to the sky line silhouetted in death. They watch the giant howitzers lift their mouths skyward and belch forth demons of devastation and death.' In total, over ninety-eight thousand residents saw the film in the first week alone. Attendance increased in the following days, as two other theatres opened in an attempt to provide sufficient seating for everyone wanting to see the film. Crowds continued to converge on the movie houses for a taste of life at the front.[50]

The visual horrors of the war, accompanied by accounts of enormous British casualties in the Somme offensive, did not make people question the war. Pictures and increased casualties translated into increased contributions to the fund. This enthusiasm helped bring the total up to $421,000 on the morning of 20 October. One more full day of campaigning, and a huge rally at Massey Hall, brought the total to $701,546 – an increase of 30 per cent over the previous year. A young man working in the Merchant's Bank of Canada in the city, H. Anson Green, wrote to his father to tell him about the campaign: 'The boys in the office gave a day's pay. This was done generally throughout the business sector.'[51] Torontonians' satisfaction with their patriotic donations was undercut, however, on 24 October when the city's largest casualty list of the war arrived, adding over two hundred new names. Also on that day, Prime Minister Robert Borden announced an upcoming tour to promote National Registration, a scheme designed to help find sufficient men to fill the military and industrial needs of the nation.[52]

When Canadian forces finally succeeded in taking and holding Regina trench, articles conceded that it was only a minor victory, however costly. Much of the attention that might have been accorded the Canadian Corps was diverted, however, when the controversial Minister of Militia, Sir Sam Hughes, resigned in disgrace and Toronto MP and businessman Albert E. Kemp was appointed in his place. Newspapers paid only passing attention to the success of the Canadian Corps in taking the support trenches around Regina trench between 20 and 22 November. From then until 28 November, the Canadians were involved in mopping up operations with relatively few casualties. Newspapers reported on one occasion that 'only' seventeen men had been killed or wounded the previous day. The gruesome attritional warfare of the Somme offensive had made the killing or maiming of seventeen Torontonians seem unexceptional. Since arriving at the Somme on 30 August, the Canadian Corps had lost 24,029 men killed, wounded, or missing.[53] It appeared as though the fighting would continue indefinitely, with no likelihood of an immediate breakthrough.

It is in this sobering context that the actions of Torontonians in the summer and fall of 1916 must be evaluated. The local population had access to a remarkable amount of information and, on the basis of the first news of the Somme offensive, interpreted it as a beginning. People understood that an important turning point had arrived, but they realized that years of fighting might still remain on the horizon. Piecing together information from Canadian casualties, papers were able to relate with reasonable accuracy the position and disposition of Canadian troops. As these men fought and died, Torontonians followed their progress.

Reports of the Somme offensive had to share space with a war effort which pervaded all aspects of life in Toronto. The growth of wartime industry had created a shortage of coal, and wartime economics translated into a steadily increasing cost of living, but local citizens tried to work through their difficulties and cope without disrupting the war effort. Criticism was directed not at the conflict itself, but at the manner in which it was being directed. While an ad hoc approach had suited the climate of a great adventure, a great crusade demanded more organization. Citizens accordingly appealed that government exert a greater influence in war planning. Governments at the federal, provincial, and municipal levels responded hesitantly by helping to organize patriotic drives and to stretch coal resources. Hundreds of local men were dead, and over a thousand others wounded, but support for the war effort did not ebb: it increased. Armed with the knowledge that the fighting would likely continue for years, Toronto was firmly set on continuing the great crusade.

The winter of 1916–17 was one of the coldest in years. All across North America, coal was in short supply. Responding to demands from their constituents, American decision makers placed an embargo on Canadian railroads to ensure that scarce resources were not shipped to Canada. Toronto struggled to cope. The city's coal supply was so limited that a prolonged spell of cold weather would pose a real hardship. Coal dealers in Canada claimed that the only way to rectify the situation was to cut down on passenger service so more attention could be paid to freight transportation. Reacting to reports of a congestion of loaded coal trucks in New York, newspapers speculated that the coal shortage was an artificial creation of American war profiteers who were giving priority to more profitable goods. Calls were again made for the federal government to take over the Ontario lines of the Grand Trunk Railway. Even Conservative papers which had earlier blamed the war for the rising cost of coal, changed their editorial opinion and blamed United States profiteers for artificially raising coal prices. Finally, the Toronto Board of Control decided to apply for legislation authorizing the city to get into the fuel business. A fund of two million dollars was earmarked to cover the cost of 'securing sites for coal-yards, scales, and other equipment.'[54]

In this context of increasing deprivations, Torontonians first learned of a peace offer. On 12 December 1916, Germany called on all belligerents to outline the objectives around which they would be willing to make peace. The Allies rejected the appeal. The press wanted nothing less than total victory. Front page articles denounced the offer and were followed by lengthy editorial condemnations. The most common observation was that the olive branch had been proffered for German home consumption. The Star's editorial on 13 December 1916 was typical in this respect, arguing that 'the offer is just as much a part of Germany's war policy as any offensive she has conducted on any front. The making of this offer is designed to have a great effect in Germany and Austria, where the people cry out against a war that bids fair to abolish the male population. Berlin now gets into position to say peace was sought and refused and that the people must fight on, must still follow their war lords.'[55]

Another prominent argument was that the Germans were seeking peace because they knew they could not win on the battlefield. In addition to arguing that an early armistice would only translate into another war in the near future, the *World* editorialized, 'Now that Germany finds that there is a limit and a climax to the brutal attacks she made on her neighbours, and that for the future she must decrease while they must increase, she is anxious to call a halt.' The *Weekly Sun* offered a simple synopsis: 'Her [Germany's] overtures have been received, here and abroad, by belligerents and neutrals, with marked disfavour.'[56] The proposal itself was short-lived, and by 19 December, newly appointed British prime minister Lloyd George condemned it; the Toronto press praised his actions.

As troops in the trenches struggled to keep warm, on 18 December 1916 President Woodrow Wilson of the United States offered to mediate. He was rebuffed by both sides. In his peace 'note,' Wilson claimed that the aims of the two warring factions were 'virtually the same' and he asked for each side to define them so that a peaceable solution could be found.[57] Both sides bitterly resented the implication that their aims were the same as those of their sworn enemy, and no diplomatic advances were made. The *Star* questioned people on the street and reported that Wilson's proposal 'has met with general and emphatic condemnation in Toronto. The citizen has yet to be found who will speak favourably of the move.' These interviews were conducted in a city which had already given 50,000 men to the Canadian Expeditionary Force, of whom 11,150 had become casualties, with 2,150 dead. Despite the tremendous human costs, the prospect of peace as Wilson defined it prompted editorial writers in both secular and religious papers to vociferously reject his offer. Echoing the opinions of British diplomats and politicians, editorials in the secular and religious press condemned Wilson for failing to see the difference between the Allies and the enemy. One writer called Wilson's move the 'prime joke' of diplomatic history, while another wondered 'whether President Wilson is an intellectual pervert or merely suffering from *cacoethes scribendi* [inadvisable desire to write].'[58]

The majority of Torontonians did not care to sign an early peace. They were dedicated to supporting the war and their men overseas. Beginning in January 1917, the city prepared itself for another patriotic drive, again for the Toronto and York County Patriotic Fund. Reflecting the growing organization that went into wartime activities, preparations were underway well before the 23–6 January campaign. A giant thermometer was set up at the corner of Queen and Yonge, fifty feet high and ten feet wide, to measure the progress of the drive on its way to securing loans of $2.5 million in four days. The papers provided extensive editorial support on the importance of the fund, outlining what it paid for, and charging citizens not to fail the families of fighting men. Once again, advertisements were a regular feature. Their slogan was 'Serve by Giving,' and they often played on the potential insecurities of those left at home: 'You work in a factory. You've got a steady job. Your folks at home get plenty to eat, go to the shows, read the clothing ads, enjoy life – but SUPPOSE YOU were to throw up your job, and go to the front, and SUPPOSE you heard that your women folks were living from hand to mouth; SUPPOSE you heard the kids couldn't go to school because they hadn't boots – *could you fight your best* [emphasis in original]?' Other advertisements were not so subtle. Comparisons were made with the cost to men at the front if they failed in their duty: 'Give – till it hurts! Give so much that you'll have to do without something. Give so much that it'll be a real sacrifice. That will put you in nearly the same class as the man at the front. It isn't charity – It's merely decent duty. And, remember – at the front if a man fails in his duty – HE'S SHOT!'[59]

Organizations all over the city promoted the Patriotic Fund, charging their membership to donate. On 18 January 1917 the Toronto District Labour Council unanimously endorsed the Patriotic campaign, and individual members were urged 'to assist in every way in making the campaign an unqualified success.' Throughout the city prominent men in political, manufacturing, financial, commercial, and labour circles came forward to endorse the fund. President Falconer of the University of Toronto advised his students on the enormity of the project, emphasizing that anything they do at home is 'far short of what is being done by those who give their lives for this cause.' The churches offered their support and ministers from the major denominations praised the fund.[60]

When the campaign opened on 22 January, the City of Toronto donated half a million dollars. The drive was off to a good start, securing $1,256,656 from other sources on the first day. All the advertisements and promotion worked well, and by 24 January the fund was 22 per cent ahead of its 1915 three-day total, reaching $2,138,959. The final tally was well over the 1915 total of $2,302,829, with residents having donated $3,258,972.14, an average of close to ten dollars for every man, woman, and child. The fund had been oversubscribed by more than three-quarters of a million dollars, and Torontonians celebrated their achievement at a giant rally at Massey Hall:

> Toronto has never before seen such a meeting as last night's. For sheer patriotic, selfless, spontaneous, exuberant enthusiasm, but there never has been such another meeting in Toronto. For once Toronto's leading citizens forgot their reserve and self-consciousness. They shouted and sang, they waived their handkerchiefs and cheered. They sang 'Jolly Good Fellow,' whenever they got a chance, and 'God Save the King,' 'Rule Britannia,' 'Keep the Home Fires Burning,' and the doxology at other times. They got on tables and made speeches, and they stood on tables and chairs and other peoples' toes to applaud the speakers. They shouted across the hall at one another; men and women vied with one another in demonstration of good feeling.[61]

The diverse support for Toronto's Patriotic Fund can be inferred from this description of the Massey Hall rally. While civic leaders were in the spotlight, they shared in the patriotic enthusiasm of everyone present. Torontonians of all classes and both genders were united in their determination to support the families of those overseas fighting for the Empire's cause.

It is small wonder then, that Woodrow Wilson's second peace initiative was rejected outright, since news of his proposal arrived in Toronto in the midst of the drive for the Patriotic Fund. In a speech to the United States Senate on 22 January 1917, Wilson called for 'peace without victory,' arguing that both sides should lay down their arms and end their dispute.[62] In the context of the opening day of the Patriotic Fund drive, editorials thoroughly condemned Wilson's speech. Some editorialists dismissed Wilson's speech as 'futile piffle,' while others remarked, 'If this be diplomacy it is malignant; if it be stupidity it is diabolical.'[63]

The war effort continued to demand more. In response, Torontonians pledged ever greater amounts of time and money. The campaign for the Toronto and York County Patriotic Fund demonstrated the willingness of citizens to pledge scarce resources to support the war effort. The methods used to secure these funds built upon previous success, continuing the process of running a more efficient and organized campaign. Even in the midst of coal shortages, rising prices, enormous casualty lists, and the promise of continued warfare, Torontonians increased their contributions.

They also reacted to the offers of peace negotiations in this context. They did not dismiss an early armistice in a cocoon of misinformation and optimism. Residents had to look no further than their kitchen table to see the demands of the war. Meat was not served as often. The warmth of a furnace was something to be celebrated, not taken for granted. Papers continued to print long lists of men who would not return. From this perspective, in this world, most Torontonians refused outright any discussion to cease hostilities. They did so fully understanding that a rejection of peace would mean months, if not years, of fighting. Their level of commitment to the war was so intense that a trade-off was not even considered. They believed that the war effort had to be continued until victory was secured. Anything which fell short of this goal was unacceptable. If there were any individuals who supported the peace proposals, they kept their views to themselves.

The Canadian Corps spent the winter of 1916–17 in a relatively quiet sector of the line, in the Arras front, training to attack the enemy's most prominent position there: Vimy Ridge. The corps was also kept busy integrating reinforcements into units greatly reduced by the Somme fighting. Even though the winter was the coldest in twenty years, the trenches were drier than previously because they now drained into the Zouave Valley. While there was little activity at the front, key events took place at diplomatic and strategic levels. After their peace feelers had been rejected by the Allies, and still suffering from the Allied blockade, Germany began unrestricted submarine warfare on 1 February 1917. Designed to starve Britain into submission, the German plan angered the United States, bringing it into the war on the Allied side on 6 April 1917. On the Eastern Front, the March Revolution overthrew the Tsar, and even though the Russian provisional government continued the war, they could not do so with as much dedication. The November Bolshevik Revolution and the Treaty of Brest–Litovsk which followed removed Russia from the war.[64]

The German stronghold at Vimy Ridge was one of the strongest positions facing the Allies in the spring of 1917. Its slopes commanded the entire sector and were surrounded by supporting trenches. The operation to take the ridge was the first time all four divisions of the Canadian Corps attacked together. Sir Julian Byng meticulously planned the assault, the troops rehearsed in mock battle zones, and artillery, aircraft, and infantry were coordinated. On 9 April, Easter morning, the attack went in, completely overwhelming German front line defenders. Resistance stiffened on the higher ground, but the Canadians continued to advance, taking the 'Pimple,' or the top of the ridge, by 10 April. The Corps established a secure new forward trench by 14 April. It was a great victory. In one day, the Canadian Corps swept forward to a depth of five miles on a four mile front. As further testament to the extraordinary success, the defenders suffered more casualties than the attackers. Victory, however, came at the price of 10,602 Canadian casualties, 3,598 of which were fatal.[65]

News of the triumph at Vimy Ridge was received in Toronto with great acclaim, rivaling the reaction to Second Ypres as the greatest Canadian achievement of the war. Headline after headline announced the advance. The press had learned of the strategic importance of the ridge, thereby adding to the laurels: 'With Vimy Ridge gone, the whole German line covering the French towns and industrial districts to the North, became a wavering one, and any leisurely retreat the Germans may have planned is made uncertain and precarious.'[66] Editorials basked in the glow of victory, and the fact that the performance of Canada's troops had been so notable that the King sent a message of praise.

Despite the accolades, there was some evidence of a growing war weariness on the part of Torontonians. Reflecting this new trend, a *World* editorial condemned the city's failure to celebrate publicly the victory at Vimy Ridge: 'Such military successes as have occurred this week in France would have been hailed in 1914 with such demonstrations, probably, as would have rivaled Mafeking night. Yet in Toronto, where thousands of her sons have gone to battle, and where the news of the capture of Vimy Ridge is the greatest event in local history, there has not been a flag raised to signalize the occasion.'[67]

Casualty reports, as usual, took over a week to begin filtering back to Toronto. The press did its best to allay fears, even as it counted the cost. Nevertheless, secular and religious magazines continued to maintain that the cause was worth the awful price. A *Canadian Baptist* article was typical, outlining a total cost of over 10 million dead or wounded resulting from the war, but still arguing, 'Some things are of more value to humanity than coin in the realm. And human life is outweighed by liberty, truth and righteousness.'[68]

This combination of glory and grief had a profound effect upon the city. Shortly after the first news of Vimy Ridge arrived, a riot took place involving soldiers and 'enemy aliens.' Returned Toronto soldiers heard that a crippled veteran had been insulted by an Austrian employee in a downtown restaurant – and they were determined to seek revenge. Over one hundred overseas men proceeded down Yonge Street between 7:00 and 8:00 p.m., calling any soldiers they passed to join them. The mob leaders entered Child's restaurant where the insult had allegedly taken place and insisted that the Austrian be brought before them. When their demands were ignored, the soldiers ransacked the establishment, overturned tables, smashed crockery, and were only halted when the manager stood on a table waving the Union Jack, pleading with them to stop. In the meantime, a large crowd gathered outside the restaurant, blocking streetcar traffic.

The soldiers' search yielded up one Russian and one Swiss employee, mistaken in the heat of the moment as enemy aliens, who were taken by the men to police headquarters. A mob mentality had taken over, however, and soldiers left Child's restaurant and went to another Yonge Street establishment just above Queen Street 'carrying pandemonium with them,' looking for other enemy aliens. Provost-Marshal Alexander Sinclair ordered the crowd to disperse, but little attention was paid to him. The soldiers continued moving from restaurant to restaurant, seizing alleged enemy aliens as they went. As word of the disturbance spread, Gen. William A. Logie was hurried away from dinner to take charge of the situation. Logie had considerable experience dating back to his pre-war militia days. He was born in Hamilton in 1866 and established a reputation as a distinguished student, eventually being called to the Bar in 1890. While pursuing his academic career, he had developed an interest in the military. He joined in 1883 and rose steadily to the rank of Lieutenant-Colonel in January 1909, after which he gained experience in charge of 15th Infantry Brigade, Western Ontario Command. He continued to perform and to be rewarded during the war, promoted Brigadier-General in September 1915, and Major-General in May 1916. He had been the officer in command of Toronto's Military District since 1 January 1915. He immediately recognized the seriousness of the situation downtown, and he dispatched a picket of fifty men from the 220th Battalion stationed at Exhibition Camp to quell the disturbance.[69]

Once the disorder was under control, military and police officials took turns blaming each other. General Logie argued, 'I think the police should do their part to quell disorder and restore conditions by keeping the general public moving.' Inspector Samuel Dickman of the Toronto police also shrugged off responsibility: 'There was no profane language, no damage was done to property, and no necessity for the police to take action against any civilian. I did not intend to precipitate a riot by giving a wrong order.' Ultimately, enemy aliens were blamed. The next day, Mayor Church sent a message to the Chief of Police: 'Cannot something be done by the commissioners to require the downtown restaurants to file returns showing the number of alien enemies in their employ? A restaurant is no place to employ Austrians and Germans, as their very presence tends to a breach of the peace at times. I think these downtown restaurants should be notified that some action will be taken by the commissioners unless they get rid of these men.' The City Council took action only days later. With unanimous approval, the chamber moved that any enemy alien who used seditious language be deported after the war. In addition, councillors promised to enact legislation barring enemy aliens immigrating to Canada in the future.[70]

Torontonians were intolerant of those whom they perceived to be enemy aliens, but when it came to remembering Second Ypres and celebrating Vimy Ridge, they focused on the soldiers. A memorial service was held in St Paul's Anglican Church, Bloor Street East on 22 April. The service had a twofold purpose, first to honour the brave dead from Second Ypres, and second to offer thanksgiving for the victory of Vimy Ridge, thus embodying both the glory and the grief of Toronto's war effort. Under the auspices of the Great War Veterans' Association, over nine hundred veterans were led by Col. John A. Currie, MP, commander of the famous 15th Battalion which had fought so valiantly at Ypres. Returned soldiers had become a prominent feature in the city since late 1915. In October of that year, City Council had ordered that the Toronto General Hospital reserve space to take care of returned men 'at the expense of the city.' Many of the veterans who marched on this day of remembrance lived at the military hospitals established by the city. In the early days of the war, the resources needed to care for wounded soldiers had been modest. Old Bishop Strachan School on College Street had been refurbished with $1,954 of civic money to serve as a permanent hospital, with a capacity for twenty-five men. The city paid the taxes and insurance. By April 1917, however, the needs of returned men had grown exponentially, prompting City Council to pay $10,000 per year to lease the Toronto General Hospital to the military until two years after the end of the war. Eager to show veterans their thanks, citizens gathered in their thousands to watch these former soldiers march, hobble, and limp to a densely packed St Paul's.[71]

A huge Union Jack decorated the back of the church, while the flags of the Allies hung along the edges of the balcony. The nave was reserved for veterans and representatives of the city regiments, while the public occupied the aisles. Among the dignitaries in attendance were Ontario premier William Hearst, Mayor Church, General Logie, Lieutenant-Governor Sir John Hendrie, N.W. Rowell, and members of City Council. The process of filling the church was slow, as men who had previously attended in prime condition made their wounded way to their seats: 'Empty sleeves, crutches; here a soldier, both of whose legs were gone, and who was carried by his comrades; there one whose sight was partially destroyed, told the tale with silent, sorrowful eloquence.' Once all were seated, and with the early spring sun shining through the windows to rest on the veterans, the service commenced with 'Mendelssohn's Funeral March.' The Reverend Archdeacon Cody conducted the service, led the singing of the national anthem, and stood at attention during the sounding of 'The Last Post.' After the benediction, 'many of the bereaved women dropped into the seats to shed a few quiet tears, before following the veterans into the sunshine of a peaceful Toronto Sunday.'[72] This description was a metaphor for Toronto's war effort; once sacrifice was made and tears shed, those who survived the struggle could exit the cauldron of the Great War into a brighter future.

The demands of the war would continue, however. Shortly after the memorial service, troops that had wintered in Toronto began their departure for 'points East.' On 24 April, two battalions departed Toronto, the 220th and 176th, to be followed by the 208th (Irish) battalion on the 26th. After the exodus, Toronto's Exhibition Camp was virtually empty. Journalists noted that a 'sort of holy calm has descended upon the headquarters of Military District No. 2.'[73] Almost three years of feverish activity had culminated in the despatch of yet another contingent of several thousand troops. This achievement did not, however, mark an end to troops being raised in Toronto. Voluntarism had run its course, but Torontonians were awaiting a federal announcement regarding conscription. After over three years of sacrifice, they believed, it was up to the government to provide the necessary impetus to continue the war.

3

Enlistment and Recruiting: Sending Citizens to War

Enlistment and recruiting were local phenomena; the national experience was of little concern to Toronto recruiting officers. They believed in voluntarism and worked to ensure that local men recognized their duty and went willingly to the front. The way that officers approached recruiting, however, changed over time.

Any examination of enlistment must begin with an assessment of the number of potential recruits available. The population of Toronto in the 1911 Census was 376,538,[1] while the 1921 Census records 521,893[2] residents. In the 1921 Census, the number of men between 19 and 40 was 100,853, or 19.3 per cent of the total population. Applying that same percentage to the 1911 total population yields 72,672 potential recruits. The number available during the war years lies somewhere between these two extremes, the middle point being 86,723. Very little information is available from military sources, but an August 1916 document reinforces this interpretation, listing the total population of Toronto at 470,444, and the total number of eligible men (including those who had gone overseas) at 87,300.[3] Each year of the war, new recruits became available as men turned nineteen, but this rise was largely offset by other men becoming too old to serve.[4] The military figure of 87,300 will be used to place the total number of Toronto volunteers in context.

The enlistment rush characteristic of the opening days of the war continued through September and October 1914. Even as papers carried reports of the British retreat from Mons and opposing sides began to dig the trenches that would be their home for months and years to come, Toronto men rushed to the colours. By the end of September, the Queen's Own Rifles was 200 over its peacetime establishment, the Royal Grenadiers over quota by 150, and the Highlanders were only 200 shy of their maximum despite having supplied a battalion for the First Contingent. In early October, Prime Minister Borden's announcement that a Second Contingent would be required sent a 'patriotic thrill across Canada.'[5] The University of Toronto responded by calling students to join the University Battalion.

These appeals were met by a broad constituency, including more than just Protestant British and Canadian men. Throughout the war, Irish Catholics from both the working and the middle classes came forward just as readily as their Protestant neighbours. Before the voluntary period of enlistment ended, over thirty-five hundred local Catholics joined up, approximately 8 per cent of Toronto's Catholic population. Italian residents also strongly supported the war, demonstrating their patriotic enthusiasm by volunteering, and by taking to the streets in parades where shouts of 'Viva l'Italia, Viva il Canada' rose above the crowd. Ukrainian men also answered the call, even though their status as 'enemy aliens' barred them from service in the Canadian Expeditionary Force. The desire to serve was so strong that many reported Russian ancestry to enlistment officers. By the end of the war, more than seventeen local Ukrainian men had died in service of their adopted country.[6]

When the quotas for the Second Contingent were announced, local regiments were disappointed. Toronto was to supply only 938 of the 16,000 men required, and had over 5,500 men from which to choose. On the first day they were eligible, 200 members of the Royal Grenadiers volunteered for active service even though the regiment could only send 120. The 48th Highlanders encountered a similar rush, with over 275 men volunteering to fill 150 places. Forced to select from this large pool of recruits, officers gave preference to men who had already seen active service. This provided a considerable advantage to men who had served in the British Army. When this criterion still yielded too many recruits, those with the greatest amount of service were enrolled.[7]

Against the backdrop of patriotic enthusiasm and the desire to measure up and be part of the 'great adventure,' men had a decision to make. Would they try to join the CEF? Were they physically strong enough to pass the stringent medical tests?[8] The common thread in these questions was individual choice. Enough men would surely be secured, so it was not a question of the necessity to volunteer. Each man elected to serve the Empire. This public expression of patriotic enthusiasm was the result of hundreds of private decisions, prompted by the needs and aspirations of each individual.

The Canadian army, however, began to show signs of strain as it exploded from a small pre-war militia to a fully fledged overseas infantry division within months. Canadian soldiers suffered through the miserable winter of 1914–15 training on England's Salisbury Plain struggling with inferior Canadian-made equipment until it was discarded and replaced with more serviceable British kit. Historians have argued that Minister of Militia Sam Hughes was at the root of the problem. Even while pressing for an overseas command for himself, he appointed officers on the basis of political, not military, ability. He also awarded contracts to powerful friends, often accepting inferior products for Canadian troops, resulting in boots that virtually dissolved in the squalid conditions of Salisbury Plain where it rained for 89 out of the 123 days the Canadians were stationed there.[9]

Despite the stories of corruption and mismanagement, the Toronto press foresaw no difficulties in securing the required recruits. The real difficulty would be selecting a contingent from the thousands of men clamouring to serve. It would not have been surprising if all the negative stories from Salisbury Plain had prompted a drop in local recruiting. However, when Prime Minister Borden announced in early January 1915 that recruiting would begin immediately for a Third Contingent, militia officers again had the luxury to select only the best volunteers. The entire city was to supply just one battalion, leaving space for 908 new men after surpluses from the previous contingent took the first two hundred places. The ranks were filled in a matter of days.

After the Third Contingent left, there was a lull in recruiting as local officers awaited orders from Ottawa. Events from the battlefield brought home a sense of urgency. The six thousand casualties at Second Ypres at the end of April 1915 affected military personnel as profoundly as it had civilians, and militia units held ceremonies to honour their comrades. The 48th Highlanders took part in the funeral procession for their Captain Darling, and the Queen's Own Rifles held a ceremony on 5 May to honour their fallen, parading 1,166 strong, accompanied by 97 new recruits. Commanding officer Lt.-Col. Arthur Godfrey Peuchen addressed the men regarding the solemnity of the occasion before introducing the regimental chaplain. Standing between two lines of flashing swords held in the hands of the unit's officers, Archdeacon H.J. Cody spoke of having expected losses, but never such an overwhelming blow. He promised, however, that even though 'the great cup of sorrow has been pressed to the lips of our Canadian people we shall strive to drink it with calm courage, with endurance, with self-control.' After a short prayer for the dead, Cody retired, and commanding officer Peuchen gave the order, 'In honour of the dead, present arms!'[10] As the rifles raised, and officers' swords rose, circled and pointed downward, the band began 'The Dead March,' followed by the 'Last Post.'

Official ceremonies like this one and the one for Captain Darling established Second Ypres as a turning point in the war effort. Torontonians had had their first encounter with the demands of modern combat and this experience formed part of their evolving memory of glorious deeds done together. Second Ypres cemented the already strong commitment of Toronto and its citizens to the war effort with the glory and blood of its soldiers and the grief and tears of its citizens. Recruiting was influenced by the scale and scope of the sacrifice because additional men would have to enlist to ensure that the ideals which had prompted this sacrifice were upheld.

Fallen soldiers had to be replaced. Preoccupied with the cost in soldiers and with marking the passing of *Lusitania* victims, militia regiments continued to prepare to meet Ottawa's new call for recruits. Meanwhile, more Canadians fell in action – 2,468 were killed or wounded in a largely diversionary attack at Festubert on 23–4 May 1915. Replacing these escalating casualties would take more men, and on 26 May the Militia Council ordered the mobilization of a Fourth Contingent of ten thousand men. The Toronto Divisional Area was to supply one battalion, the 58th; Lt.-Col. Harry A. Genet, a sixteen-year veteran of Brantford's 38th Dufferin Rifles, was given command. Disappointment was expressed that Toronto could only supply 8 officers and 253 non-commissioned officers and men; it had been hoped that the city would contribute the entire battalion. Even in the face of the dire news from Second Ypres, the numbers called did not reflect the much larger the number of men who wanted to serve.

Filling this call for recruits, however, prompted an innovation that remained a fixture on the streets for months to come: the recruiting sergeant. In late May 1915, the 109th Regiment sent recruiting sergeants marked by red, white, and blue rosettes in their caps out into the streets, drawing volunteers after them to their Armouries at 73 Pearl Street. Even though medical officers turned down many applicants on the basis of physical defects, the ranks were filled quickly. Recruiting passed into a new stage, however, when military officials changed the way they interacted with prospective soldiers. No longer content to announce enlistment details and wait for volunteers to come forward, recruiting officers actively pursued men, making them justify why they were not enlisting, rather than allowing their own consciences to serve as guide. Recruiting drives were taken out of the private and thrust into the public realm.

Recruiting efforts increased considerably after 9 June 1915, when Sam Hughes announced from Montreal that thirty-five thousand more men would be required immediately for the Fourth Contingent. Three new battalions would be raised in Toronto: the 74th, 75th, and 76th. To meet these demands, recruiting became an ongoing process. No longer would recruiting offices be open only long enough to secure enough men for the latest contingent: recruiting continued for the duration.

Before the campaign began, however, there were signs that the city would be required to send even more men. Rural areas surrounding Hamilton and Toronto in Military District No. 2 had failed to meet their numbers, forcing Toronto to fill vacancies left in the 58th Battalion. In the face of such a radical increase in the number of men demanded, officials re-examined the stringent physical requirements for service in the Canadian Expeditionary Force. The first target was the dental standard, which military dentists claimed accounted for the rejection of many men who were otherwise fit.[11] While awaiting reduced standards, however, recruiting shifted into high gear. Plans were put in place to open a central recruiting office at 215 Simcoe Street, the former military headquarters of the district, with Lt.-Col. R.C. Windeyer of the 36th Peel Regiment in command.

For the first time since the war began, there was a noticeable drop in the enthusiasm and the number of men volunteering. The 109th Regiment reported that there was only 'a little more life at the Armouries' in the wake of Sam Hughes's call for thirty-five thousand men. In addition, the Canadian 1st Division suffered the loss of another 366 men killed or wounded at Givenchy-lez-la-Bassée on 15 June. Despite the obvious need, men were not coming forward in sufficient numbers. Recruiting officers knew that Britain had had success with posters, and the Royal Grenadiers experimented with a text-only poster to appeal to local men: 'Canada's New Army for Overseas. Recruits wanted. Apply at once to Royal Grenadiers Orderly Room. Come, boys, do your bit by rallying around the flag of freedom.'[12] This poster was typical of the appeals in the early stage of recruiting. It was at base an announcement of the need for volunteers, and allowed men to make their own decision about whether or not to enlist. Reference was made to the justice of the cause, but there was no overt pressure to join: it was a call to become part of an elite club.

On Dominion Day 1915, recruiting sergeants spread out into the streets, with each militia unit aiming to secure two hundred new men. The results were disappointing. The common obstacles of defective teeth and poor eyesight were compounded by the fact that very few men volunteered. Throughout the city, fewer than thirty recruits were attested. Recruiting sergeants reported that crowds avoided them, and that potential soldiers were defiant when confronted. 'They can get along without us,' was the response of a pair of likely men to a sergeant on Yonge Street. The sergeant explained that their country needed them. 'They won't get us,' came the reply.[13] These men resisted being told their duty, providing evidence that the call of Britain and Empire was not enough to overcome their obligations to self, family, or employers. They were among those who made a personal decision not to enlist and resented the pressure placed on them by the early pleas of recruiting sergeants. It would take something more persuasive than reason to encourage such men to join the colours.

The Royal Grenadiers, however, secured twice as many volunteers as the other regiments; their success was attributed to the use of recruiting posters and active campaigning. Local initiative produced returns, resulting in a dramatic increase in activity, and a new phase of recruiting beginning around 3 July 1915. Rather than pushing men into service directly, recruiting officers now sought to create an atmosphere which promoted service and involved the local population. Returned soldiers spoke at rallies, stressing the need for volunteers. Religious leaders emphasized to their congregations the virtues of signing up. Bands played martial music at street corners to help gather an audience. Militia regiments established recruiting offices downtown: the Mississauga Horse opened a branch at 111 King Street West; the 36th Peel Regiment adapted offices at 1425 Dundas Street and 28 Adelaide Street West; the 12th York Rangers set up at St Paul's Hall, Yonge Street, and at 58 King Street West; and the 48th Highlanders even erected a large tent at the foot of University Avenue to serve as a temporary recruiting office. Gen. William A. Logie, commander of the Toronto Divisional Area, called a meeting of local officers to coordinate efforts. They hoped that the minimum height requirement would be lowered from 5 feet 3 inches to 5 feet 1 inch, and that the chest measurement would be reduced from 33½ to 33 inches. In upcoming campaigns, recruiting posters would play a much more prominent role, along with streamers flown across principal streets.[14]

Another fundamental difference in these new recruiting drives was the target group. Enlistment in Toronto had stalled because earlier drafts had taken either intensely patriotic or unemployed men, leaving behind those who had jobs. Militia officers told reporters that they would now specifically target this previously untapped source of recruits. This new tactic, they hoped, would create a climate in which employed men would come forward. To this end, recruiting officers planned a big parade through the downtown, accompanied by every military band in the city. They solicited the aid of the City of Toronto and were granted the use of City Hall and other public buildings.

Enlistment boomed. The sudden increase in the number and scope of appeals prompted many men to come forward, leading officers to report that their drive was 'crowned with success.' Captain Wandless,[15] recruiting officer of the 36th Regiment, greeted men walking by his station on Adelaide Street West, saying, 'Step inside my boy, the doctor is in there waiting to see you.' His efforts secured roughly 2 per cent of the passing men. Other units scoured the city looking for advantageous locations, the 9th Mississauga Horse selecting the Labour Temple at 167–9 Church Street. With the exception of a small sign tacked up in the poolroom in the basement, there had been no concerted attempts by recruiting officers to use the buildings. Accordingly, the Mississauga Horse left behind a number of officers and men to appeal for volunteers. No longer were the Toronto battalions willing to wait for men to come to them; throughout the city, young men were constantly appealed to by the military.[16]

Men volunteered by the hundreds. Between 3 and 10 July 1915, over one thousand were attested. In the wake of these dramatic increases, regiments continued to experiment with new methods. Capt. D.F. Keith of the Mississauga Horse suggested a special badge be given to those who came forward but failed the medical. Doing so would allow rejected volunteers to avoid the stigma and reproach of failing to serve and would aid recruiting officers in their search for 'shirkers.' A variety of such badges were adopted. The Queen's Own Rifles capitalized on the appeal of the automobile, taking 'gaily decorated cars' down to the Exhibition grounds, securing eleven recruits. The Queen's Own also paraded fourteen hundred officers and men through the downtown. Two battalions marched up University Avenue to College, turned east to Yonge Street, went down Yonge Street to King, turned west onto Bay Street, following it up to Queen Street and then back to the Armouries. Thousands turned out to watch.[17]

The Queen's Own parade was just part of the general move away from individual appeals and towards creating a climate in the city which would encourage young men to volunteer. Officers took advantage of whatever opportunities presented themselves, using a home leave visit by Col. John A. Currie to arrange a patriotic rally on the lawn in front of City Hall. Recruiters correctly assumed that thousands would turn up to see the man who had led the Toronto Highland Battalion (15th) at Second Ypres. The band of the 10th Royal Grenadiers played the anthems of the Allies to the delight of a 'vast crowd.' When Colonel Currie rose to speak, he was greeted by a chorus of cheers. Popular songs were played, and once the martial spirit of the men had been raised, the recruiting sergeants got busy. The clergy also helped the campaign, organizing a Toronto Ministerial Association meeting on 16 July for the specific purpose of taking steps to aid recruiting. It was decided to print a letter for local ministers which stressed the importance of the war and asked them to encourage enlistment from their pulpits. Local labour officials also endorsed recruiting activities, sending representatives to Militia Headquarters to discuss arrangements. Even the Institute of Chartered Accountants of Ontario passed a resolution that 'suggests and urges upon its members as well as their clerks and students that all who are physically fit should at once enlist.'[18]

The high point of this new tactic was General Logie's 20 July monster rally at Massey Hall. Designed to raise the profile of recruiting and to launch the Toronto Recruiting League, the rally promoted the fact that the league had members from many prominent local organizations: the Board of Trade, the Manufacturers' Association, the Trades and Labour Council, the Speakers' Patriotic League, the Canadian Defence League, the City Council, and representative clergy.[19] This new appeal was broadly based and made use of organizations representing the working, middle, and business classes.

Anticipating more people than the four thousand seats at Massey Hall could accommodate, organizers also planned an overflow meeting two blocks away outside City Hall. With a captive audience, over one thousand recruiters would get to work. The actual size of the crowd exceeded even the most optimistic projections. Massey Hall was filled to capacity, men occupying most of the seats on the main floor, while women gathered in the galleries. Soldiers served as ushers. The platform was taken up by the band of the Queen's Own Rifles. Behind them were draped the flags of the British Empire, along with posters that urged men to do their duty and enlist. The program was scheduled to begin at 7:30 p.m., but all available seats were filled well before that time. The rally was so successful that by ten o'clock Lieutenant-Governor Hendrie could announce that ninety-two volunteers had been secured.

To the cheers of the crowd, Provincial Secretary W.J. Hanna declared that future recruiting efforts would be defrayed by a provincial gift of $25,000.

For those not fortunate enough to get a seat in Massey Hall, there was another, larger rally at City Hall. While citizens walked the few blocks south and west, military bands gave concerts at the main downtown corners. An enormous white banner greeted them: 'You said you would go when you were wanted. You are wanted now.' Even before the patriotic speeches began, over twenty men volunteered. Carefully lined up at the east side of the platform, the ranks of the recruits grew steadily, totalling over one hundred and fifty by evening's end. The patriotic spirit of the crowd of fifteen thousand was cultivated by regimental bands stationed on the stone platform in front of City Hall. As each man stepped up to the platform to offer his services, the crowd cheered him along to the nearby recruiting tent. The results shattered all previous records: more than five hundred men had been attested and joined the Canadian Expeditionary Force in one evening. Sir George Foster, MP, recorded in his diary that the 'meeting was a great one.' The whole evening, he noted, 'combined to a climax which will never be forgotten by those who participated ... It will have a great effect on recruiting.' [20]

These giant patriotic rallies marked a remarkable turnaround in recruiting fortunes. When sergeants went after men individually during the first few days in July their efforts were largely unsuccessful. However, when they shifted their focus to creating a climate conducive to enlisting, men volunteered by the thousand. Even with the poor results in the first days of July, by 21 July the city had recruited over 3,000 men. The 9th Mississauga Horse alone managed to raise 1,143 men and a full complement of officers in only three weeks, thereby completing the 75th Overseas Battalion. Success translated into the authorization of another battalion, the 81st, to be filled with surpluses already enlisted for other battalions. Local elites serving in the Recruiting League also got down to business. Toronto Labour representative T.A. Stevenson asked the organization to have a band and parts of military units join in the Labour Day parade 'in order that some of the boys might get enthused enough to join the colours.' [21]

Giant patriotic rallies were now staged all over the city. Enjoying the crest of another successful recruiting wave, new units were authorized as quickly as they could be filled. The latest additions were the 83rd and 84th Overseas Battalions, to be commanded by Lt.-Col. Reginald G. Pellatt and by Lt.-Col. W.T. Stewart of the 109th Regiment, respectively.

To help recruiting officers meet their goals, physical standards were relaxed: the minimum height dropped to 5 feet 2 inches, and a chest measurement of 32½ inches was now acceptable for young, growing men.[22]

Local businesses began to feel the effects of such dramatic recruiting increases. An employee of the Merchant's Bank of Canada, H. Anson Green, wrote to his mother to tell her that the recent campaign had resulted in the enlistment of many bank employees. Green himself tried to enlist, but suffered the same fate as almost 40 per cent of those who volunteered: he was rejected on medical grounds. He had reason to hope, however, as the medical officer informed him that if he had an operation, he would likely qualify. Green underwent surgery, at his own expense, only to be told by his employer that the bank could not afford to lose any more men to the army. Unfortunately, Green's letters do not state the nature of the physical defect which prevented him from being accepted in the first place, nor the nature of the corrective operation. After making a full recovery, he applied for a commission despite the pleas of his manager. Tired of waiting, he enlisted in November 1915 as a private with the University Corps. For all his efforts, Green's military career was relatively short. He was sent overseas in April 1916 and was commissioned a lieutenant in England. He proceeded to France as part of the Royal Canadian Regiment, but was severely wounded soon after his arrival. He recuperated in England and was discharged as medically unfit in 1917.[23]

As Green struggled to find a place in the army, other formations were authorized. In early August 1915, another Highland battalion, the 92nd, was slated to be filled by Toronto and Hamilton men, with the 48th Highlanders assigned to recruit all but one company. Commanded by Capt. George Chisholm, an eighteen-year veteran of the militia unit, the 92nd would serve as a replacement unit for the Highland battalions already in the line. Recruits continued to come forward in significant numbers, filling the ranks of these new units. On 4 August, the medical officer of the Royal Grenadiers passed fifty-three men while his counterpart at the Queen's Own passed another fifty-two.[24]

Even organized labour took part in the big recruiting campaign, demonstrating that support for the war was not just a middle-class phenomenon. The Street Railway Men's Union, and the Builders' Labourers Union, and the Typographical Union were among many unions who continued to retain hundreds of members who had enlisted, 'carrying them at a great financial sacrifice in good standing on their books.'[25]

Organizers on the Labour Day Committee specifically asked the Citizens' Recruiting League to make full and complete use of the Labour Day parade to help stimulate enlistment.

Throughout the city, rallies were organized by the Citizens' Recruiting League. Beginning on 7 August 1915, these efforts became a common sight. One of the first rallies was highlighted by the Queen's Own Rifles band playing at the corner of Logan and Danforth Avenues. The assembled crowd of eight thousand was addressed by Lieutenants Nicholl and Rogers, two men recently back from the front.[26] As always, sergeants were available to escort men to recruiting offices, thirty-three taking advantage of the opportunity.

The largest of these gatherings took place at Riverdale Park on the evening of 9 August 1915. Originally scheduled to mark the anniversary of the declaration of war, the rally was delayed five days because of rain. Once the weather cooperated, Riverdale Park became the scene for the 'vastest and most spectacular patriotic military demonstration which has been held in Canada since the outbreak of war.'[27] Between one and two hundred thousand people lined the natural amphitheatre formed by hills sloping down from Broadview Avenue to the Don River. Looking up from the platform, even the crest of the hill a thousand yards away was filled with people. Several hundred square feet was cordoned off for a tattoo by all the military bands of the city, led by Bandmaster Lieutenant Waldron of the 10th Royal Grenadiers. Boy Scouts acted as torch bearers and behind the platform, hundreds of automobile lights twinkled in the darkness.

Even the process of amassing such a great crowd was not without incident. People began arriving as early as six o'clock; Broadview Avenue and other streets leading to the Park were soon choked with spectators. Unfortunately, the small footbridge over the Don River was not equipped to handle more than a few hundred people at a time. Police officers were on hand to ensure that the sheer weight of the fifty thousand people who passed over it would not overwhelm the bridge's supports. Police constables Fairweather and Townsend, along with Park Constable Butler, managed the other difficulty – the level train crossing of more than four sets of tracks which people had to pass over to get to the rally from the west. Southbound trains advanced unseen from around a curve and, to make matters worse, no one had stopped rail traffic for the occasion. At any given point in time, between four and five hundred people were slowly moving across the tracks. Tragedy almost struck at 8:25 p.m. when an engine backing up from the south, with no headlight visible, bore down on the crowd. There was a very real danger of a panic, with the engine thundering near and the water of the Don River below. A Royal Grenadiers recruiting officer, Private McGowan, averted the tragedy: 'He slipped out without commotion and with the utmost coolness split the crowd in two, crushed it back on each side of the track, and a panic or worse was avoided.'[28] In the interests of safety, McGowan stood watch until he learned that all trains had been notified to slow down.

The tattoo began at 8:00 p.m. with the Queen's Own Rifles Bugle Band sounding 'First Post.' A combined march was conducted by all the bands, followed by the separate marching of each, culminating in a massed concert. Traditional martial songs and hymns were rendered: 'The Maple Leaf,' 'Rule Britannia,' 'O Canada,' 'The Buffs,' 'Tipperary,' 'Boys of the Old Brigade,' 'Soldiers of the King,' 'Onward Christian Soldiers,' 'Oh God, Our Help in Ages Past,' and 'Abide with Me.' Report after report in the papers remarked on the power and poignancy of the thousands of voices joined together in song, particularly during the singing of 'Abide with Me.' Accompanied by the skirling pipes of the 48th Highlanders, fireworks began at half past nine.

The whole extravaganza had been organized to encourage enlistment. A giant electric sign, erected in the centre of the valley, beamed a large coloured Union Jack, over which was printed in lights: 'Your King and Country Need You. Enlist Now.' Organizers had arranged to have speakers address the crowd, but the sheer size of the gathering made that impossible. Mayor Church and Colonel Peuchen were among the dignitaries scheduled to speak, but they were content to watch the ceremony along with the thousands in attendance. Recruiting sergeants found the density of the crowd daunting, restricting their efforts to the immediate area surrounding their tents until the crowd began to disperse. Organizers dubbed the evening a success, securing over four hundred volunteers, and successfully promoting the participation of local residents in recruiting drives.[29]

Recruiting was no longer about personal decisions made by individual men in the comfort of their own homes, according to their own consciences. It was now a public phenomenon, drawing half the city's population to a rally to help promote enlistment. Men now had to justify to themselves as well as to others why they were not in khaki. Sitting with friends or family on the hillside overlooking the rally, watching the military tattoo, and seeing other men cheered as they stepped forward to enlist must have exerted a profound pressure on the men still in civilian clothes. Recruiting was no longer about choosing the best because only a few could go; it was now an ongoing process the goal of which was to fill the ranks as quickly as possible. Gone were the days of private patriotism and the privilege of serving: recruiting was now very publicly about patriotism and duty.

The military continued to seek ways to keep up the momentum, opening the Toronto Recruiting Depot on 16 August 1915. Located in a large new suite of offices at the University Avenue Armouries, the depot allowed new recruits to go through the entire enlistment process in one place, from signing attestation papers to passing final medical exams. A staff of twenty-two men, and one woman, were to handle all the medical exams and paperwork.[30]

Volunteers overwhelmed the staff the first day. Patriotic spirit encouraged by rallies coupled with curiosity prompted seventy-five potential recruits to line up hours before the 9:00 a.m. opening. They buried recruiting officers in application forms, attestation papers, and medical certificates when finally admitted. The demand was so great that two hours after opening, depot officers called for reinforcements, prompting Lieutenant Le Grand Reed to send for another half dozen clerks to assist. The first hurdle for the would-be soldiers was the medical exam, which saw doctors passing judgment on the fitness of volunteers in forty seconds. One-quarter were dismissed for poor eyesight or varicose veins. Other men were rejected because of poor teeth and flat feet. Those who passed the medical filled out insurance forms, attestation papers, and were assigned to a local battalion for training. The frenetic activity continued well past official closing at 10:00 p.m.; it took until 10:30 p.m. to examine each man. By the end of the day over 500 men had volunteered, but only 143 had passed the medical exam and been sworn in as members of the Canadian Expeditionary Force.[31] Recruiting was an increasingly centralized and organized activity. Paralleling the attitude of Torontonians about the need to better organize the war effort, militia officers worked to ensure as efficient a recruiting system as possible.

Recruiting officers were struggling against more than just winning the hearts and minds of potential soldiers. Although the medical standards were relaxed, they still posed an insurmountable barrier to a significant number of men. Successfully passing only 143 out of 500 potential recruits, only 30 per cent, was not atypical. This large body of men who were willing, but unable, to serve with the Canadian Expeditionary Force, has escaped the attention of historians. Typically, for every ten men who volunteered, three or four failed the medical exam, but it was not unusual for six or seven to be rejected. These ratios constitute an important example of the willingness of local men to serve overseas.

Enjoying high levels of success, recruiting officers continued to innovate. Noon hour rallies at City Hall were organized by the Citizens' Recruiting League in cooperation with the T. Eaton and Robert Simpson companies, whose directors agreed to release their men from store duties on 17 August 1915 to attend. A large tent was set up to enlist immediately any men persuaded by the speeches of the Rt. Rev. Bishop James Fielding Sweeney, and Colonel Henry Brock, the chief recruiting officer for Toronto. Innovations also removed previous obstacles to enlistment, the latest casualty being the requirement for a husband to secure the consent of his wife to enlist. The second day at the Recruiting Depot built upon the success of the first, with another 194 soldiers passed for overseas service.[32]

Recruiting continued to proceed at the pace of a battalion per week. Between 1 July and 21 August 1915, the city raised over 7,000 men for overseas service. By 27 August, the Toronto recruiting total for the entire war had risen to over 25,000. Given that at this point in the war there were about 125,000 Canadians under arms, Toronto was providing one out of every five recruits for the Canadian Expeditionary Force. The figure of 25,000 men, however, does not include those who volunteered but failed the medical exam. Given that between 30 and 40 per cent of those who voluteered were rejected, securing 25,000 fit recruits meant that between 35,714 and 41,666 men came forward. Even using the lower number to account for the number of men rejected as medically unfit, in just over one year of the war, more than 40 per cent of the *total* number of eligible Toronto men had volunteered for war: more than one man in every three.[33]

Recruiters continued to take advantage of every opportunity to appeal to young men, and the Toronto Exhibition was the perfect venue. Throughout the fall fair, one recruiting officer and two recruiting sergeants from each militia unit staffed a tent at the south-west section of the grounds. Recruiters also took advantage of the opportunity to march in the annual Labour Day parade, demonstrating the continued support of organized labour for the war effort. The 1915 parade was smaller than in previous years, owing to the sheer number of union men who had joined the army. For those who did march, their ranks were 'shot through with the King's uniforms,' and each local carried a board showing the number of men at the front or working on munitions.

Recruiting dominated the parade. Twenty motor cars were filled with children of working men serving at the front. Many carried banners reading: 'Daddy's at the Front. Why Not You?' 'Daddy Loves His Union and Serves His Empire,' 'Our Daddy's Fighting for Peace and Fair Wages,' and 'Our Daddy Carries a Union Card and a Rifle.' Other appeals to patriotism were plastered on the carriages of the Citizens' Recruiting League. The parade took about an hour and a half to reach the Exhibition grounds, arriving just before noon, having passed an estimated crowd of two hundred thousand. Once again, local battalions benefitted from the enthusiasm, securing another one hundred recruits. To allow for the training of all these new men, City Council granted permission to close University Avenue from 9:00 a.m. until noon and from 2:00 to 5:00 p.m. weekdays so that the thoroughfare could be used for drill purposes.[34]

There were limits, however, to the number of men who could be reached through general patriotic appeals. Even as the 2nd Canadian Division was joining with the famous 1st to form a Canadian Corps on 13 September 1915, it became clear that recruiting numbers were dropping again. It was the end of a summer of bad news for Allied forces, typified by the disastrous Gallipoli campaign. On the Eastern Front, things were little better as the Russian forces teetered on the brink of collapse. The combination of these two factors forced the British into an agreement with the French that the war would be won on the Western Front. A combined assault at Champagne and Artois from late September to early November 1915 advanced the line but little. The casualties of this offensive included an administrative one; the directors of the war effort fired British Commander in Chief Sir John French and replaced him with Sir Douglas Haig.

Despite the bad news, enlistment had boomed in Toronto up to the middle of September. The news from the front provided the backdrop for recruiting, but did not exert as great an influence as the successful campaign to promote a climate that would persuade men to come forward. When they did enlist, men did so knowing that the deadlock at the front was now over a year old. As with any recruiting campaign, however, there were limits to the number of men willing to come forward. By the middle of September, the numbers began to drop and recruiting officers searched for new ways to re-energize their tactics. During July and August daily totals had been measured in the four to five hundred range; in September and October daily totals rarely broke the one hundred mark.

Concerned about the decline, General Logie called a meeting of prominent recruiting officers, Colonel Brock, Major Le Grand Reed, and the commanding officers of the city regiments to discuss the situation. They decided to further systematize their efforts. At the start of October, the city was divided into thirty-two 'posts' chosen from the most populated sections of town. Each militia regiment contributed four recruiting sergeants to be moved each day to a different post, thereby covering the entire city and allowing each regiment equal access. Once a man enlisted, he would immediately be taken down to the Central Recruiting Depot for examination so that 'an applicant will not have a chance to forget or change his mind about reporting at the central Depot.'[35]

Despite the new system, recruits did not come forward as they had done in July and August. Further innovations followed, including appealing to men at picture shows. Proprietors granted military personnel the use of their property on Sunday nights, free of charge, to hold rallies.[36] Recruiting still did not pick up. It was at this point in late October 1915 that Sam Hughes announced a new scheme for attracting volunteers. Modeled after Lord Derby's British plan, Hughes authorized the creation of individual battalions to be raised by prominent locals. Although the minimum number required was only twenty-five men, Hughes authorized whole battalions this way throughout the Dominion. The rationale was that locally appointed lieutenant-colonels chosen from among prominent residents could appeal to their communities in a more personal way, thereby re-energizing recruiting. This increase was necessary to meet the new ceiling on the maximum size of the CEF: 250,000 men.

For Toronto, the new scheme meant six new battalions. The Queen's Own Rifles, the 10th Royal Grenadiers, the 36th Peel, the 48th Highlanders, and the 109th Regiment were responsible for raising one battalion each. The Governor General's Body Guard and the 9th Mississauga Horse, two cavalry units, would unite to organize a sixth battalion of infantry. Militia officers, however, were conscious of the difficulty of having several battalions compete for recruits. To avoid that problem, General Logie and recruiting officers decided to raise one battalion at a time, with all militia units working together. After securing the necessary complement of men for Lt.-Col. R.K. Barker's 95th Battalion, authorized on 2 November, Col. W.B. Kingsmill of the 10th Royal Grenadiers would raise the next one, the 123rd. The new method increased the number of volunteers. Local men now had the opportunity to serve under a commanding officer they knew, and they could choose the battalion and the men with whom they wished to enlist. For thousands of Torontonians this incentive was enough to prompt them to offer themselves for service.[37]

As volunteers filled the ranks, officers capitalized on the return of thousands of soldiers from summer training at Niagara Camp to stimulate recruiting. Hoping that the sight of old friends in khaki would encourage others to come forward, recruiting officers planned an enormous twelve-mile military march through the streets.[38] Beginning at the Exhibition grounds, over ten thousand soldiers marched north up the slight rise of Dufferin Street to King Street, passing block after block of two-storey townhouses. Units then turned right onto King Street and proceeded down a slight grade towards the downtown, passing St Andrew's Presbyterian Church at King and Simcoe and the massive St James' Anglican Cathedral at King and Church. At Jarvis Street, the parade swung north, uphill and away from the lake, passing St Michael's Cathedral at Shuter Street. At Wellesley Street the battalions marched west and proceeded towards Queen's Park before heading down University Avenue to Queen Street, west back over to Dufferin and south to Exhibition Camp. Accompanied by no fewer than sixteen military bands, the soldiers marched with all their war equipment, including field kitchens, ambulances, transports, and the big gun carriages of the field artillery. The troops were reviewed from a saluting base in front of the Parliament Buildings at Queen's Park by Sir Sam Hughes, Ontario premier William Howard Hearst, Mayor Tommy Church, and other prominent citizens. Crowds began to gather two hours before the parade arrived at Queen's Park; young citizens climbed monuments or sat on the window sills of the Legislative Building to get a better look. As always, recruiting took centre stage. Motor vehicles in the parade carried signs, 'Your King and Country Need You. Step on Board.' By the time these mobile depots arrived at Queen's Park, they were filled with young volunteers waving to the cheering crowd.

As a testament to the importance of the event, the Board of Education gave its students a half holiday, while business was practically suspended altogether. The whole parade route was decorated with flags hanging from homes, offices, and businesses. Automobiles, too, were outfitted with Union Jacks, and men, women, and children carried miniature flags. People arrived in crowded street cars, hanging off side rails, cheering. Every time the parade stopped, the populace roared and showered the soldiers with gifts of 'sweet meats,' cigarettes, and tobacco. Keeping with the spirit of the occasion, officers 'gazed solemnly in another direction' while troops gathered their prizes. Practically the whole city saw the march, citizens crowding six or seven deep over the entire route, while others sought better vantage points from roof-tops, trees, and the roofs of automobiles. With the sheer number of flags, 'the avenues of humanity made a veritable Union Jack through which the soldier boys passed.'[39]

The military was taking advantage of the two most important elements of Sam Hughes's recruiting scheme: familiarity and peer pressure. Not only would prospective recruits know who their commanding officer would be, but they had the chance to volunteer with colleagues and be initiated to the rigours of military life surrounded by friends. In addition, men still in civilian clothes had to watch parades such as this one and witness the praise accorded to servicemen. Seeing old friends or classmates parading to the cheers of tens of thousands must have caused many men to further question their decision to stay at home. Surely the whole city must be correct, they might have reasoned, in its support of those heading overseas; after all, even in a wartime economy business had been all but halted out of respect for them. The pressure to join must have been enormous.

The combination of the parade and the new recruiting scheme prompted another rush at the Central Recruiting Depot. The depot had its best day yet, successfully enrolling 172 men. For the three days after the parade, the daily average for recruits once again exceeded 100. The 95th Battalion quickly came up to strength. By 10 November, just eight days after being authorized, its complement was up to 825. Each day the battalion marched through the streets, drumming up support and appealing to men it passed to join: it took less than two weeks to fill its ranks. It was then the turn of Lt.-Col. W.B. Kingsmill and the Royal Grenadiers to move to centre stage and recruit the 123rd. Their first day broke all previous records: 204 attested out of the 345 who offered, one-third being refused for medical reasons. Recruiting officers were securing in one or two days the number of volunteers that had taken a week in October. To further stimulate enlistment, arrangements were made to hold meetings in city churches following regular services.[40]

During the winter, Major Le Grand Reed asked that route marches be planned through the downtown, instead of sending battalions into rural areas. This measure, he hoped, would remind civilians of their duty to enlist. Lieutenant-Colonel Kingsmill used a much more direct approach. Beginning in December, those already serving in the 123rd Battalion instituted a city-wide campaign to appeal to men directly in their homes. 'Flying squadrons of soldiers' were also sent to factory districts to interview men at their desks and workbenches. Each soldier was equipped with patriotic tracts to serve as reminders even after they had gone. To ensure that no man could plead ignorance of the 123rd's campaign, over five thousand postcards were mailed to likely prospects. Kingsmill promised that 'the young men will be approached at meetings, in the restaurants, at work and at play.' He also sent letters to each of the eighteen hundred men who had previously volunteered for service, but had been rejected because of poor eyesight. The circulars informed these men that guidelines had been relaxed considerably, and urged them to offer themselves once again.[41]

On the first official day for recruiting by the 123rd Battalion, 6 December 1915, the Recruiting Depot set another record, enlisting 216 men. To keep up momentum, recruiting officers conducted a military census in the downtown, asking store and factory managers how many men they could spare. At restaurants, officers placed recruiting literature on each seat, and passed circulars to every man attending a picture show. As soon as they volunteered, new recruits were arranged in line, and paraded through the downtown streets carrying a banner that proclaimed, 'We Have Joined; Why Not You?' Even the Boy Scouts were used to help distribute handbills from house to house, which read:

(1) If you are physically fit and between 19 in 40 years of age, are you really satisfied with what you are doing to-day?

(2) Do you feel happy as you walk along the streets and see other men wearing the King's uniform?

(3) Do you realize that you have to live with yourself for the rest of your life? 'Gee! And have to look at yourself in the looking-glass every time you shave, too.'

(4) If you are lucky enough to have children do you think it is fair to them not to go unless you are going to leave them hungry?

(5) What would happen to Canada if every man stayed at home?

Your King and Kitchener and 100,000 more Canadians at the front are calling you.

These circulars played on the insecurities of the remaining young men by making volunteering a cure-all for a host of doubts. Volunteering would provide job satisfaction, a sense of purpose, the self-confidence needed to look oneself and one's children in the eye, and a place in the great struggle of the Empire: heady stuff, and evidently very appealing.

The first Saturday of the 123rd Battalion's campaign provided a great opportunity to appeal to downtown crowds. While one half of the Royal Grenadiers' home service regiment paraded, the remaining Grenadiers and the 123rd men patrolled the streets making personal appeals to every man not in uniform. In just one week, the 123rd had secured 712 volunteers, over 400 additional men having been rejected for medical reasons. General Logie, District Commander, wrote to Sam Hughes, confirming for him what military officers had known for months: 'the fact remains that a personal appeal must be made to individuals who may be wavering as to whether they will join or not.'[42] Even with these efforts, more than one-third of those who volunteered were denied the chance to serve because they failed to meet the medical standards.

This new style of recruiting, however, cost money. Lieutenant-Colonel Kingsmill spent his entire budget for the recruiting of the 123rd Battalion in one week. Once those resources were exhausted, Kingsmill made public appeals through the press for more money: 'I cannot organize a battalion and carry on a recruiting campaign at the same time without funds, so I have decided to call in all my men who have been engaged in recruiting work, and they will start to drill instead.'[43]

Without the strenuous campaigning of the 123rd Battalion, enlistment numbers dropped immediately. On 14 December only eighty-seven volunteers were attested, compared with 123 the previous week. Recruiting officers once again met to discuss strategies, debating the merits of a gradual return to competition between battalions. They believed that this approach would dissuade local militia regiments from discouraging their members to join overseas units organized by other battalions. In the meantime, recruiting continued for the 123rd Battalion, newly energized by a $1,000 donation from the Sportsmen's Patriotic Association. Numbers immediately improved, owing to the renewed presence of the 123rd on city streets.[44]

At a further meeting, recruiting officers decided to reintroduce competition beginning 15 January 1916. This decision was made after careful consideration. The confusion of having several battalions recruit at once was deemed acceptable if it was accompanied by an increase in volunteers. Once the 123rd had completed its establishment, Lt.-Col. Vaux Chadwick could begin recruiting the 124th Battalion, which was the combined responsibility of the 9th Mississauga Horse and the Governor-General's Body Guard. Chadwick would have until 15 January, then the 48th Highlanders and Queen's Own Rifles would begin recruiting their overseas battalions, followed by the 109th Battalion on 25 January.

Kingsmill, however, was having difficulty getting men to enlist just before Christmas because they wanted to be at home for the holiday.[45] Confident that he would ultimately succeed, however, he allowed Chadwick to begin recruiting the 124th Battalion on 22 December.

Chadwick's campaign had a different emphasis than did Kingsmill's. While the latter directed a street-by-street sweep to promote enlistment, Chadwick simply advertised that friends could serve alongside each other. Dubbing his battalion the 'Pals Battalion,' Chadwick asked friends to enlist together. After a lull during Christmas, men rushed to join the 124th Battalion, several hundred enlisting on 27 December. Even without much advertising, the men came forward. On 28 December sixty-four men volunteered for the 124th Battalion, while only eight men signed on with the 123rd, now up to one thousand one hundred.[46]

At the front, events guaranteed that still more men would be needed. As soldiers suffered through a cold and wet Flanders winter, word was received on Christmas Day 1915 to prepare for the arrival of the 3rd Canadian Division. Canadians now had three times as many men at the front than during Second Ypres, with the consequent potential for much higher casualties. The ceiling of the CEF was also increased. In his 1916 New Year's address, Prime Minister Borden announced that the authorized strength of the CEF was to be raised to 500,000 men, just two and a half months since 250,000 had been set as the goal. Whether or not Borden was using this gesture as a lever to increase Canada's voice in Imperial affairs remains subject to debate.[47] For Toronto, as for the rest of the country, it meant recruiting would have to be increased. Local minister S.D. Chown wrote to Borden to commend him on his decision to increase the allotment and to promise that he could 'depend on the Methodist church contributing its full share of recruits until the victorious end.' Toronto MP George Foster also wrote to congratulate Borden on his 'support of our forward movement in the defence of the Empire.'[48]

Lieutenant-Colonel Chadwick's 124th Battalion appeared up to the task, recruiting half its complement in one week. The honeymoon for the 124th continued in the first days of 1916, as it regularly secured more than one hundred men a day. At the Recruiting Depot totals were at record levels, consistently exceeding two hundred. The police attempted to help the process by conducting their own military census of available recruits. Some business leaders, however, were unwilling to cooperate, arguing that recruiting efforts should be directed at those men without employment before drawing even more men from the workforce. Cards left at the T. Eaton Company were accepted, but Sir

John Eaton made no promises that they would be distributed. 'We have sent approximately 1,400 men to the front from this store,' Eaton argued, 'and while I am not prepared to say that we will not have a census taken among our employees, I believe that it should be taken at the homes.' Similar objections were made by other employers throughout the city. Chief Constable Henry James Grasett defended the choice of recruiting at businesses, maintaining that a house-to-house canvass to distribute forty thousand cards would be too time consuming. The police census was dubbed a farce, with only 30 per cent of the forms being completed, even fewer having been properly filled out. In citing their reasons for not enlisting, many men were quite candid, replying 'Safety First' and 'It's dangerous.' Others referred to family obligations and the fact that there were still plenty of single men available. Police officials blamed the press for criticizing the campaign and for publicizing the fact that it was strictly voluntary.[49]

The response to the police census, however, illuminates the thoughts of men on the war effort. Their reasons for staying behind clearly demonstrate that they understood the nature of the fighting, no doubt aided by the graphic letters published in the papers. Enlisting meant a real chance of being killed or wounded. Men also understood that the war would be a long one, and that if they enlisted it would have a significant impact on the lives of their families left behind. High enlistment totals were not an expression of the ignorance of volunteers but the result of the skill and persuasiveness of local recruiting officers who presented the call for men in a way which stressed the importance of the war effort over and above the demands of safety and family.

Despite the known dangers, the message continued to get through in January 1916: recruiting record after recruiting record was shattered. At the forefront of this drive was the 124th Battalion, growing to 736 men in only nine days. Another massive parade of 13,000 soldiers wound its way through the downtown on 7 January. The week ended with the largest recruiting total for one week ever, over 1,200 offering and 844 being accepted. Once again, for every two men taken into the CEF, another man was refused for medical reasons. Just two days later, the Pals Battalion (124th) was complete, having secured its 1,200 men in two weeks.[50]

As a result, recruiting for the new Queen's Own Rifles and 48th Highlander Battalions was moved up to 12 January. Lt.-Col. Duncan Donald of the 48th Highlanders was responsible for the 134th Battalion, while his Queen's Own Rifles counterpart, Lt.-Col. R.C. Levesconte, raised the 166th Battalion. Buoyed by the success of the 95th and 123rd Battalions, new units continued to use innovative methods to secure recruits. The 48th Highlanders hung giant posters throughout the downtown. At the end of the first day of recruiting, the Highlanders and Queen's Own Rifles were in a dead heat, each securing fifty men. Recruiting successes, however, brought with them new problems. During the winter months, there were not enough buildings to accommodate the new battalions. Various suggestions were made to rectify the situation, the most common being to rent space in unused factories, particularly the Conboy Carriage Factory on the Don River near Queen Street East, and the Crown Stopper Company Factory at King and Parliament Streets.[51]

While these proposals were debated, City Council took action. Military officials accompanied Mayor Church and members of the Board of Education to examine the newly constructed School of Commerce on Shaw Street as a potential barracks. The board decided later that afternoon to open the building to the 123rd Battalion, with the proviso 'that the building shall be returned to the Board in proper condition.'[52] Recruiting officers also extended their pleas to include appeals to manufacturers to release men for service. At a meeting of the Board of Trade, General Logie requested permission for recruiting sergeants to address employees during working hours for ten minutes. He also asked that employers guarantee the positions of men who enlisted until their return. Most employers did so.

In the midst of all this activity, a grand military review before the Governor General the Duke of Connaught and his family took place on a cold 17 January 1916. The Duke inspected 10,000 Toronto troops at Queen's Park and University Avenue. The day after this event, a record number of 247 men were attested.[53] These men were needed to help reinforce the 3rd and 4th Canadian Divisions that Prime Minister Borden had authorized. By late December 1915, the 3rd Canadian Division had been formed and moved to France. The 4th Division spent the early part of 1916 organizing, eventually moving into the line in April 1916. Canada now had four times as many men at the front as they had during Second Ypres, and the continued 'wastage' at the front made ever-increasing demands on recruiting at home.

As the demand for men increased, the scope of recruiting drives continued to expand. The newly authorized 169th Overseas Battalion, raised by Lt.-Col. J.G. Wright of the 109th Regiment, appealed for recruits during regular Sunday church services. In thirty-six churches and twelve Bible classes of various denominations, recruiting sergeants spoke directly to congregations. One hundred and thirteen men volunteered as a result. They were quickly ushered out into motor cars waiting to take them to recruiting headquarters. Another major innovation was to recruit methodically in places of business. Officers of the 169th had been given permission by the Canadian Manufacturers' Association to appeal directly to employees at local companies. On the first day, recruiting officers visited Nielsen's Limited, Langmuir Manufacturing Company, and WR Johnson Company. The result was the largest recruiting day since the first day of war, 544 men offering themselves for service. Officers further planned to speak to men at three large warehouses or factories each day for over a week. By mid-week, over 1,000 had offered to join, 197 on Wednesday alone. At the end of this most successful week of recruiting in the war, 1,257 men were attested out of the almost 2,000 who volunteered for service. Recruiting officers for the 169th Battalion even stopped a dance at the Pavlova Dancing Academy at 212 Cowan Avenue on Saturday night, addressing about 200 'young male fairies' and inviting them to leave the revelry and enlist.[54]

Additional units were authorized and entered the recruiting arena immediately. Provincial Crown Attorney Richard H. Greer was given command of the 180th Overseas Battalion, named the 'Sportsmen's Battalion.' Greer, now a Lieutenant-Colonel, entered the recruiting ring in late January, advocating a strategy similar to the one used so successfully by Chadwick's 124th Battalion. He appealed to sporting associations, asking men to take advantage of the opportunity to serve with former teammates. In this way Greer enlisted many Toronto athletes of national and international quality. The high calibre of his recruits translated into above average showings by the 180th in inter-battalion sporting competitions.[55]

January 1916 proved to be the best month for recruiting in the war. The weekly totals climbed from 628 in the first week, to 790, 840, and 1,257 in subsequent weeks. The grand total for January alone more than doubled those for November and December combined. And still the momentum continued, thanks in large part to the appeals made by the 109th to the employees of Toronto's biggest firms. The Ford Motor Company at 106–10 Richmond Street West, Gunn's Limited at 25 Toronto Street, Gunday Clapperton and Company at 61 Albert Street, and the Swift Canadian Company at St Clair and Keele, all closed down their works so that recruiting officers could address their employees. At Ford, of the 90 men gathered to listen to appeals, 8 offered to enlist even though they were paid an average salary of $1,200, almost three times that of an enlisted man.[56]

Unit after unit was authorized. Lieutenant-Colonel Le Grand Reed was given command of the 170th Battalion, to be raised under the auspices of the 9th Mississauga Horse. The former editor of the *Canadian Courier*, Capt. John A. Cooper, was given the provisional command of another battalion, the 186th. Lt.-Col. E.W. Hagarty, principal of Harbord Street Collegiate, proposed to call his 201st Battalion the 'Toronto Light Infantry,' referring not to its equipment but to its temperate character. Also entering the competition was the 204th Overseas Battalion, to be commanded by W.H. Price, MPP for Parkdale. Preliminary discussions were conducted on the possibility of organizing a Bantam battalion, to be made up of men who failed to meet the minimum height requirements. In addition, the 208th Battalion was authorized, also called the Irish Fusiliers.[57] By the middle of February, nine overseas battalions were competing with one another for recruits in Toronto, and only three were anywhere near full strength: the 134th (Highlanders), the 166th (Queen's Own Rifles), and the 169th (109th Regiment).

Innovations continued, however, and men were found to fill the ranks. Lieutenant-Colonel Greer held a rally at Massey Hall for his Sportsmen's Battalion that began with boxing matches, wrestling, and bayonet contests. After the festivities, Greer spoke to the assembly, concluding with an appeal for volunteers. As the first men came forward, other recruiting officers shouted at the audience for reinforcements. When it was all over, 325 responded to the call, forming the basis of another daily record total of 574 men. Despite the success, there was concern about the high level of competition between units. The chief recruiting officers and officers commanding newly authorized battalions decided to restrict competition by giving the 180th (Sportsmen's) and 170th (9th Mississauga Horse) Battalions exclusive rights to recruit until 7 March. It was expected that these units would be complete no later than 14 March, at which point the 201st (Light Infantry), the 204th, and the 208th (Irish Fusiliers) would enter the arena together. The other unit seeking recruits was Lt.-Col. F.L. Burton's 216th Bantam Battalion, which recruited throughout the period since it could only accept men too short for service in the other units.[58] These efforts continued strongly through to the end of February 1916, with daily totals regularly approaching the two hundred mark.

This enlistment boom continued amidst gloomy news from the front. The Germans attacked at Verdun on 21 February 1916, and the papers were soon filled with tales of hundreds of thousands of German and French casualties. Toronto, however, had every reason to be proud of its contribution. The full scale of the winter's recruiting was displayed to its citizens in a massive parade of local soldiers on 1 March 1916 to mark a visit by Sam Hughes. Described by papers as the 'greatest military parade in the history of Canada,' eighteen thousand men marched twelve miles through the downtown on a clear winter day. With Hughes at the front, followed closely by the senior 74th and 75th Battalions, the parade left Exhibition Camp at one o'clock. When the column reached Queen's Park, Hughes dismounted and took his place on the reviewing stand. It took almost an hour and a half for the five-mile stream of khaki to pass. Accompanying each unit was one of thirty-one bugle, pipe, trumpet, and fife bands. New recruits, still in civvies, marched alongside the soldiers.

A half-holiday had been granted to practically the entire business section of the city and tens of thousands lined the parade route. Even after months of feverish recruiting activity, Torontonians continued to take a keen interest in the success of their city's efforts and in the need to reinforce their loved ones already at the front. Over three hundred policemen were assigned to keep the crowds back, four being stationed at almost every intersection. Some children clung to their parents' shoulders for a better view while others availed themselves of vantage points from store windows, houses, and factories. One of the most remarkable sights was the passing of four artillery batteries complete with their full complement of 16-pounder and 12-pounder quick-firing artillery pieces. Each time the parade stopped and soldiers were ordered to 'stand easy,' spectators showered them with cigarettes, chewing gum, and candy kisses while the troops responded with cheers and camp songs. The crowd got considerable amusement out of an incident at the corner of King and Yonge Streets. One of the men from 48th Battery was 'carrying on' with several young ladies watching from a second story window when he was thrown from his gun carriage seat as the carriage bounced over the streetcar tracks.[59]

Recruiting continued well in the wake of the giant parade. Overseas, on 2 March 1916, Britain imposed conscription to reinforce its troops already at the front.[60] In Toronto, innovations continued in an attempt to keep up voluntary enlistment, including rewarding soldiers if they successfully recruited a friend. The 95th Battalion, short sixty men lost through attrition during training, unleashed its men on the city, promising an extra day's leave to any man who brought forward a recruit: seventy-eight were secured.[61] By 14 March, the 134th (Highlander) Battalion was full, and the 180th (Sportsmen's) and the 166th (Queen's

Own Rifles) had 1,051 and 1,048 men respectively. With those units almost complete, recruiting officially began for Lt.-Col. W.H. Price's 204th Battalion, headquartered at 155 Richmond Street West. Upon joining, each man in the unit signed a pledge to secure another. Circulars were also given out to residents asking them to find a recruit before 1 May 1916. Price believed that personal appeals would go farther than patriotic demonstrations, so he attempted to turn every citizen into a recruiting agent. He asked that each person in a position to appeal to a man to enlist should do so, be it at the dinner table, the church meeting, or the union hall. Price's campaign was another example of the ever-expanding scope of recruiting drives that attempted to touch the nerve that would prompt men to take the final step and enlist.

Other units tried different methods. After setting up headquarters at 13 Queen Street East, Lieutenant-Colonel Hagarty began recruiting for his 201st Toronto Light Infantry, hoping that the temperate character of his unit (and its hard line against members consuming alcohol) would attract many of the better-educated of the younger generation. Another MPP, Lt.-Col. T. Herbert Lennox, began recruiting for his 208th Irish Fusiliers, supervising events from his offices in the Stair Building at the corner of Bay and Adelaide Streets. Lennox began recruiting on St. Patrick's Day, and signalled the beginning of the campaign by having each factory whistle in the city sound at 10:00 a.m.[63] As had been the case with previous recruiting booms, the success of this latest one also began to fade as the number of men moved by its style was exhausted. Despite the publicity accorded each of the battalions in the middle of March, daily totals were now consistently under the one hundred mark, producing weekly totals around six hundred, lower than the weakest recruiting week in January.

Sam Hughes's battalion scheme, however, had re-energized recruiting. Instead of ministers preaching the virtues of the Allied cause, officers appealed directly to congregations. Rather than accosting men in small groups, recruiting agents spoke to hundreds at their workplaces. Battalion commanders used 'niche marketing techniques' to secure volunteers, appealing to friends, teammates, or temperance advocates to enlist together. This recruiting phase was focused around public appeals, public rallies, public parades and celebrations, and public pressure. Local initiative was supported by a continuous supply of money for recruiting purposes. When the money dried up, however, as was the case with the Sportsmen's Battalion, enlistment slowed. The dwindling numbers at the end of March and into April prompted a switch once

again in the sphere in which recruiting was conducted. Up until this
point in the war, men could take refuge from recruiting campaigns in
the privacy of their own homes. That would soon change as recruiting
officers continued to expand their tactics to target men not only at work
and at play, but at home.

These personal recruiting attempts took place against the backdrop
of renewed Canadian activity at the front. On 27 March, near St Eloi,
the British exploded six giant mines under the German lines, hoping to
pour troops into the breach. Unfortunately, the gaps were quickly filled
and the fighting focused instead around newly created craters, around
17 metres deep and 60 metres across. German artillery had a clear view
of Canadian positions, resulting in terrible carnage. The fighting continued until 16 April, costing over one thousand Canadian casualties.

While Canadian soldiers struggled under German artillery at St Eloi,
recruiting efforts in Toronto relied increasingly on individual appeals
directed at men in their homes. In early April the 204th Battalion sent
recruiting sergeants to visit every resident in the East End to allow each
man to have the 'opportunity' to tell them just why he thought he
should not be in khaki. The canvassing process was painstaking, but
general appeals made in a climate of patriotic enthusiasm were no
longer effective. Recruiting officers surveyed Enderby Road and discovered there were eight eligible men living there. Similar surveys revealed
there were thirteen men on Main Street East, three on Lyall Avenue,
one on Kimberly Avenue, and so on.

The Bantam Battalion also reached out directly, believing that recruiting had reached the point where only 'the direct personal appeal brings
results.' The unit arranged for a house-to-house canvass in the section of
the city bounded by Queen, Bloor, Yonge, and Sherbourne Streets.
Only three recruits were secured, along with eight hundred names of
men who could be approached later. The Bantam's personal expedition
revealed why recruiting was dropping: 'the canvass along All Street
reveals the fact that, with the exception of two or three houses, every
house on this Street has given at least one man for active service, and
throughout the entire evening it was the rule rather than the exception
to find that one or all of the eligible men in house after house had
already enlisted.'[64]

There could be no doubting the efforts of local recruiting officers to
secure volunteers. Lieutenant R.V. Jones wrote to W.H. Price, commander of the 204th Battalion, to inform him of a confrontation which
had taken place involving a recruiting officer and a prospective soldier:

Pte. James Brown stopped Mr. Drummond and in a polite and unoffend-
ing way asked if he had any desire to sign up to-day, at the same time laying
his hand on Mr. Drummond's arm. Mr. Drummond attempted to walk on
but Brown persisted and again asked him if he would care to join up to-day,
and for some apparent and unknown reason [Mr. Drummond] lost his
temper and made a remark, 'To Hell with all of you,' and again attempted
to proceed along his way, but Brown held onto his coat and Mr. Drummond in an effort to tear himself loose tore a button off his coat. Brown
picked up the button and offered it to Mr. Drummond, but he [Mr. Drum-
mond] was still offensive in his manner and language and Brown said, 'I'll
just keep this button now seeing that you are so fresh.' Now I would point
out that Mr. Drummond is a young fellow not over 25 years and he appears
to be physically fit and eligible and he has not at any time offered a good
reason for not enlisting, nor has he shown the recruiters a rejection slip. I
am of the opinion that Mr. Drummond owes to and should offer an apol-
ogy to Pte. Jas. Brown for his nasty insulting remarks.[65]

The letter reveals much of the climate of Toronto for the young men
still resisting the call to serve. The aggressor, Pte. James Brown, was
excused, while Mr. Drummond's lack of patriotism was blamed for the
entire incident.

Toronto papers recorded that 25,000 men had left the city by August
1915. Between August 1915 and March 1916, another nine battalions of
infantry were filled, adding a further 10,800. The resulting total of
35,800 men does not include those who volunteered for artillery batteries, pioneer or construction battalions, or the Royal Flying Corps. Nor
does it include men essential to war industry who could not leave their
jobs, nor those unable to reach the minimum height or physical standards who never attempted to enlist. In addition, it must be remembered that the number of men who came forward was usually one-third
higher than the number accepted, meaning that some 53,700 had to
volunteer just to fill the infantry positions, let alone the ancillary places.
Comparing this number with the 87,300 eligible men provides a tremendous record of achievement for Toronto recruiters: more than 60 per
cent of the eligible men had volunteered. Rather than demonstrating
that their patriotic enthusiasm of Toronto's men had run out, recruiting officers were discovering that their appeals had been so successful
that there were very few men left to recruit. Recruiting officers were
fighting, not the recalcitrance of local men, but their own previous success in calling men to the colours.

With the arrival of spring, the battalions quartered in the city for the winter prepared to leave, either for the front or for further training at Niagara Camp. To keep recruiting at the forefront of life, there was one final mass public ceremony involving men recruited over the past year and a half. The largest divine service ever staged in a Canadian city was held on 1 May 1916 at Queen's Park for the more than eighteen thousand men leaving for the front. The day dawned bright and crisp, the early spring growth just beginning to emerge on the trees in the park. Troops filed in between 9:15 and 9:30 a.m., each unit having taken a different route. On the streets through which the units advanced, crowds had congregated, particularly on University Avenue. There was a sharp divide between civilian and soldier, the dull khaki tones of the soliders standing in stark contrast to the Sunday best of the civilians. An estimated crowd of one hundred thousand framed the troops, as children scampered up trees to get a better view. Just before ten o'clock, the Duke of Connaught and his family, accompanied by Sir John Hendrie and other dignitaries, including General Logie and Mayor Church, moved to their reserved places. As they arrived, the massed bands played 'God Save the King.'

Honorary Major G.H. Williams, Senior Chaplain, assisted by the chaplains of the 92nd and 95th Battalions, led the service from a flag-draped enclosure placed on a slight rise at the northern end of the park. Standing beside the Union Jack, Williams began to speak as church bells rang out throughout the city, calling the city at large to join with the men in their supplications. He chose as his text the words, 'Think not that I am come, to send peace on earth. I came not to send peace, but a sword.' Due to the size of the crowd, most of the troops and spectators could not hear the service, but everyone joined in the singing of the hymns: 'Old Hundredth,' 'The Son of God Goes Forth to War,' 'Oft in Danger, Oft in Woe,' 'All People That on Earth Do Dwell,' and 'God Save the King.' After the service was complete, there was a crush of civilians moving in to see their favourite soldiers. While the police did their best to control the situation, three women fainted in the press, prompting members of the St John's Ambulance Association to step forward to care for them.[66]

With the coming of spring, the units proceeded overseas. Again, thousands of Torontonians turned out to watch each battalion march through the streets one last time before boarding trains. Over five thousand citizens turned out at Riverdale Barracks to take their leave of the 92nd Highland Battalion. Men from the Sportsmen's and the Queen's

Own Rifles Battalions were assigned the task of keeping soldiers and spectators separated; they were only partially successful. Several hundred relatives and friends rushed through the assembled guard to say good-bye. Civilians and soldiers continued to fraternize until policemen and soldiers broke up the crowd at the junction of Queen Street and the railway. 'I didna' think the 92nd had so many friends,' remarked one Highlander when asked about the size of the crowd. Almost twelve hundred officers and men boarded thirty-four train cars and headed for 'points East' while the notes of 'Auld Lang Syne' were played by pipers.[67]

If troops were not proceeding overseas, they were heading to Niagara Camp after its official opening for the season on 13 May. While troops departed, their future replacements thinned, a week's recruiting in the middle of May yielding only 359 volunteers. The needs of the Canadian Expeditionary Force were competing with full employment and high wages, making it more difficult to convince men to enlist. Recruiting numbers continued to drop, with daily totals now hovering at or below the fifty men per day mark, and weekly totals rarely surpassing three hundred.[68] Although these were still remarkable results, they were undeniably lower than earlier in the year. The Bantam Battalion conducted a new house-to-house canvass, tabulating the total number of eligible men still in the city. Different recruiting sergeants approached each local man three times. The names of eighteen thousand men of military age were duly recorded, fifteen hundred of whom were eligible only for the Bantam Battalion.[69] It was obvious that the current system of securing recruits was not yielding results, leading to criticisms of the battalion scheme.

Even as papers reported in early June 1916 that Field Marshal Kitchener had drowned as a result of a German submarine attack and that the Canadian Corps was engaged at Mount Sorrel, officers in charge of recruiting for Military District No. 2 met at Niagara Camp to discuss the enlistment slump. They decided that no further units should be authorized until present ones were up to strength. Many officers believed that some form of government registration would be of material benefit to recruiters.[70]

Organization after organization pledged its support for some form of conscription. The Anglican Synod of Toronto unanimously passed a resolution that supported conscription under the Militia Act, the Defence of the Realm Act, or 'otherwise as may seem advantageous, for the more complete and effectual mobilization of the entire resources of Canada in men and materials.' A similar resolution was debated and passed at the

Toronto Methodist Conference in Carlton Street Church calling for a more effective and equal scheme to raise recruits, by conscription if necessary. Women crowded into Massey Hall for a patriotic rally, endorsing a resolution calling for national registration and conscription if necessary. The Board of Trade was also supportive of national registration as a more efficient way to run the war effort. The Speakers' Patriotic League passed a resolution that the people of Canada would stand behind the Government in 'any plan ... as may seem most advantageous for the more complete and effectual mobilization of the entire resources of our community in men and materials.' All these appeals began to have an effect. On 16 June papers reported that Prime Minister Borden had promised that a more effective way would be found to recruit.[71]

Public opinion leaders made another push to fill up the ranks using voluntary enlistment. The Clerical Patriotic Association sent a circular to all religious leaders in the community, reminding them that 'it is imperative that the Canadian Division now in action be kept at full strength.' To help military officials with recruiting, the association unanimously approved the setting aside of 18 and 25 June 1916 as 'Patriotic Sundays,' when ministers were to appeal to the people and emphasize 'the spiritual aspects of the call to sacrificial service for our Empire.' The letter closed by reiterating the holy nature of the war, and the necessity for 'all Christians to make every possible contribution, which, under the blessing of God, will help to bring victory and a righteous peace.'[72]

General Logie also made a public appeal for recruits on the front pages of the daily papers, addressing his letter to the Citizens of Toronto: 'Speaking with authoritative knowledge of the immediate need for men, I make this appeal to the City of Toronto. Toronto's quota required to complete her Battalions now authorized is 2440 men. This City has never in its history failed to rise to its full responsibility. Surely the women, the Churches, the Board of Trade, the Canadian Club, and other Patriotic and Fraternal Societies, and the business interests will, by one last united effort, give the men so urgently needed.' The result was a 'big day' for recruiting in Toronto, ninety-three men being attested. Despite the best efforts of recruiting officers, the numbers underlying a successful recruiting day had changed. In the boom time of the battalion recruiting scheme in January 1916, a big day meant over five hundred volunteers, whereas by June 1916, it meant only one hundred. A civilian committee appointed to deal with the question of further recruiting was frustrated. Made up of representatives from women's organizations, the Board of Trade, the Labour Council, the Sportsmen's

Patriotic Association, the National Service Week, the Orange Order, the Recruiting League, and other organizations, it passed the following resolution: 'This committee is of the opinion that a whirlwind campaign to raise recruits is not practicable at the present time.'[73]

The officer in charge of recruiting the 170th Battalion agreed. Lieutenant-Colonel Le Grand Reed wrote to General Logie about the situation. His letter encapsulates the struggles of recruiters over the previous months and reveals the depths of the efforts to reach every man in town:

> Since I organized the Toronto Recruiting Depot, 1st August 1915, there have been Recruiting Meetings, District Recruiting Meetings, Free Moving Picture attractions, Visits to men in their places of employment, Free Sunday Theatres, Church Rallies, Political Branch Meetings, Boxing Bouts, Midnight Shows, Burlesque Theatre Performances, The Police Census, Political and other centralizations of personal appeal, Fetes and entertainments of all sorts carried on with the last degree of human effort and every one of those mediums completely exhausted and depleted of results. The cost of all their work has been borne by certain and numerous private citizens of Toronto who have thus generously expressed their loyal support of the Recruiting Cause ... During the last few months the streets of Toronto have been overrun with thousands of untrained men in uniforms accosting with such manner and expressions as have aroused constant indignation. These men perforce of circumstances untutored in their duties, have done their best. I claim that there is not one civilian man in each thousand in Toronto who has not been most strongly and continuously urged to join the colours. The Press, the platform and the Pulpit have informed everyone of the need and yet since February 7th, despite the cost to the private purse and to the Government, with these thousands of paid soldiers daily roaming the streets, it has been impossible to recruit the men needed ... [It is time to consider] what has been obviously the unwisely postponed, the only equitable and, now and finally, the only possible medium for raising more men – conscription, or at least Registration.[74]

The news of the Allied advance at the Somme on 1 July 1916 changed nothing. Even though Torontonians celebrated the offensive as the beginning of the 'big push,' it did not move young men to enlist. At a Sunday evening recruiting rally at Loew's Theatre at 189–91 Yonge Street, only six men came forward at the end of the night. In the context of a mass recruiting drive and reports of Allied advances, a mere fifty men were attested on any given day. Recruiting had dropped off so dramatically that securing fifty men was now considered a 'big day.' A week later, recruiting dropped even more markedly, with only twenty-three obtained on 12 July. The following day was even worse, the four battalions still recruiting in Toronto (201st, 204th, 208th, and 216th) having to share the *ten* men who were accepted for service with the 69th and 70th Batteries, No. 1 Construction Corps, the 238th Forestry Battalion, and the Canadian Army Service Corps.[75]

Dismal recruiting results were reported throughout the summer of 1916. When Canadian units were engaged in offensive action at the Somme in September, enlistment numbers continued at very low levels. Both Liberal and Conservative papers printed editorials which attempted to shame local men into joining up and appealed for some form of compulsory service. The physical standards for the CEF were once again dropped, allowing men with good sight in only one eye to be accepted. Recruiting officers once again took to the streets to appeal for new men, pushing totals back up to nearly forty per day, but they quickly dropped off again.[76]

In the charged atmosphere of daily casualty lists from fighting at Courcelette, the increased cost of living, and a war which would continue well into the foreseeable future, Torontonians looked for scapegoats. Someone or something had to be held responsible for allowing daily recruiting totals to drop to one-fifth the average daily casualties. The most likely target was the province of Quebec and its poor recruiting totals. As Canadian soldiers fought for Regina Trench, editorials in secular and religious papers raged that 'the people of Quebec have not taken the part in the war which their allegiance and their racial origins seemed to require.' Torontonians read that the cost of imposing conscription would be divisive to national unity, but most supported whatever measures were necessary to back up the troops at the front. Stating what had become a truism, the *Christian Guardian* remarked, 'There is no use beating about the bush or ignoring the self-evident. Quebec constitutes one of Canada's outstanding problems.'[77]

Borden's solution to the recruiting problem was a scheme called National Registration, a plan similar to the British National Registration Act implemented in August 1915. National Service Cards were to be distributed to each man between the ages of 18 and 65. The cards would request information on occupation and fitness for service and would be returned to military authorities. This process, it was hoped, would retain those men in essential war-related industries and provide recruiting officers with the names of other men eligible for overseas service. Newspapers and representatives of various organizations were skeptical. An editorial in the *Globe* was typical: 'It is difficult to understand what effective steps can be taken under the registration Order in Council to make slackers of this sort do their duty. They have been subjected for more than two years to moral suasion, and if in that time they have not been aroused to a sense of their obligations as citizens there is little hope that any pressure short of compulsion will send them either to the front or to the munition factory.'[78] A private letter by prominent Torontonian J.M. Godfrey to the prime minister echoed these sentiments. Godfrey warned Borden that he would find National Registration 'totally inadequate and an utter failure' for several reasons: it had no legal strength; it requested incomplete information; it targeted men already enlisting; it failed to take into consideration the failure of the voluntary Police registration scheme; and it did not make use of civilian recruiting organizations.[79] Borden did not answer the letter.

Throughout October, while the infrastructure of the National Registration program was put in place, citizens dedicated themselves to the British Red Cross Fund. Volunteers continued to enlist in small numbers, but large recruiting drives were a thing of the past.

In stark contrast to the results of a referendum in Australia which had rejected conscription,[80] Recruiting rallies in Toronto were evolving into public expressions of support for conscription rather than appeals to the patriotism of local men. At a 29 October rally at the Hippodrome Theatre, to the 'vociferous applause' of the crowd, Mayor Church emphatically advocated conscription as the most fair and equitable way to obtain recruits. At a meeting of the chief officers from Military District No. 2, it was decided that 'the voluntary system of recruiting has about reached its limit, and some form of compulsion will have to be introduced if Canada is to obtain the hundred thousand men recently called for by Prime Minister Borden to reinforce the divisions now at the front.' Prominent religious figure S.D. Chown 'boldly and with pride openly confessed his conversion to conscription as a national necessity.' In a private letter to a colleague, Chown defended conscription: 'Does it not appear to you as a most horrible thing that our boys should become voluntary murderers? Would it not be much better for their character if they should kill only at the stern compulsion of the state?'[81] Even before National Registration was undertaken, papers and civic leaders believed in the ultimate necessity of conscription.

In this increasingly tense atmosphere, Sir Sam Hughes was fired. Dealing with a growing manpower crisis at home, rising Canadian casualties from the Somme offensive, and Hughes's penchant for wild public statements, Prime Minister Borden no longer had the patience to deal with Hughes's antics. On 9 November 1916 Borden demanded his resignation, which he received along with a list of complaints.[82] Hughes symbolized the voluntary spirit which had until now dominated the Canadian war effort, but his firing was partially the result of a recognition that the time for voluntarism was passing. The war's demands were too great for ad hoc measures and few people lamented his dismissal. Most people viewed it as a positive sign that the government was taking a firm grip on recruiting.

Before withdrawing at the end of November to rest and train for spring offensives, the casualty totals of the Canadian Expeditionary Force clearly demonstrated the pressing need to solve the manpower dilemma. Casualties greatly exceeded enlistment. It was in this context that Torontonians undertook what would become their last major recruiting drive of the war. The Clerical Patriotic Association helped recruiting officers secure the almost seven thousand men needed to fill up the units that had already been authorized in the district. The basic tactic was 'moral compulsion' to push men into service. The needs of individual men no longer took precedence; at stake was the patriotic reputation of the city and its ability to live up to its commitments. Patriotic appeals were largely dispensed with and citizens openly attempted to shame men into service.

The centre of this campaign was a new unit to be raised by the Queen's Own Rifles, the 255th Battalion, commanded by Lt.-Col. George L. Royce. Advertisements were run in the papers announcing the 'Give Us His Name' campaign. Recruiting officers hoped that citizens who knew the names and addresses of potential recruits would send this information to the regiment. The following advertisement was designed to secure the aid of local citizens: 'GIVE US HIS NAME. We ask You to help our Men at the Front. We ask You to Help Win this War. We ask You to Perform An Urgent Duty. Nearly everyone knows of ONE MAN who should be in khaki to-day. We ask you to give us his name so we can call upon him and give him this opportunity to join an Overseas Battalion – the 255th Q.O.R. [Queen's Own Rifles]. Reinforcements for the 3rd Battn [Battalion].'[83] At the bottom of the form was a 'coupon' that asked for the eligible man's name, address, business address, and occupation. Respondents were asked to mail the form to the Queen's Own Rifles. Despite the effort, recruiting did not pick up.

The winter of 1916–17 saw the Canadian Corps free of any major operations. Units engaged in trench raids and trained for the upcoming 1917 offensives. Throughout December, Torontonians were preoccupied with the ever-increasing cost of living, the discussions about Germany's and President Wilson's peace proposals, and the upcoming visit of Robert Borden to Toronto as part of his cross-country tour to promote National Registration. On 22 December, the prime minister spoke to a crowd which did not even fill Massey Hall, appealing for support of National Registration as one last attempt to avoid conscription. Imposing conscription, he warned, would divide Canada precisely at the moment when it had to be united.[84] In the wake of his visit, editorials debated the merits of National Registration. For their part, the Conservative *World* and *Telegram* did not support it, arguing that the system was flawed because it was not compulsory, and that Canada should emulate Great Britain and introduce conscription outright. Other papers and religious periodicals, however, said that voluntary enlistment was worth one last try.

Beginning on 29 December, National Service cards were circulated to every male resident in Canada between the ages of eighteen and sixty-five. Respondents had three days to fill out the cards, at which point postmen would return to retrieve them, forwarding to Ottawa the names and addresses of all those who refused. Civic and religious leaders urged Torontonians to fill out their cards, as did Labour leaders. The end of National Service Week also saw the end of some voluntary recruiting associations. The Citizens' Recruiting League ended its tenure as the leading organizer of patriotic speeches, formally disbanding on 12 January 1917. There was no turbulent discussion in the wake of the end of National Service Week. Nationally over 1.5 million cards were returned, roughly 80 per cent of the number circulated. However, over 200,000 of these were blank or only partially complete. After deducting essential workers and the disabled, the National Service Board determined that just over 250,000 men were still available for service. Very few of these men volunteered; they were willing to wait for the state to compel them to serve. In Toronto, the subject was quickly dropped and the people and the papers focused on the upcoming patriotic campaign to raise money for the Toronto and York County Patriotic Fund.[85]

Towards the end of January, as the city at large conducted the drive for the Patriotic Fund, militia officers met in the University of Toronto's Mining Building to discuss recruiting. The 'Give Us His Name' drive had failed to fill the ranks of the 255th Battalion and the meeting favoured conscription. The more than two hundred officers present believed that all single men and widowers without families 'should be taken completely away from their ordinary avocation and trained in the same manner as overseas troops.' The conference asked that an Order in Council be passed by the Dominion government to enforce the Militia Act.[86]

Global events proceeded rapidly while the Canadian government hesitated over imposing conscription. On 1 February 1917, Germany declared that it would begin unrestricted submarine warfare. The March Revolution toppled the Tsar in Russia, weakened the Russian war effort, and threatened to pull it out of the fighting altogether. This loss was partially offset by the entry of the United States into the war on 6 April, but it would take months to assemble and ferry an American force across the Atlantic. As these global events unfolded, many Torontonians lobbied for conscription. Their pleas escalated in the wake of the Canadian attack at Vimy Ridge in April 1917. Editorials in secular and religious publications blasted the Canadian government for failing to realize that National Registration had failed and that voluntary recruiting was no longer viable.

With the coming of yet another wartime spring, those battalions recruited over the winter began to depart. The 208th (Irish) Battalion left in a downpour on 26 April 1917; other units followed over several weeks. While the spring of 1916 had heralded new recruiting attempts, such renewed energy was not forthcoming in May 1917. After five months of recruiting, the Queen's Own Rifles 255th Battalion had secured only 385 men, with only 54 coming forward in the last month, less than 2 men per day. While Exhibition Camp stood largely empty, Torontonians waited for the return of Prime Minister Borden from his trip overseas: it was widely expected that he would then announce his intentions with regards to conscription. Meanwhile, City Council again put itself on record as supporting conscription with a resolution that argued that the voluntary 'system is not now sufficiently effective for our military requirements, and therefore [the Council] urges upon the [Canadian Government] to enforce our present militia act, and to forthwith call out class No. 1.'[87] Headlines on 19 May marked the end of one chapter in Canada's history and the beginning of a new one. They read: 'Conscription for Canada.'

Voluntary recruiting had succeeded in securing approximately 40,000 Toronto men before conscription was announced.[88] Since one-third of those who volunteered were rejected on medical grounds, at least 60,000 must have offered to serve King and Country overseas. Placed alongside the total number of men available, 87,300, we can see that more than two-thirds of Toronto's eligible men had volunteered for duty. The behaviour of thousands of local men underscored the persistent level of dedication of the people of Toronto to do what was necessary to win.

At this point, Torontonians had an option. They could have acknowledged that even though sufficient volunteers were no longer coming forward, conscription was too alien and divisive a measure, and they could have scaled back the war effort. But the majority could not accept this path. The memory of thousands already sacrificed in battles like Second Ypres made breaking faith with the dead impossible to countenance. Recollections of thousands of Toronto's soldiers marching in columns through the downtown were too strong to be dismissed. The men who had made the sacrifice and left for the front demanded that their ranks be replenished as necessary. Appeals to reject conscription for the sake of national unity given the strong opposition of French-Canadians fell on deaf ears; Quebec's poor recruiting totals epitomized precisely why conscription was supported. Resolutions were passed by City Council, representative churches, women's organizations, political leaders, and militia officers endorsing conscription as the only available way to secure more men for overseas. In the context of May 1917, it appeared as the only way to continue the war.

Recruiting was not, however, uniquely a male preserve. Throughout the two and a half years of voluntary recruiting, women were closely linked with the success and failure of voluntarism. Organizing tag-days to supply the money required for local recruiting, appealing to young men to enlist, taking places of men who left their jobs for the front, or marching in patriotic parades to promote enlistment, Toronto's women formed a visible and active part of the war effort. Their experience with the struggle to win closely paralleled the recruiting drives, shaping their contributions and making demands on them previously unheard of in Toronto.

4

Women and War:
Public and Private Spheres

In August 1914, women's first patriotic duty was to allow husbands, lovers, or sons to enlist. Consenting to let loved ones serve the Empire was viewed as the epitome of selflessness and women were praised for their patriotism when they did so. While women demonstrated their enthusiastic support of the war in this way, many also wanted to play a more active role in the war effort outside of the home. Nursing was one avenue which provided a chance to go overseas, but the competition for places was intense. Nationally, in August 1914 the Red Cross had positions for one hundred nurses, and over six hundred applicants. This disproportionate ratio underscores women's support for the war effort. At the same time, the newly formed Women's Patriotic League held emergency meetings to confront the tragic Belgian situation and organized the shipment of relief supplies to that war-torn nation.[1]

After three months of war, the leading women's periodical, *Everywoman's World*, took stock of women's role in the war effort. This literary magazine catered to the social and economic elite. Established in 1913 and published monthy by Continental Publishing in Toronto, most issues contained forty pages, with three or four columns of text per page, allowing for large, clean print. *The Canadian Newspaper Directory* claimed that *Everywoman's World* was 'the dominant national magazine, far over-topping all others in Canada in point of circulation, proven buying power of subscribers, high quality of editorial contents and reader influence.' Its circulation exploded during the war from 67,570 to almost 120,000 by 1915, almost twice the distribution of *Maclean's*. According to a poll of more than 25,000 readers, 52 per cent of subscribers had an average worth exceeding $8,000, 12.1 per cent owned automobiles, and another 15.9 per cent were in the market to buy one. One out of every four English-Canadian households subscribed.[2]

The November 1914 issue asked what Canadian women had done to support the war. At the forefront of the list was the fact that they had 'sent Britain the flower of their nation. Then, knowing that while it was man's pitiable duty to go forth to slay, it was women's duty to succour, they instantly set about their work.' The August 1914 campaign for a hospital ship and offers to serve as nurses were the immediate manifestations of the desire to aid in the effort. In the same month the Toronto Women's Patriotic League established itself in the residence formerly used by Casa Loma's Sir Henry Pellatt at 559 Sherbourne Street; the property quickly became 'a ceaseless hive of activity.' On the third floor, twelve donated sewing machines were in use for all but a few hours of each day. On the second floor, volunteers ceaselessly packed the garments destined for the city's poor, the Belgians, or the Red Cross. On the main floor, a labour bureau recorded the names of any girl or woman needing work, serving as a link with wartime employers in need of help. Mrs L.A. Hamilton, a suffragist dedicated to the war effort, served as head of the league's social service branch. She oversaw the process of dividing the city into twenty-five districts, each with a captain on the lookout for cases of distress which required immediate aid.[3]

The league also organized 'home work' for women able to knit for the Empire: 'And not alone are white-haired grandmas at it. Stern ladies with college degrees who scorned such elemental things are hard at work. Lonely women on farms are knitting long into the night, Society women take their knitting to theatres and concert halls. Everywhere women have got back to their needles.' Female support for the war, as was true for the male half of Toronto, was not tied to a particular class. Once Exhibition Camp was set up, women donated pies and knitted socks to ease the burden assumed by the city's soldiers. The Women's Liberal Association, one of the highest profile women's organizations in the city, created a hospital to administer to the needs of the men at the camp. Upon hearing of British casualties at the front, other women organized a campaign to supply the wounded with cigarettes. The work continued to appeal to women of all classes, and campaigns were conducted to secure knitting and sewing material for those unable to supply their own, but willing to donate their time.

Few personal diaries from this period are available, but those that survive demonstrate that the private sentiments of many women were in accord with public expressions. Most conceived of the war as an honourable struggle for the survival of the Empire. *Everywoman's World* carried an editorial in September which argued that the Empire was engaged in 'battles of righteousness.' References were also made to keeping faith with ancient British traditions, as women strived to be 'worthy of the race of Nelson.'[4] A lengthy article on what women wanted from the war quoted the views of several locals. Mrs Willoughby Cummings, President of the Toronto Women's Patriotic League, was a long-time visible member of the community. She had worked as a correspondent for the *Globe* and the *Winnipeg Free Press* during the 1893 World's Fair in Chicago before serving on the editorial staff of the *Globe* for ten years. A tireless worker, she was the 'backbone of the National Council of Women' in her capacity as member of the executive. She believed that while everything had to be done to win the war, 'It [was] altogether too soon to attempt to define what will be, or may be, the outcome of a war that may last for years, when it is only three months old.'[5]

Local artist, great-niece of an aide-de-camp to Queen Victoria, and descendent of United Empire Loyalists, Elizabeth A. McGillivray Knowles added her voice to the discussion. Well known for her artistic achievements, not the least of which included displaying several of her paintings in the National Gallery, Knowles hoped a better world would result from the struggle: 'Will sorrow soften, will the desire to help foster unselfishness, will the discovery of that joy which is born of loving service make the striving after extravagant social display seem futile and wearisome? One might at least hope for this result.' Just before Second Ypres, women's groups were firmly behind a war effort which was engaged in a struggle with 'the armed criminal whose liberty is a menace. In such a conflict neutrality has no merit.' Women's public discourse was similar to that of the rest of the population. They were part of an epic struggle, and hoped that they would live up to the examples set by their ancestors.[6]

Women shared the glory and grief with the rest of the community when news gradually filtered back about the six thousand Canadian soldiers who had been killed or wounded at Second Ypres at the end of April 1915. In addition to grieving in the home, women publicly carried out their role as nurturers of the sick and wounded. A towel drive was conducted to secure enough fabric to make bandages for wounded combatants: 'There they lay, those men you have known and loved, in the fields of France, bleeding, dying for the Empire, while their comrades in arms, to avenge their death, to keep clean Britain's – Canada's honour, swept along determined on the victory which is theirs.'[7] Women endorsed the necessity of continuing to fight for the same reasons offered in the mainstream press: to keep faith with those already sacrificed and to support the honour of the country and the Empire.

Within days of the battle, prominent women again demonstrated their support of the war effort. Jane Addams, president of the International Congress of Women at the Hague, requested delegates from Canada to attend an international women's peace conference. One of the most accomplished women in Toronto, Mrs H.P. Plumptre, responded. She spoke with an eloquence born of years of experience. A social worker by training, she had studied at Oxford before degrees were granted to women. She settled in Toronto where she taught history at Havergal College, and was a lecturer in social service at the University of Toronto. A dedicated supporter of the war effort, one of her contemporaries remarked, 'There have been few if any women who have stuck closer to patriotic service than Mrs Plumptre.' Plumptre worked for the Canadian Red Cross and was a member of the executive of such organizations as the National Council of Women and the Young Women's Christian Association. On this occasion, however, she replied to Addams's request on behalf of the National Committee of Women for Patriotic Service in Canada: 'The committee is composed of the presidents, or their representatives, of the nationally organized societies of women in Canada. Many women represented on this committee have received invitations to be present or to elect delegates to represent them at the [peace] congress. None have felt able to accept the courteous invitation, because they believe that the time for peace has not yet arrived, and therefore no women from Canada can speak as representing the opinion of Canadian women.'[8] Only one person attended the conference, unofficially, as a Canadian delegate – Laura Hughes, the niece of Minister of Militia Sam Hughes. A consistent anti-war activist, Laura Hughes was harassed by the public wherever she went. Even her anti-war stance, however, has been overplayed. By her own admission, her efforts to establish a peace league were not part of a 'stop the war movement,' but rather an attempt to 'ensure that there never was another war.' Laura Hughes notwithstanding, it is a remarkable demonstration of the commitment of Canadian women to the war effort that 'Canadian women's groups were hostile and refused invitations to send delegates to The Hague.'[9]

Plumptre's response to Addams also included a commentary on her reasons for rejecting peace. First and foremost was the memory of the German atrocities in Belgium. These had galvanized the Allied nations in support of the war effort, and continued to do so even in the face of the casualties from Second Ypres: such was the level of international outrage at the behaviour of the conquering German army. Plumptre also maintained that the spiritual losses which would accompany a premature peace would far outweigh the physical and material losses of continued fighting. How could the international community, Plumptre asked, sign a peace agreement which sanctioned the destruction of a country whose 'sole crime was her geographical position?'[10] The war had to be continued for the sake of the Empire, whose soul had been pledged when it drew its sword to defend Belgium. Failure to endure the war's demands would mean the Empire's failure.

In the midst of new-found grief and determination, women increased their efforts, steadily extending the idea of the 'nurturing role.' Prominent women's organizations spearheaded a project to provide for the comfort of Canadian soldiers in France, which created a threefold approach to help wounded soldiers: first, to create home-like surroundings which would allow convalescents to recover quickly and return to the front; second, to establish a refreshment canteen with recreation and reading rooms to see to the comfort of the soldiers; and third, to distribute refreshments and comforts to wounded soldiers passing through to neighbouring railway stations.[11] The place selected for the Canadian rest home was a little-known town the name of which would have enormous resonance with Canadians a generation later: Dieppe. Women were supporting a more effective war effort by creating mechanisms to get men back to the front as soon as possible.

After learning that the German Army was using asphyxiating gas, women secured authorization from the Militia department to make respirators. Directions appeared on the women's pages of newspapers on how to construct a gas mask; a pattern was available at the Women's Patriotic League. Women who could not make respirators were asked to help defray the cost of purchasing materials by sending donations.[12] There was no naivety about the consequences of a man being caught without a mask when a gas attack commenced. Women understood the importance of the introduction of gas to the front and the demands that it would make on the lives of their loved ones. They worked to provide the equipment necessary to survive it.

Women were also encouraged to refrain from wearing their traditional black mourning clothes in the wake of the casualties from Second Ypres. The National Council of Women appealed to women 'to refrain from wearing the conventional mourning, and to wear, instead, a band of royal purple on the arm, to signify that the soldier they mourn died gloriously for his King and Country.'[13] This appeal was done for two reasons: the first was to save women the expense of purchasing mourning clothes. The more important reason, however, had to do with recruiting. Toronto's women, along with their national organizations, feared the negative impact on recruiting of thousands of wives and mothers walking through the streets in black. The solution was to change both the fabric and thereby the meaning of traditional mourning. The royal purple arm band was an innovation that associated bereavement with sacrifice, glory, and the cause of the Empire, rather than with loss and sadness. Thus, this badge of honour could circulate through the city and stimulate further recruiting, calling upon people to live up to the sacrifice of others.[14]

Women's reaction to the news of Second Ypres paralleled the behaviour of the city at large. Although women worked to care for soldiers, they did so with a view to returning them to the front. The mechanisms created to oversee this process were similar to the ad hoc arrangements used elsewhere at the time. Women reacted to events from the front, demonstrating their patriotism and commitment to the war, but they did so in the spirit of the amateur enthusiasm which Torontonians believed would see them to victory. All these efforts demonstrated their commitment to the war effort and the necessity of continuing what had become a great crusade.

In the months after Second Ypres, the grim news continued. Thousands of women took part in the public mourning for Captain Darling and attended his funeral. Others lost loved ones on the *Lusitania*, which further drove home the ability of the war to affect their lives. More of their husbands and sons were killed at Festubert later in May 1915, and they watched as recruiting sergeants took to the streets for the first time to fill the holes left by the fallen soldier-heroes. New contingents were authorized in June 1915 and recruiting became an ongoing process, providing further evidence that the war would not be short. In late June 1915 enlistment was at a low point, but recruiting officers changed their approach and involved the men and women of Toronto in helping to secure volunteers. They were enormously successful.

Changes in recruiting strategies altered the way women participated in the war effort. In July 1915 recruiting became a public phenomenon, and an increased role for women was central to this new campaign. The giant recruiting rally at Massey Hall on 20 July featured the first overt participation of women in promoting enlistment. The Women's Patriotic League received a request from the military to help organize the rally. In response, the league drafted plans and appointed a committee of sixty women from different patriotic organizations to distribute literature before the meeting and to consider participating in recruiting after the speeches were over. Two days later, a meeting of 'representative women' was held at City Hall in the Council Chamber to further discuss how women could help. Mrs Willoughby Cummings presided, and a resolution was adopted which suggested that women offer their services to the recently formed General Committee and work in 'whatever manner this committee felt would be best' to facilitate recruiting.[15]

Although it was a major change to involve women in promoting enlistment, women's groups and recruiting officers initially decided to keep women's public involvement to a minimum. Women formed a part of the 20 July rally, but they served as helpers, distributing literature before the meeting opened. The military decided that women could best help at the fringes so that attention could be focused on prospective recruits, rather than on the novelty of women serving as recruiting sergeants. Women were expected to promote the virtues of enlisting, but they were to do so in private, in 'a quiet way,' among their friends and acquaintances rather than out in the public sphere.[16] Nevertheless, they were early participants in the drive to ensure sufficient volunteers for the Canadian Expeditionary Force, and an important precedent was set. As the demands of the war increased, women would assume a greater role in promoting campaigns, moving to an ever-increasing degree into the public sphere.

In the meantime, in the wake of the 20 July rally at Massey Hall, a column in the *News* reported on the big meeting from a woman's point of view. Commenting on Sir George Foster's assertion that it was a privilege to be living at this time, the leading women's columnist for the *News*, Helen Ball, wrote, 'Yes, it is a privilege.' That privilege was based in the possibility of helping to make history of a more vital character than 'any since the days when the first Christians began to teach humanity.' Referring to the glory of General Brock at Queenston Heights, Ball reiterated appeals to women to play their part in sending their men to the Recruiting Depot, and praised the creation of a women's auxiliary to the Recruiting League. Women knew that they would be ashamed, she argued, if the men belonging to them were not among those who had upheld the honour of Canada: 'Yes, even if they were left lying in rough graves in France, you knew last night you could bear it better than having a shirker by your side.' The ultimate sense of pride was felt by a woman at the rally, Ball related, when she could look up and see 'her husband or her son, little more than a boy, standing facing that vast throng of people, while they cheered him to the echo.' Ball reminded Canadian women that they were of the stock of Laura Secord, could endure hardships unflinchingly, and could not allow their men to be shirkers by tying them to apron strings.[17]

Women were an integral part of the new recruiting scheme, which depended upon creating a climate conducive to enlistment. For recruiting drives to succeed, men had to be pushed from both the public and the private sector to join the forces. If women had not supported the idea of continuing the war effort, this new strategy could not have worked. A man might be willing to endure public pressure, if privately he could retreat to the home and have his convictions supported by the woman in his life. Many women, however, willingly participated in the recruiting drives and publicly committed themselves to work within the private sphere to promote enlistment. By their urging, men who had previously declined to enlist, or failed to secure a place, did so by the thousands.

To celebrate the securing of over five hundred men for overseas service the day of the Massey Hall rally, over three thousand women and children whose men were already at the front gathered at Massey Hall the next day. These dependants of the Toronto and York County Patriotic Fund held a rally of their own. The doors opened at three o'clock, but long before that a 'line of mothers, most of them bearing babies in their arms and leading small children by the hands – a line of infinite tragedy never before seen in Canada, stretched back as far as Yonge Street.'[18] The hall was filled within a matter of minutes. The front row was occupied by forty-two small children who scrambled about restlessly, despite the best efforts of their mothers to keep them quiet. The band of the 48th Highlanders entertained the crowd, accompanied by a series of 'lantern slide pictures' of Canadian and British soldiers at the front.

The keynote address was given by Sir William Mulock, president of the Patriotic Fund, who took as his theme the necessity of being thrifty during wartime. He warned that following the war, there would likely be a depression, so women would be well advised to save now against the possibility of a downturn later. Representing the Women's Patriotic League, Mrs L.A. Hamilton asked assembled women, 'Are we downhearted?' The answer was a resounding 'No!' Hamilton addressed the crowd, telling the women that they must 'show the world that we are not tired of our duties. A good nation is the nation that has good women. Canada will be a good nation because the women are doing their part, not only in giving, but in thinking of the future and in caring for the nation's children.'[19]

This meeting was not about blind patriotic enthusiasm, but was rather about ensuring a calm and rational approach to the demands of the war. Women understood that the deprivations associated with the war would likely last longer than any victory parade and were told to prepare against that possibility. They were soldiers on the home front, and the war effort depended upon their ability to stretch scarce resources. Thus, sheltering their families in the home would contribute to the public process of winning the war. The lantern slides from the front prompted cheers from some women, tears from others. There were no illusions about the potential cost of the fighting. Women were determined to continue the war because they believed in the cause and in the necessity of keeping faith with the men already sacrificed for its sake.

As the summer of the 1915 progressed, women continued to play a prominent role in helping to create a climate conducive to recruiting, and men continued to enlist. At the enormous patriotic rally at Riverdale Park on 9 August to mark the anniversary of the declaration of war, women played a public part. Half of the two hundred thousand people who filed into Riverdale Park were women, demonstrating that they were as inclined as men to attend military festivals and recruiting rallies. A few of these women used the occasion to push men into service. Mimicking the actions of women in Britain who shamed men into service, two young women paraded through the crowd with a torn pillow, presenting white feathers to men not in uniform.[20] Elsewhere in the crowd, two women placed chicken feathers from the sofa cushions they carried on the lapels of those men still wearing civilian clothes. The *Star* described the process as a deadly method of attack: 'You would be standing with strained neck watching the bands in the valley. Someone would brush past and quietly lay something white on your lapel. It did not dawn at first what the white thing was. Then when you saw, in the dim light, your single violent impulse was to crawl, on hands and knees, out of the crowd and climb a tall tree.'[21] What made this attack so devastating was that women had not yet previously participated so publicly in the campaign for recruits. Men were unaccustomed to being publicly shamed by women, and would do virtually anything to avoid it, including enlisting. It was partly the fear of public ridicule and the desire to avoid the social stigma of failing to do one's duty that prompted so many men to come forward that night, and in the days and weeks to come.

Throughout the rest of the summer, women's activities paralleled those of the war effort in general, gradually moving away from an ad hoc approach to a more organized one. Rather than waiting to react to an event, women began organizing campaigns to address future needs.

As early as the middle of August, a 'tag day' was discussed as a way to raise recruiting funds. On 13 August, representatives from various women's organizations met at City Hall to confer with the finance committee of the Citizens' Recruiting League. Labour representatives, Mayor Church, and women's groups decided that Labour Day provided the best opportunity as a large number of people could be canvassed while they watched the parade. The preparations for a tag day demonstrated the increasing efficiency of women in responding to the war's demands, but it also showed that they understood the nature of recruiting campaigns. Creating a climate conducive to recruiting required money to purchase advertisements in the papers, to print posters, and to equip the military bands that paraded through Toronto's streets.

Women working for a wage began organizing their own campaign to raise money to purchase a machine gun or a motor ambulance. Newspaper articles estimated that by August 1915 some forty-five thousand women were employed in 'every sort of labour open to the sex.' The idea originated among stenographers, who sent out over two thousand letters urging fellow workers to donate money to purchase machine guns. When they discovered that enthusiasm for the scheme was widespread, they merged their efforts with the Business Women's Club. A call went out to all wage-earning women in Toronto to attend a meeting at 114½ Yonge Street on 24 August to help arrange a mass meeting to be held towards the end of September.[22] This campaign raised the profile of women working in the public sphere and demonstrated that their organizations continued to parallel the war effort, becoming more and more centralized as the demands of the conflict grew. Moreover, the earlier focus of women's groups on nurturing and comforting those harmed by war had shifted. This campaign was not directed at equipping hospital ships, running towel drives, or outfitting convalescent homes; rather, it aimed to equip the soldiers at the front with the weapons necessary to win.

Women continued to rally in support of the war effort by forming a visible part of the 1915 Labour Day parade. The vast majority were members of the working class. As union members marched from Queen's Park down to Exhibition Park in front of hundreds of thousands of spectators, women were front and centre. The wives and children of union men who had joined the colours filled twenty motor cars donated by the Ontario Motor League. The Women's Patriotic Association also entered a float that featured women making toys for the children of departed soldiers or sewing for soldiers. The float was decorated in red, white, and blue to show support for the Empire. The Belgian colours were displayed as well, demonstrating the degree to which the trials and tribulations of the Belgian nation had penetrated the consciousness of Torontonians.[23]

The tag day discussed in August was put into motion in November 1915. This effort was conducted in a climate of bad news from the front. There were now two Canadian divisions in the line, Allied efforts at Gallipoli had been a fiasco, the Russian army was in disarray, and new fall offensives on the Western Front advanced the line only marginally, at great cost. Sam Hughes authorized the creation of new battalions in late October and re-energized recruiting, but put even more demands on local resources. Women understood that recruiting in Toronto would cost an enormous sum of money and set about organizing their tag day to coincide with the massive parade of ten thousand soldiers through the downtown.

The parade marked the anniversary of the late King Edward's birthday and formed part of 'Khaki Day,' which took as its slogan, 'Keep Toronto Ahead.' A small army of twenty-five hundred women volunteered to sell the tags. Even before the date arrived, women raised the profile of the event by driving motor cars decorated with banners announcing the upcoming campaign and displaying recruiting posters. The tag was in the shape of a shrapnel shell, with the words 'King Edward VII, Memorial, Khaki Day,' emblazoned across it. The flag of Britain was featured prominently, and at the bottom was a picture of a Canadian soldier with bayonet fixed, along with the words 'In aid of regimental recruiting.' Anticipating a big day, 350,000 tags were made, one for almost every man, woman, and child in town.

On the day of the parade, women fanned out in the chill of an early November morning to cover the city. By eight o'clock, at each transfer corner in the city, a captain in an automobile oversaw ten other women. In the downtown area, virtually every corner had a unit appealing to citizens to 'Keep Toronto Ahead.' Each woman carried a tray made of red cardboard with a money box attached, and patrolled up and down the street until she encountered a tagger from another car. At this point, the two women exchanged progress reports and turned back. Only soldiers were not to be tagged: they had already demonstrated their patriotic enthusiasm by donning a uniform. Young men wearing a tag, therefore, formed a visible target for recruiting officers.

The Khaki Day was a resounding success. Almost all the tags were sold within hours and virtually everyone going to work could be seen wearing one. By noon hour, there were no tags left; women resorted to pinning small British flags on those who donated money. One woman raising funds at the corner of King and Bay Streets reported that of all the citizens she had approached, only two refused, and the cause was lack of money. Another woman scaled the scaffolding of a new hydro station being built at the corner of Carlaw and Gerrard Streets, tagging brick layers, mechanics, labourers, firemen, and architects alike. In another incident, a woman reported encountering only one unwilling donor all day about whom she commented, 'I just begged his pardon and said I hadn't known he was a German.'

At the end of the day, the women in charge of different sections of the city proceeded to the main corridor of City Hall, which had been made available to count the money. Tables were placed in the hall, each one bearing a number corresponding to the district covered by its captain. Forty bank tellers were in charge of the counting. By nine o'clock, all the returns were in, and a cheque made out for the amount received was given to Sir Sam Hughes, to be turned over later to Mayor Church in his capacity as chairman of the Citizens' Recruiting League. Over $34,000 was raised in a single day, surpassing the previous record established by the campaign for the hospital ship in August 1914. This number was added to by the City of Toronto and the Ontario Government to bring the total up to $50,000, and was announced at a patriotic gathering at Massey Hall to a chorus of cheers.[24]

Khaki Day was the first time that women organized a campaign which contributed directly to prosecuting the war, as distinct from working to ensure the comfort of soldiers. It demonstrated that public and private spheres of activity were beginning to blend as the demands of the war grew. The day also showed that Toronto women had made advances in conducting an organized campaign. In contrast to the early ad hoc arrangements, this tag day was thoroughly planned months in advance and was the most successful in the history of Toronto. Judging from the reaction of citizens to appeals for donations, they continued to show overwhelming support for the war effort. It was a day for youth, with the city's young men parading in uniform, and its young women securing the funds necessary to continue recruiting. While the flower of Toronto actively promoted the war effort, the rest of the population supported them by attending the parade and generously oversubscribing to the tag day fund. Collectively, the people of the city understood the voracious demands of the war, and were working together to ensure they provided their share of the cost of victory, in terms of men and money.

In the wake of this successful tag day, the Central Ontario Women's Institute Convention held its meeting on 10–12 November 1915 at the Central Technical High School at 275 Lippincott Street. The reports for the convention emphasized the enthusiasm for patriotic work on the part of local women. They were more than living up to their motto, 'For Home and Country,' the aim of which was the 'betterment of home and the advancement of the nation.' Gathered to celebrate women's work for the Belgians, the British Red Cross, and to plan future activities, the convention heard from a Private Cockburn who had been in the fighting with the Toronto Battalion at Second Ypres. He spoke of how the enemy's trenches were only 150 yards from the Canadians'. He described how men walked to the front line, the dangers they faced, and how the trenches were organized. He also spoke of the desperate need to aid the Belgians and to supply new socks and comforts to the soldiers. He concluded with an appeal to women to tell their men that their King and Country needed them: 'Please tell the young men to come down off the fence and play the game.'[25]

Private Cockburn's speech typified the patriotic activities expected of women at the end of 1915. They understood the nature of front-line fighting, and knew that more men were needed to fill the places of those killed or wounded. Their patriotic duty was to work to ease the damage inflicted by the war on civilian and soldier alike, even as they pressed loved ones to volunteer to fill the depleted ranks.

In the coming months, the distinction between private and public spheres of activity continued to blur. The demands of the war had a great deal to do with this transformation as a third Canadian division prepared to enter service at the front in December 1916. In Toronto, as large numbers of men left their jobs during the recruiting boom between December 1915 and February 1916, the first reports began to circulate of women participating in the workforce in non-traditional jobs. Women's organizations like the Local Council of Women, and the Liberal and Conservative Clubs, recruited women to fill the ranks of wage earners who had enlisted. The Local Council of Women represented a federation of seventy-two other women's groups. Under its guidance and leadership, in addition to their regular activities, 'every one [of the subsidiary societies] has done "war work" of one kind of another, the total amount handled annually amounting to thousands of dollars.' It drew most of its membership from the middle and upper class of the Anglo-Saxon and Protestant population, and it argued that 'women and particularly mothers, had the capacity to infuse social insti-

tutions and political life with superior moral virtue and maternal qualities.' The Women's Conservative Club functioned in much the same way
as its Liberal counterpart, working hard to send over 1.4 million articles
of clothing and comforts overseas to the soldiers, in addition to '35 bar-
rels of jam, 800 pounds of sugar, and Christmas boxes.'[26]

All across town, women expressed their willingness to canvass and
drive jitneys, and some 'even registered for work as streetcar conductors
to free men conductors so that they may enlist for military service.'[27]
The language describing this phenomenon made it clear that women
were moving into these occupations because they had been left vacant
by men who joined the Canadian Expeditionary Force. The word 'enlist'
was used to describe the activities of both men and women, referring to
the fact that they would work in this capacity for the duration of the war,
but no longer. Like the men going overseas, women assumed that these
jobs were temporary, part of their patriotic duty to help the war effort.

Early December 1915 also saw women become an integral part of the
whirlwind campaign by Lieut.-Col. W.B. Kingsmill of the 124th Overseas
Battalion. Kingsmill was the first Toronto officer to conduct an all-out
campaign to secure recruits. In addition to conducting appeals downtown, in restaurants, and in the papers, Kingsmill asked that each young
woman of courting age be presented 'with a recruiting leaflet and asked
to pass it onto her young man.' The military believed that men would be
more likely to volunteer if they received a leaflet from a loved one rather
than a stranger. A few days later women walking downtown were handed
the following circular: 'Bar them out, you women. Refuse their invitations, scorn their attentions. For the love of heaven, if they won't be
men, then you be women. Tell them to come in uniform. Tell him to
join the colours while he can do so with honour. The day is not far off
when he will have to go. The old mother has issued the last call to her
sons.' Only a few days later, Kingsmill continued to press for an
increased role for women in recruiting work and in the war effort in general, arguing that 'the women will have to be organized – not only to take
positions in the factories and offices now occupied by men – but to
engage in actual recruiting campaigns. The women of Toronto must
realize, at once, that they will have to equip themselves to perform men's
duties sooner or later. A great deal will depend on them.'[28]

As the recruiting net continued to be cast further afield by the military and with the ever-increasing demands of the war, it was inevitable
that women would be called upon to help. According to Kingsmill,
women could best fulfil their role in two ways: first, by pushing men into

service by refusing to speak with those not in uniform, a tactic particularly effective when practiced by someone's sweetheart; second, by offering to take up the positions traditionally filled by men, freeing them for overseas service. Kingsmill's address spoke to a wide constituency. He warned young men that if they failed to see their duty and enlist, they would be shunned by young women. He called upon women to formally move beyond their traditional private sphere activities and assume the positions of men who could then leave for the front. Finally, he demonstrated to traditionally-minded citizens that the war effort demanded the movement of women into the workforce in an organized manner. By doing so, Kingsmill deflected criticism of women performing non-traditional work because it was seen publicly as temporary and essential to winning the war.

Christmas 1915 found women's positions in a state of flux. Citizens retained their pre-war notions of gender roles, however, which included a public recognition of the sacrifice of women to the war effort at a dinner given to the dependants of the Toronto and York County Patriotic Fund. The whole city assumed the paternalist role in the absence of so many soldier-fathers. On 23 December, two separate rallies were held at Massey Hall, entertaining ten thousand mothers and their children. The recently formed Sportsmen's Patriotic Association sponsored the event, ensuring that there was an ample supply of entertainers and a present for each child. Mothers were presented with a gift as well, although it was one that reminded them of the ubiquitous demands of the war: each basket contained wool to be knit into socks for soldiers.[29]

This rally championed the roles women were expected to play by Christmas 1915: they were to shelter their families, provide for their children, and work for the war effort. While many continued to work in the private sphere, knitting socks as part of their contribution to the war effort, by 1916 women were moving steadily into the public sphere as well. Kingsmill's recruiting drive proved prophetic: women were *required* to take the positions of men so that they might enlist. This was doubly necessary after Prime Minister Borden announced on 1 January 1916 that the upper limit for the Canadian Expeditionary Force had been increased to 500,000 men. Wartime demands made it impossible to keep a clear division between men's and women's work. Although the ultimate responsibility of fighting lay solely with men, civilian jobs that had been previously reserved for men were opened up for the first time to women.

As recruiting in January continued to set new records, women prepared to take on a greater role in the wage economy. Recruiting officers and local businessmen recognized that to maintain 'business as usual,' 'a patriotic appeal must be made to the young women to take the places left vacant wherever it is possible to substitute.'[30] A campaign was necessary because societal norms continued to exert an enormous influence on young women and their families, who believed that a woman's proper place was in the home. It took the demands of wartime to prompt many women to come forward, and to allow society not only to accept this transformation, but to encourage it for as long as it was required.

One of the first places considered for female labour was unskilled industrial work. It was believed that, with proper training, women could fill the places of several hundred young men. Clerks and salesmen, along with the provincial civil service, and many jobs in newspapers requiring editorial and reporting staff could also be done by women. Even the dangerous labour associated with the manufacture of munitions came to be considered a likely place for women to replace men. In report after report discussing possible locations for women, one word appeared again and again: 'temporary.' Women knew that they were fulfilling these roles as part of their patriotic duty, and realized that they would be asked to vacate the jobs when the war was over to make jobs available to returned soldiers. Although there was a blurring of the roles associated with the public and the private sphere, the assumption was that the distinction would be reinstated as soon as peace returned.

Reflecting the increased organization of the war effort, women from all over Military District No. 2 met at the Parliament Buildings on 14 January 1916 to discuss how they could help recruiting. The meeting promoted the sympathy and cooperation of women. Organizers recognized that if the district was to meet the quota of 90,000 men required under Prime Minister Borden's new limit of 500,000 men, it was a mathematical and economic necessity that women would have to take over men's jobs. A scheme to register those willing to do so was discussed by women from the upper and middle classes, and, judging from the overwhelming turnout at rallies, supported by thousands of working-class women. A prominent activist, Mrs A.M. Huestis, was chosen as the president of a new organization, the Women's Emergency Corps. Huestis had been active in Toronto's war effort from the beginning. In August 1914, at her 'Birchknoll' house at 1184 Mount Pleasant Road, the Women's Hospital Ship Campaign had been inaugurated. Huestis joined with local president Mrs Willoughby Cummings to spearhead the movement of women into jobs vacated by men who left for the front.[31] The following were cited as likely places for women to replace men: sales clerks, streetcar conductors, policemen, bookkeeping agents, tailoring cutters and trimmers, chauffeurs, grocery delivery people, bank employees, professional workers, munitions workers, and farmers.

There could be no mistaking this change, however, as anything other than a response to the demands of the war. The word 'emergency' in the organization's name clearly indicated that its mandate was temporary. Even as it was formed, threats to traditional men's work were downplayed. Huestis carefully pointed out that the object of the corps was not to take work away from men, but to place appropriate workers in essential jobs according to the following priority sequence: returned soldiers, men not fit for military service, suitable women. She added further, 'I want it to be distinctly understood that we are approaching this matter entirely from the standpoint of patriotic service. It has nothing to do with any women's suffrage movement in any shape or form.' The president of the local branch of the corps, Cummings, took pains to reassure Torontonians that women were assuming these positions only during wartime, and would vacate them when the fighting was over. Cummings dismissed fears that women's involvement in the workforce would reduce men's wages, maintaining that the problem would be avoided simply by paying women at the same rate as men.[32]

If the Women's Emergency Corps was any kind of a movement, it was a patriotic one. Women joined the workforce 'for the duration' just as their male counterparts joined the Canadian Expeditionary Force. Although the expectation was that everyone would resume their 'normal' roles at the end of the war, Torontonians still had some reservations about the idea of women working in non-traditional jobs. The number and extent of the disclaimers from those in charge of the Women's Emergency Corps suggest that there was a need to pacify the fear that this role change would destroy the fabric of the traditional family and undermine male wages. Nevertheless, women's experience in wartime Toronto continued to reflect that of society in general, which was becoming steadily more organized as time went by. In the midst of a recruiting boom, plans had to be made to maintain the productive capacity of industry by employing female labour. Societal norms proved to be only a fleeting obstacle. The demands of the conflict were simple: if the war effort was to be expanded, women would have to work outside the home, and society would have to accept it.

In the weeks and months ahead, the Women's Emergency Corps registered women who offered to fill the positions of men who volunteered for overseas service. Throughout the process, prominent women continued to emphasize the temporary nature of the change. In a typical statement to the press, Huestis informed readers, 'when a woman is enlisted we will make it clear to her that she will not be given a position until it has been found impossible to get a returned soldier, or another man, to do the work left by the man who enlists. Secondly, we will make it plain that her only object in taking the work is to release the man who wants to go to the front, in other words, that she holds the position only as long as the man is away.'[33] Whatever the goals and aspirations of the women's labour movement, and the drive for equality and the vote, women registering for the Emergency Corps could not have failed to hear statements on the nature of the work ahead. It was its very temporariness that rendered it patriotic. Women sacrificed their spare time and family obligations to help in the war effort just as the men had done by enlisting for the Canadian Expeditionary Force.

While women set about organizing a reserve force of labour, recruiting officers lobbied local manufacturers and the Board of Trade to restructure their businesses to allow men to enlist. Meeting with board officials in their plush offices on the 19th and 20th floors of the Royal Bank Building on the north-east corner of Yonge and King Streets, officers requested that manufacturers determine how many men could be spared, and how many women would be necessary to fill their places. It was pointed out that the employers should guarantee the positions of men when they returned.

In the meantime, the Women's Emergency Corps continued its work. In addition to enlisting women for the labour force, the organization stressed the need for women to persuade the men in their family to enlist. At its inaugural meeting, the corps passed the following resolution: 'The changing conditions due to the progress of the war having enlarged the scope of patriotic service for which women are needed, it seems desirable that the various societies whose members are already working so earnestly for those who are serving the King should co-operate in order to meet these new requirements. With this desire in view, the Women's Emergency Corps has been formed by the 2nd Military Division. The Corps is formed for patriotic service in connection with the war only, and is in no way identified with any political or other organization.'[34] This resolution demonstrates a high level of awareness of the nature of the war and its future demands. Women knew that these demands had escalated constantly since hostilities commenced, and that the pattern would continue well into the foreseeable future. There was a clear recognition that meeting Prime Minister Borden's new commitment of 500,000 men required the movement of several thousand women into wage work.

Organizers arranged to have the purpose of the Emergency Corps clearly presented to women at various meetings of women's societies and church groups. They set up central headquarters in the Women's Patriotic League and drafted a registration sheet which would give employers details on the physical and mental efficiency of the women who registered. Those targeted were from the middle class as it was believed that working-class women either would already be employed in wage work, or would not have the money or the support networks necessary to secure child support if they were to obtain such work. Moreover, many of the positions to be filled required levels of education that women of middle- or leisure-class backgrounds were more likely to have. The process of linking labour vacancies with suitable female workers involved the alumni of various colleges who had contacts with the business world and could place women in employment efficiently. Meanwhile, business leaders met to discuss the ideal female labourer. The general opinion was that they needed healthy women with good educational backgrounds who were able to work steadily and regularly in clerical and other responsible positions. Middle-class women most closely approximated this ideal.[35]

Society, however, did not suddenly abandon working-class women who were dependent upon the Toronto and York County Patriotic Fund for survival. Caring for the wives who had given their husbands to the Canadian Expeditionary Force remained one of the focal points of patriotic enthusiasm. On 24 January 1916, the largest formal reception ever held in the city took place, a tribute to those whose husbands were in France. By this time citizens had become accustomed to thousands of men parading through the streets in khaki, but they had never before witnessed such an awesome testament to the demands of the war as they watched more than ten thousand women and children left behind by departing soldiers converge upon City Hall. The building was decorated with giant British flags, which draped down over the arched entryway. Thousands gathered to watch the arrival of Lieutenant-Governor Sir John and Lady Hendrie. The band of the 83rd Battalion played 'God Save the King' and the lieutenant-governor and his wife proceeded inside.

For the next three hours, mothers and their children streamed into the city buildings, through the guard of honour provided by the 83rd Battalion, up the wide marble staircase and down the corridor to the Council Chamber. Expecting a large crowd, organizers had placed an orchestra in the Upper Hall to entertain the guests while they waited. The Council Chamber was decorated with ferns in each window sill and the flags of the Allies. There was a festival atmosphere, but interspersed with the light-heartedness of the reception were the signs of mourning, silent testimony to the cost of war. In the Council Chamber, thousands of tiny citizens, accompanied by their mothers, were received by Sir John and Lady Hendrie, and by Mayor Church and his sister. The official announcer from Government House called out the name of each woman as she came into line. After exchanging greetings with the lieutenant-governor, women left by way of the members' corridor out into the Upper Hall along to the west side of the building, downstairs to the Terauley Street exit, and out into the fresh air. The entire route was lined with soldiers.[36]

Even during this week, the most successful for recruitment in the city during the entire war, residents were constantly reminded of increasing demands. As this massive group of more than ten thousand women and children were received by the lieutenant-governor and his wife, the wives and children of more than one thousand other men were taking leave of their husbands who had enlisted for overseas service. Another thousand women said goodbye the following week as recruiting records continued to be set, and so the process of feeding the demands of the war effort continued.

It was in this context that the Women's Emergency Corps continued the process of organizing female labour. It did so under increasing pressure from recruiting officers who were agitating for the mobilization of women, boys, and retired men to take the places of those who enlisted. In addition, a special Emergency War Corps of the Boy Scouts was organized to place boys on farms in any capacity that would relieve the labour shortage that accompanied the growing size of the Canadian Expeditionary Force. The question of just how many women would be required to work in munitions continued to be debated, but by early 1916 manufacturers and citizens alike had accepted the fact that continuing industrial work would require female labour.[37]

Recognizing the organizational efficiency of the Women's Emergency Corps, several banks requested women to serve as bank tellers because some branches had been closed due to the lack of clerks, over two hundred having enlisted. Bank officials wanted well-educated women, thereby reinforcing the parameters for eligible women workers set down by the Emergency Corps. They also wanted reassurance that the women taking these positions would realize that they held them only for the duration of the war, after which men would return to their former jobs. Within the context of wartime Toronto, citizens did not have the luxury of slow societal change, but they continued to cling to pre-war notions of gender divisions of labour.

Throughout March and April, the precise nature of women's involvement in the wartime economy continued to be debated. As the mines at St Eloi exploded in another costly military disaster, enlistment slowed again. Recruiting officers became bolder, confronting men in their homes if they failed to show at the depot. The efforts of recruiting officers were complemented by organizers at the Emergency Corps who continued encouraging women to come forward and work. In conjunction with the Toronto Manufacturers' Association, the corps sent forms to factories requesting employers to provide information on how many skilled workmen they required, and how many positions could be filled by women.

In the meantime, the Emergency Corps participated in campaigns to secure recruits. At a meeting of the corps in St Margaret's College, Bloor Street, women listened to presentations by the commanding officers of different battalions. The general consensus was that the present system of recruitment was not meeting demands. Women were asked to speak to the parents of eligible young men and make them see the need for their sons to do their part. As military canvasses were conducted throughout the city, many women joined the census-takers. As the recruiting situation became progressively more desperate, women's organizations paralleled the activities of the city and took increasingly extreme measures to stem the decline in enlistment. The Women's Emergency Corps decided to set a good example by passing, without a dissenting vote, the following resolution: 'no woman will preside at its meetings, and no speaker will be sent out under its auspices who has male relatives who are shirking their duty.'[38]

The expansion of women's public roles did not lessen or replace expectations of their duties as nurturers and protectors. Time and time again women proceeded to the trains to watch the departure of loved ones. Society demanded that women not impose their concerns and fears upon the men leaving to fight the Empire's battles. A stiff upper lip was required when taking leave of soldier-husbands and sons. The departure of the 83rd Overseas Battalion on 25 April 1916 was typical as the unit marched through the downtown, shadowed by loved ones who knew they would not see these men until after the war – if at all. Mothers passed parcels to the soldiers through the cordons of the 92nd and the 169th Battalions, society women bade farewell to officers, and sweethearts took what might be their last look at beloved enlisted men. Tears, however, were shed in private, not at the station: 'It was a British farewell.'[39] Invoking the imagery of the first major engagement by the Canadian Expeditionary Force, one newspaper report argued that the scenes at the train station were women's Second Ypres.

These sacrifices were made by women in the name of the Empire. As they continued to move into traditional male jobs, or participated in further recruiting campaigns, the backdrop to their activities was the all too common scene at the train station. By taking leave of loved ones for a period of years, and possibly forever, women became ardent supporters of the war effort. The war effort meant keeping faith with those men who had already sacrificed their lives and supporting the men still at the front. Women believed that the harder they worked, the sooner the war would be over, and the sooner their loved ones would be able to return. Women continued to play a large role in securing funds to continue with recruiting drives. Just a few days after the large religious ceremony in Queen's Park for the departing soldiers, another $22,000 was raised by women in a tag day held on 4 May 1916.[40]

By June 1916, monthly recruiting totals were still much lower than during the previous January. The 204th Battalion made an appeal at its noon hour rally at Yonge and Temperance Streets for women to enlist with the battalion for recruiting purposes. The new scheme was to raise several platoons of women to accompany recruiting sergeants in approaching those whom they thought should be in khaki. The officers of the 204th suggested that women visit places of employment. When they found a young eligible man doing work that a woman could do, one of these female recruits was to volunteer to hold his position until he came back from the war. In two hours, 108 women came forward and gave their names.[41] The distinctions between public and private spheres continued to blur. At the beginning of the war, a woman was considered patriotic if she supported her man in the private sphere and took care of his children. By June 1916, women were entering the public sphere to push men to do their duty, something that would have been abhorred in August 1914. Within the framework of mid-1916, it was celebrated.

Preparations were also underway for a rally of women at Massey Hall. After twenty-two months of war, they gathered for the specific purpose of ensuring that their efforts were organized and coordinated in a manner best suited to helping the war effort. The impetus for the meeting came from Gen. W.A. Logie, director of Military District No. 2. Mrs Willoughby Cummings was put in charge of the arrangements. All women were invited, particularly those with relations at the front. Massey Hall was filled to capacity on 12 June 1916; most of the audience knitted for soldiers throughout the meeting. On the platform sat representatives from women's organizations, as well as the wives of the commanding officers of the city battalions. While commemorative speeches were given in honour of the men who had fallen for the cause, the primary focus of the meeting was to interest women in recruiting. It was not a time to mourn losses, but rather 'to see how still more useful women might become along other lines of patriotic endeavor.' The focus was on duty and victory. By night's end, Cummings informed the crowd that the Women's Emergency Corps had registered over three hundred women who were willing to take men's places to release them for enlistment, but more were required.[42]

Several resolutions were passed, including one that called upon the Canadian government to enact National Registration in order that the country might more efficiently prosecute the war effort. Such a scheme would prevent the departure of a skilled labourer with a wife and small children, and ensure that an unskilled labourer working as a shop clerk would be required to serve. Another resolution recognized that the call to patriotic service came as insistently to women as to men, and women pledged to do their utmost to set free every eligible man. To this end, Mrs Huestis encouraged women to come forward and temporarily take over men's jobs. Women need not be concerned, she argued, about having to work longer than the duration of the war: 'We are not looking for women to replace men permanently; we are not looking for a position that a returned soldier could fill; we are not looking for a position that an unfit man holds; but we are looking for positions that are held by men who ought to be in khaki.' Col. G.H. Williams, a prominent recruiting officer, reinforced this point by telling women that if they failed to come forward and take men's places, these positions would have to be filled by enemy aliens.[43] Given the general feelings towards enemy aliens, this was something to be avoided at all costs.

Having secured female volunteers willing to work in positions typically held by men, the last obstacle to employing women was the attitude of manufacturers. This small group of men was as much the intended audience of the resolutions passed at this meeting as were the women in attendance. It was likely for their benefit that the Women's Emergency Corps and prominent patriotic speakers stressed the temporary nature of war work, and the need to use returned soldiers and unfit men first. Women were fighting on two fronts: first, against Germany; second, against traditional societal norms.

The turning point in the latter battle was announced during this meeting. The Munitions Department at Ottawa had given permission for over four thousand women to work in munitions in Canada in the coming months. This relaxation of employment restrictions was absolutely the product of the demands of the war. Both women and men at the forefront of the struggle had been clamouring for the government to increase its involvement in recruiting and the war effort in general. Women's organizations and recruiting officers recognized that women would be required to work in non-traditional jobs. Gradually, between January 1916 and June 1916, manufacturers had been persuaded of this necessity, a change in attitude that culminated with the above announcement stating that women's labour would be required in munitions plants. Women celebrated this official recognition of the role they could play as a victory for the efficiency of the war effort.

Over the next several weeks, women continued to move out into the public sphere. As part of a general search for areas of employment where women could replace men, it was decided that hotel management was uniquely suited for female employment. Not only could women put their considerable knowledge of running a household to good use, it was reasoned, but they would also be better suited than male managers to make the adjustments necessary when the Temperance Act came into force in September 1916. Prior to the mass meeting of 12 June, the number of women who enlisted to take men's positions were counted in hundreds. In the wake of the meeting, over one thousand women offered their services. Arrangements were also begun to have women march on 1 July 1916, Dominion Day, as a public demonstration of their support for recruiting and the war effort. Several hundred women's societies were expected to take part, resulting in a parade of several thousand women. As preparations continued, requests from manufacturers filtered in to the Women's Emergency Corps asking for those willing to work in factories. At a meeting of the corps in the private dining room of the Robert Simpson Company, a letter was read from John Bertram of Dundas requesting seventy-five women to work in his factory. Along with the request came in invitation to the members of the corps to visit the factory and see the women making 18-pound shrapnel shells.[44]

On the same day that British troops began the Somme offensive on the Western Front, women took to the streets to promote recruiting. Papers were filled with accounts of the parade. At three o'clock, the drums of the 170th Battalion announced the start of the march. Over three thousand women participated in this public appeal for recruits. On a beautiful summer day, Queen's Park was filled with spectators waiting to see the procession, the chief interest being the mothers, wives, and children of the soldiers marching at the front of the parade. Wanting to demonstrate their ability to sacrifice and endure the demands of the war, most women walked, with motor cars provided only for the elderly. On Canada's national holiday, women were the principal actors in a patriotic display promoting greater participation in the war effort. Throughout the entire length of the parade route, residents cheered the marching women. It was hoped that the most conspicuous result of the parade would be a renewal and an expansion of their patriotic work.

The order of the procession was determined by the level of sacrifice of the participants. Mothers who had given sons to the cause led the parade, carrying a banner that read 'Our Sons Serve.' Next in the hierarchy came the wives of men serving overseas, followed by children holding a sign which read 'Our Fathers Serve.' Following behind the women and children who had given loved ones to the cause, were those serving on the Women's Auxiliaries of the Toronto battalions. Behind these followed various women's patriotic organizations, including the Imperial Order Daughters of the Empire and the Women's Patriotic League. Next walked the women involved in church groups organized to see to the welfare of soldiers, followed by Liberal and Conservative political associations, Temperance societies, and the women's auxiliaries of various unions. Towards the end of the parade, the connections between the war and organizations represented became less marked, as women from various musical clubs and Christmas associations participated in support of recruiting. Next to last walked members of the Women's Emergency Corps and women who had registered for service. Those without links to any of these organizations marched last.[45]

According to the hierarchy established by the order of marching, the greatest contribution a woman could make was to provide one of her sons for the war effort. It was considered a greater sacrifice to part with a son than to surrender a husband or a father. These women were demonstrating to those watching that the single most important patriotic activity they could perform was to ensure that the men close to them recognized their duty and went to the front. All other patriotic duties, in employment, in patriotic societies, in religious groups, and in other organizations, were secondary to the all important task of securing recruits. Next in importance was to draw attention to the tasks performed by women who had been serving in an auxiliary capacity with Toronto's battalions for the past several months. These women were accorded the honour of marching before those attached to patriotic societies. Thus, the parade reinforced the notion that it was more important to serve directly than to belong to an organization that only supported the war. It is interesting to note that secular patriotic societies were placed in front of church groups, suggesting that secular reasons for fighting took precedence over religious justifications.

The fact that the Women's Emergency Corps and those who had recently registered for service were marching towards the end of the parade speaks volumes about societal attitudes towards women working in non-traditional jobs. The fact that they had a place in the parade indicates growing acceptance of them, but in a march to promote recruiting, these women followed far behind others who had donated loved ones to the cause. The hierarchy of the procession thus reflected contemporary visions of a woman's duties. Her first duty was to offer up her family, followed by serving in an auxiliary capacity to traditional male occupations, and then by participating in societies designed to promote the war effort. Even in a parade organized by women, those working in non-traditional jobs were not recognized as having sacrificed as much as those performing in traditional areas. After all, the Women's Emergency Corps was only temporary, and after the war – it was still assumed – the hierarchy embodied in this procession would be resumed.

In the wake of the Dominion Day parade, women moved increasingly into non-traditional jobs, and newspaper articles commented on the novelty. *Saturday Night* observed that 1916 had become a year of plentiful employment for women anxious to work. Along with recognizing that having women performing these duties was unusual, the article praised the adaptability of modern women in adjusting to life as munitions workers.[46] Thus, while there may have been some opposition to female labour in the public sphere, when it was clear that women could perform their duties adequately and aid the war effort, citizens offered their support.

Throughout the summer and fall of 1916, women read about the Somme offensive at the front and followed the activities of the Canadian Corps closely when it returned to the line in September. Local units continued to finish their training and march one last time through the streets before proceeding overseas. The emphasis on maintaining a cool composure and stiff upper lip remained the norm, as women and children again performed the pitiable task of saying goodbye to loved ones. In the middle of September, women took stock of the number and value of the articles that the Women's Patriotic League had sent to Europe in two years of war. All told, just under 4 million articles at an estimated value of $429,000 had been shipped from the city: surgical supplies, sheets, towels, socks, cigars, cigarettes, and canned vegetables.[47] Shipping this much material required careful organization at the local level, demonstrating that women increased their efficiency as the demands of the war effort grew.

The public focus of women's activities, however, continued to be shaped by the now difficult recruiting situation. The casualties the Canadian Corps was sustaining at Courcelette greatly exceeded the intake of new recruits, and articles proclaimed Quebec's failure to do its duty. In this tense atmosphere, it was clear that voluntary enlistment was not working well enough. Recruiting officers responded by appealing to employers and potential employees to move women into the workforce as soon as possible to release men for the front. Editorials appeared in Liberal and Conservative papers extolling the virtues of women moving into the workforce. In response, women transferred into war work by the thousands. Only one certificate was required: a note from their doctor attesting to the fact that they could bear the burden.

Despite the attention accorded to women performing non-traditional tasks, they continued to work in the public sphere as an extension of their more private roles. The 17–19 October 1916 campaign for the British Red Cross owed much of its success to the more than fourteen hundred female workers who did most of the campaigning. Women who attended church encouraged donations from other members of the congregation. Over two hundred automobiles were donated to help women in their city-wide campaign. The work of local women, and the generosity of citizens, ensured that the Red Cross Fund enjoyed a 30 per cent increase from its 1915 total, successfully raising over $700,000 in three days.

Even while the British Red Cross campaign was being waged, the organization to move female labour into war industries was being enhanced. The federal government declared that it would employ 'inspectresses' in munition plants and appealed to women with education to volunteer. Suitable candidates must have spent one year in high school, take one week of special training at a technical school, sign for a period not less than six months, and be willing to go to whatever part of the country where they might be sent. Their railway fees would be paid for them along with their hotel bills for two days while they secured lodgings. In banks, too, women were an increasingly common sight. Gazing through the windows of any downtown banking office, one could see the profound changes the war was having on the workforce. Women now occupied the places of desk clerks who had enlisted, and the banks were actively recruiting their staff from the city's female population. These changes had taken place in a remarkably short period of time, not having begun in earnest until January 1916.[48]

Despite the movement of women into the workforce, recruiting numbers continued to decline, and many organizations and citizens began to openly support conscription. Various women's organizations supported the move towards conscription as well. Representing seventy-two societies, the Local Council of Women put itself on record in favour of conscription on 21 November 1916.[49] Independent women's groups followed its lead. For its part, the Women's Patriotic League announced that the efforts directed at universal suffrage should wait until the end of hostilities, and declared itself in favour of conscription.

As another winter of war settled over the city, it was obvious that the place women had taken in the struggle was dramatically different from the previous year. While Christmas 1915 had seen a banquet for the dependants of the Toronto and York County Patriotic Fund, the Christmas season of 1916 witnessed a gathering of women's munition workers. Throughout Canada, four thousand women were employed in munitions, twenty-five hundred of whom worked in Toronto. Just under half of these turned up on New Year's Eve for a banquet that was held for them in the Transportation Building at the Exhibition grounds.

Coloured electric lights and hundreds of flags decorated the building. To ward off the cold, huge stoves were set up and 'awning walls' were stretched around the tables. At the south-east corner, a dressing room was arranged where women could take off their wraps before forming in line and marching to the table reserved for their munition plant. The regimental bands of the 198th and 204th Battalions entertained the workers, and men from these battalions served as waiters. At the conclusion of the evening, Rebecca Church, famous for spearheading a campaign to raise funds for the Great War Veterans' headquarters, rose, raised her glass, and said, 'Ladies, the King!' Just as the officers of a battalion rise after mess dinner at the word of their commanding officer, over twelve hundred women rose to the toast while the band played 'God Save the King.'[50]

This remarkable banquet celebrated the very public work that women were doing to help win the war. A dramatic transformation in the number and scope of women working in the public sphere had taken place within a single year. In January 1916, women were in the opening stages of organizing to work in non-traditional jobs. The demands of the war had outweighed the requirements of societal norms and the reservations of manufacturers, and by the end of 1916 female labour was an essential part of the munitions workforce.

The beginning of 1917 saw the public discourse about women working in munitions factories develop further. The head of the Imperial Munitions Board, Sir Joseph Flavelle, argued that fully 95 per cent of the munitions work in Canada could be done by women. Despite this, there was no relaxation of the demands placed on women to serve as nurturers and protectors, requiring them to maintain the home as a place of refuge. Women were now expected to work, if they were able, in addition to their traditional duties, and they continued to support public patriotic campaigns as well.

In the January 1917 campaign for the Toronto and York County Patriotic Fund, women were actively engaged in soliciting funds, accounting for 1,842 of the 2,052 campaign workers. In addition, they were targeted for donations themselves. One campaign poster illustrates the widening of possibilities for women wishing to participate in the war effort: 'WOMEN OF TORONTO! FOR THE SAKE OF THE BOYS IN KHAKI LEND THIS CRUSADE YOUR HELP! To the women who have made the sacrifice of giving a man, to all who know what the sacrifice means, we particularly appeal. Every woman has a two-sided opportunity. She can serve by giving money, and she can serve by giving work and money.'[51] Although the greatest contribution a woman could make remained the donation of a man close to her for the war effort, such a sacrifice was no longer considered a sufficient demonstration of patriotic dedication. Women now had to give more. Their choices were to give money, to work, or to do both where possible. The choice was theirs, but there was no mistaking the increased demand on and the new options available to them to fulfil their duty. As Canadian troops rushed to victory at Vimy Ridge in early April 1917, they owed their success in no small part to the sacrifices and work of women at home who functioned as an integral part of the collective response to the demands of the war.

5

Conscription: A Decided Commitment

As the federal election polls closed on the evening of 17 December 1917, thousands of people began to gather around Toronto newspaper offices to wait together for both the local and the national results. Despite the cool temperatures, the crowd was good humoured, confident that the voters of English-speaking Canada would endorse the cause of conscription by electing Unionist members. Toronto, as we shall see, voted overwhelmingly for candidates pledged to support the Military Service Act. Despite three long years of ever more costly war, Torontonians were virtually unanimous in their support for conscription.

When Prime Minister Robert Borden announced in May 1917 that he intended to introduce a bill to conscript not less than fifty thousand men, he knew that he could count on the editorial support of all of the Toronto papers. From the Liberal *Star*, which described the action as 'absolutely necessary,' to the Conservative *Mail and Empire*, the daily press offered ringing endorsements of the new policy.

Religious periodicals were also fully supportive. An editorialist from the *Canadian Churchman* was 'certain that it was with a sigh of relief that the vast majority learned on Saturday last that it [conscription] was really coming. The need of reinforcements, coupled with the lamentable falling off in recruits, made it inevitable.' Even as they waited for the bill's details, public opinion leaders endorsed the decision: University of Toronto president Robert A. Falconer, Sir William Hearst, Newton W. Rowell, Gen. William A. Logie, and Archdeacon H.J. Cody were among those prominent citizens who endorsed the idea. On 28 May 1917, City Council declared itself in support of compulsory military service without referring the question to the people. At their annual meeting, the Woman's Christian Temperance Union declared itself in support of conscription, but argued that the wealth of the nation should also be made to serve. At their annual meetings, Anglicans and Baptists also recorded their endorsement. At the club rooms of the Great War Veterans' Association at Church and Carlton Streets, the announcement was cheered. One of the more than thirty-four hundred members of the local GWVA commented, 'We are tickled to death that the powers that be have realized their duty and the pressing need of the time for men and still more men.' At recruiting meetings all over the city, 'every mention of conscription was received with cheers and applause by the audience.'[1]

There was one section of the community, however, that was not entirely pleased with the announcement. Labour leaders agreed to support conscription provided the government also conscripted wealth. They did not object to the idea of conscription. They objected to a conscription policy that was, in their eyes, not broad enough. Labour leaders said they wanted not just a centralized military manpower scheme, but a centralized economic one as well. James Simpson, vice-president of the Trade and Labour Congress of Canada, was also upset that Borden had not consulted with labour leaders before announcing conscription. This long time political activist, past member of the Board of Education, unsuccessful 1908 mayoral candidate, and prominent pre-war labour movement supporter,[2] however, did not object to conscription. He became a strong supporter of the measure after a meeting with Borden in Ottawa.[3]

While public opinion leaders put themselves on record, ordinary citizens of military age responded by heading to the Toronto Recruiting Depot to enlist in the local battalion of their choice. Men lined up hours before the examination centre opened, and by half past nine a considerable crowd had gathered. Clerks and medical officers had not anticipated such a demand on their services. As a result, the depot became quickly filled with men in various stages of the attestation process. By ten o'clock, over 60 men had been assigned to local battalions for training. By the end of the week, 968 men had applied to serve, though less than half of these, 408, had met the medical standards and been attested. The mere announcement of conscription had accomplished what months of cajoling had failed to deliver, but the sudden rush to enlist turned out to be short-lived, and recruiting totals soon declined to normal levels.

The public discourse on conscription during the summer of 1917 demonstrated that Torontonians were determined to influence events, not simply react to them. Initial anger at Laurier's decision to reject a coalition with Borden led to a conviction that English-speaking Canadians must now have their way. Citizens turned out by the thousand to support conscription. At a mass rally at Queen's Park on 2 June 1917, under a glorious blue sky, ten thousand men, women, and children endorsed a resolution supporting conscription. The crowd also demanded that the government 'take immediate steps to put down sedition in Canada.' The gathering was so large that it was addressed from two platforms. Cheer after cheer was raised when one speaker demanded that the government 'put a revolver to the head of the fit man who refuses to go.' The strongest cheers were for the more than two hundred khaki-clad former soldiers who had limped, beneath the banners of the Great War Veterans' Association, to their seats surrounding the dais. Mayor Tommy Church presided, and after the speeches, the entire crowd sang, 'Oh God, Our Help in Ages Past.'[4]

A large group of returned soldiers decided to put down 'sedition' on their own by confronting a socialist anti-conscriptionist meeting at the Labour Temple. The veterans forced their way into the hall where around five hundred men and women, including many 'foreigners' of non-British descent, were meeting to condemn the Military Service Act. The veterans demanded that the first item of business be the singing of the National Anthem. The Finnish band outraged them by refusing to comply. At that point, these former front-line troops attacked tables and chairs with their crutches and sticks. Furniture was sent spinning around the hall. Spurred on by the soundings of a bugler, the veterans knocked down anyone who had the temerity to resist. They chased protesters through windows, over roofs, and down fire escapes, and sent bodies rolling down stairways and crashing through doors. A large crowd gathered during the altercation, filling both sidewalks from Queen Street to Wilton Avenue, and cheered the veterans. After the building had been cleared, Sergeant-Major Lowery addressed the men from the steps, led the cheers for conscription, and paraded the troops to City Hall. On the way, however, another incident took place. A man dressed in German colours threw a bottle at the procession. He was chased to St Michael's Hospital where the veterans deferred to staff and police to locate the man, out of respect for the patients.[5]

Labour and union leaders stated 'very emphatically' that they had no sympathy with the objects of the socialist meeting, and that it had been organized by extremists. Caretaker William Fordham declared that there would be no more such meetings at the Labour Temple, telling reporters, 'If I had known what was going to take place last night,

Socialists never would have got the hall.' Chief Constable Henry James Grasett claimed that Toronto police were powerless to stop indoor meetings. British subjects were allowed freedom of speech, he said, and he would protect that right. However, enemy aliens were accorded no such privileges, and he promised that any anti-conscription rally involving enemy aliens would be shut down immediately. Grasett blamed the victims for precipitating the conflict, arguing that they were 'foolish to try to hold anti-conscription meetings when the people are so excited over the matter.'[6]

A week later, the Labour Temple was the site of a very different meeting. The Greater Toronto Labour Party met to pass a resolution that endorsed conscription based 'upon the principle of equal liability to service and the policy of controlling finances, food and resources in Canada to prosecute the war.'[7] This rally was part of a feverish few days of activity which coincided with the tabling of the Military Service Act in the House of Commons on 11 June 1917. Since Laurier had rejected coalition on 6 June, Borden decided to push the Act through Parliament before it was dissolved. The Act made all men between twenty and forty-five years of age liable for military service. Given the Conservative majority in the House of Commons, the Act's passage was a certainty, but it was still debated vigorously in the House.[8]

During this period, Toronto demonstrated little of the division apparent in Ottawa. Massey Hall was the site of a bipartisan rally on 10 June, involving prominent politicians from both the Conservative and the Liberal parties. The unity of the two parties was symbolized by the joining of hands by N.W. Rowell, the leader of the Ontario Liberals, and Sir William Hearst, the Conservative premier of Ontario. Soldiers who had returned from the front were once again a prominent feature of the pro-conscription rally, as several hundred veterans were accorded a place of honour by the platform. As they hobbled forward on crutches or were pushed in wheelchairs, the crowd erupted into a chorus of cheers. The gathered thousands adopted a resolution that gave the government a blank cheque: 'This mass meeting of citizens of Toronto ... places on record its conviction that our people, irrespective of party or of creed, are ready to support any immediate legislation as promised by the Prime Minister of Canada to provide through some equitable system of compulsory selection the necessary reinforcements for our Canadian Divisions now so heroically battling at the front.'[9]

Torontonians were not only in favour of conscription, the vast majority supported measures that made it difficult, if not impossible, to organize opposition to it. A second anti-conscription meeting was arranged at the corner of Queen and Bathurst Streets for 10 June by the Social-Democratic Party. There were fewer people at this rally than at the Labour Temple meeting, likely due to the fear of reprisals from veterans and citizens. When the police heard of the rally, plainclothes and uniformed officers arrived quickly, took over the platform, ordered the speaker to be silent, and examined 'every individual with a view to finding out how many were naturalized British subjects, how many [were] alien enemies, and how many [were] alien enemies without the necessary qualifications to be at large.'[10] True to his promise to clamp down on seditious activities, Chief Grasett arrested eighty Ukrainians and Austrians. Grasett told reporters that it was his duty to stop meetings which were anti-government. Attending an anti-conscription rally at this time was proof enough of anti-government activity.

Throughout the summer of 1917, the Military Service Act wound its way through the House of Commons. The situation heated up on 5 July 1917 when the House passed the bill through a second reading. The voting was cast along linguistic, not party lines, with a large majority of English-speaking MPs voting for conscription, and all French-speaking members opposing it. Laurier's forces were bolstered by the desertion of nine Quebec Conservatives, but were hurt by the crossing of twenty-five English-speaking Liberals to the government side. Ultimately, the Act found its way to the Senate, becoming law on 28 August 1917.[11]

At the front, the newly Knighted Sir Arthur Currie, now commanding the Canadian Corps, clashed with Sir Douglas Haig over a proposed attack at Lens, France, in July 1917. Currie argued that if the Canadians took the town, the Germans could shell them from nearby Hill 70 with impunity. Currie argued that the Canadians would be better served by taking Hill 70 and destroying the inevitable German counter-attacks in an attritional battle. Haig reluctantly agreed, and the Canadian Corps spent July preparing for the assault. The assault began on 15 August 1917 as the Canadians fought their way onto Hill 70 and then defended it against wave after wave of German counter-attacks. The cost of the fighting was nine thousand Canadian casualties compared with over twenty thousand on the German side. By the standards of attritional warfare, it was a victory. The Canadian Corps spent the rest of August and September in front-line duty, recuperating and absorbing replacements.[12]

As Canada's soldiers prepared to attack Hill 70, Toronto hosted the 'Win-the-War Convention,' on 2 August 1917. All public-spirited citizens were urged to attend and offer suggestions 'as to the way in which the war may be speedily brought to a close with a victory for the Allied nations.' Meeting at the arena, the convention opened at three o'clock with the 'people of Ontario' listed as the speakers for the first three hours. These patriotic speeches would later be followed by a concert by the Queen's Own Rifles, speeches by veterans, and addresses by Sir William Hearst and N.W. Rowell.

More than six thousand people filled the arena to capacity. Miles of 'fluttering green paper grasses' hung from huge supports up near the roof. Streams of electrical lanterns were strung from the floor to the ceiling. Bands were stationed on either side of the platform to entertain the audience. The whole assembly stood on its feet and cheered as more than two thousand veterans marched in to take their place of honour at the front. The speeches targeted Quebec and its failure to provide as many recruits for the army as had the English-speaking provinces. 'Don't call them French. They're not French,' one ex-soldier exclaimed, 'they're traitors!' The audience also opposed any discussion of the motivations behind Sir Wilfrid Laurier's rejection of the conscription bill. When Liberal Hugh Guthrie attempted to explain his break with Sir Wilfrid over conscription, he was met by a chorus of boos, and shouts calling Laurier a 'traitor.' Despite repeated appeals for order, Guthrie was unable to discuss Laurier. He shifted his focus back to winning the war and endorsing conscription, and was rewarded by a chorus of cheers.[13]

On the evening of 3 August, the arena was taken over by the women of Toronto for a mass meeting to support the continuation of the war. Advertisements announced that 'Every woman who has a Husband, Father or Relative at The Front or in training in Canada, Every Patriotic Society worker, every Red Cross worker, every Woman engaged in Munition or other work connected with the war is urged to attend the meeting, so that all women's efforts may be further unified and greater inspiration *to go on* may result from this first Mass Meeting of Ontario Women [emphasis in original].' Mrs A.M. Huestis presided, calling for conscription as soon as possible. Over two thousand women crowded into the arena, many of whom maintained their commitment to the men overseas by knitting throughout the meeting. Resolutions were passed which endorsed pleas for unity and for the effective mobilization of the country's resources to prosecute the war effort. An election, it was argued, would only slow the process of supplying the needed recruits and was, therefore, rejected.[14]

The Win-the-War Convention demonstrates that there was a large and growing pro-conscription and anti-French-Canadian sentiment. The unwillingness of the crowd to allow Hugh Guthrie to explain Laurier's actions speaks volumes of the mood in Toronto. Leading this condemnation were members of the Great War Veterans' Association. These men had fought and been wounded at the front, and would not tolerate anti-conscription talk. Far from being on the periphery of civic life, they were physically present in great numbers and were quick to voice their opinions. Veterans were ardent supporters of conscription, branding all those who opposed it as traitors. In addition, the mass rally continued the process of placing women in the same public space occupied by men. Both participated in the campaign to secure conscription as soon as possible.

This public support for conscription took place in a climate that was increasingly demanding of the resources and emotions of citizens. As the war effort continued to exact its toll, it also placed a considerable strain on the food supply. The summer of 1917 had yielded a good crop, but the labour shortage was such that there were not enough workers to bring in the harvest. Premier William Hearst wrote an open letter to the people of Ontario, under the heading '10,000 Men Needed Now: Ontario's Crop Must Be Harvested.' Directed at the urban population, it asked employers to release employees to be put to work wherever they were needed.

In response, Toronto organized a complement of four thousand workers. Articles in the daily papers stressed the need for volunteers to serve on the farms. The Canadian Manufacturers' Association and the Retail and the Wholesale Manufacturers met to discuss the situation, endorsed the necessity of supplying farm hands, and agreed to work with all haste to procure them. At this point, the issue of what the workers would be paid by the farmers was dismissed as of secondary importance. Initial attempts were successful; a canvass at the T. Eaton Company yielded three hundred volunteers.[15]

Advertisements appeared in the papers emphasizing the necessity of helping the farmers. Men were asked to register at the War Production Club, 15 King Street East, and 'Help Build the Bulwark against Famine!' This slogan accompanied a picture of two farmers struggling to bring in the fall harvest as another man in urban clothes arrives, taking off his jacket to assist them. All three men are standing behind a pile of harvested wheat, forming a bulwark to fend off the grim reaper stalking them from the other side of the barrier. Another advertisement showed a farmer and an urban worker shaking hands in a field, while across the divide, as a result of their work, a soldier is able to stand his post.

Two weeks after the campaign was launched, it appeared that men newly recruited to serve on the farms were doing well. In interviews, farmers expressed surprise at the effectiveness of urban workers, but were concerned about the high wages they were paying for these amateur farm hands. Over the coming days, this friction over wages resulted in fewer men volunteering than were needed. By 21 August, over six thousand men had volunteered provincewide: just over two thousand of these came from Toronto. Still more men were needed, but low pay remained a major obstacle. The high cost of living had driven wages upward, and farmers found it difficult to pay the rates demanded by urban workers.

The shortage of labour was so pronounced that more than 50 per cent of the seven thousand Boy Scouts in Ontario were already engaged in some form of war production. The strain on farm labour capacity was so great that farmers' wives came to the city to take workers back with them to help with the harvest. 'They say men are scarce,' one farm wife told a reported, 'but I started out to get a man to help my husband, and I am going to keep looking until I find one.'[16]

The difficulty of bringing in the fall harvest provides ample testimony to the scarcity of labour in Ontario in the summer of 1917. It had nothing to do with lack of patriotism and everything to do with the high cost of living and the demands of the war on human resources. The city attempted to confront the labour shortage in an organized fashion, pulling together representative employers and employees to discuss the situation. Unfortunately, the demands of the war were so great that Torontonians had to face the fact that not everything helpful to winning it could be done. There were only so many projects that the city could take on at any given time. The imposition of conscription would further stretch these resources, but even in the face of the ever-increasing demands of the war, the people did not falter in their support for it.

In September 1917 Borden's Conservatives created the War-Time Elections Act, a political manoeuvre by the prime minister to bolster support for his party. The Act disenfranchised recent immigrants (who typically voted Liberal) and enfranchised women who had relatives serving with the Canadian Expeditionary Force. Having increased his chances of being re-elected, Borden dissolved Parliament on 6 October and called an election for 17 December 1917. On 12 October Borden announced the formation of a Union coalition of prominent Conservatives and Liberals.[17]

At the front, the British were embroiled in the fight for Passchendaele, a battle that began in July 1917 and continued on into November. In September 1917, however, the Canadians were not directly involved. They were engaged in the familiar trench routine 'characterized by mud, boredom, disease, and misery, sometimes punctuated by the excitement and terror of an occasional trench raid or artillery duel.'[18] At the same time, much of Toronto's attention was directed at the Canadian National Exhibition, as it drew its largest crowds ever. On Labour Day, the Trades and Labour Congress of Canada used the Exhibition to announce its full support of conscription. Spokesmen pointed out that labour had done its part in the war, although they continued to point out that they would be even more supportive if wealth was also conscripted.[19]

Conscription had become law with the passage of the Military Service Act on 28 August 1917. The Act, however, did not suddenly erase all of the war's other demands. Food shortages remained, and just as residents had participated in harvesting the fall crop, they now turned their attention to stretching those resources. What had been a private sphere concern for women – feeding families – suddenly became a public issue for the entire city as women directed a thrift campaign. Advertisements appeared in the papers which portrayed women doing their part for the war effort. One image showed a long line of women carrying platters of food which they passed across the Atlantic to the outstretched arms of Canada's soldiers struggling under shellfire. Printed instructions told readers the nutritional value of fish, and explained the necessity of substituting such 'nutritious foods' as peas, lentils, and potatoes for beef and bacon.

These advertisements were supplemented by an open letter by Food Controller W.J. Hanna to the women of Ontario. Hanna announced that there was a worldwide shortage of beef and bacon, precisely those commodities most required by the troops. He requested that women 'not use beef and bacon on two days a week or at more than one meal on any other day, that they reduce their consumption of wheat bread by one-quarter, and that they use perishable and non-exportable products to the greatest possible extent as substitutes for the staple foods required for export.'[20] The centrepiece of the thrift campaign was the distribution of the food service pledge card to every household. Women volunteers asked other women to sign the pledge, and display the card prominently in their windows: 'To Win the War, This Household is Pledged to Carry Out Conscientiously the Advice and Directions of the Food Controller.'

In the middle of September 1917, women fanned out over Toronto to distribute cards. Canvassers reported that most women signed and displayed the food service pledge gladly. Planners had hoped to secure twelve hundred volunteers to do the canvassing, but they received over fifteen hundred applications. At the end of the first day, thirty-two thousand signatures had been secured. At one house, the canvasser was greeted by a woman who insisted upon showing her tiny vegetable garden and her little two-and-a-half-year-old baby who had never seen its soldier-father. The woman signed eagerly.[21]

The thrift campaign was assisted by the publication of numerous advertisements in the papers. One illustration showed a tall woman shielding Canadian soldiers behind her by standing with her arm outstretched to ward off the grim reaper. Another advertisement showed a line of women proffering the food they had saved to soldiers in bunkers in France. Each advertisement urged women to participate: 'For All We Have and Are – Serve Our Heroes – Sign and Live Up to Your Food Service Pledge;' 'Will They Let Famine Fight against Us? Sign The Food Service Pledge before It Is Too Late;' 'Waste Not That He May Want Not, Grant That You May Be Worthy of His Sacrifice.' At the bottom was a list of practical housekeeping hints, informing women about how to use leftovers to stretch food resources, how to care for food, how to can fruits with sugar, and how to shop effectively.[22]

By the time the campaign was over in early October, more than half of the pledge cards had been signed by the city's women. Organizers felt that even more success had been achieved in driving home to women the necessity of economizing at home in order that men not starve at the front. The campaign also illustrates the context in which support for conscription occurred. Even as they faced an increasing demand on the manpower of Canada, Torontonians understood that the war had pushed the resources of the nation to the limit. Further, they understood the sacrifices involved in continuing the struggle and did not flinch at implementing them. Women were not simply forced to economize; campaign workers explained why they had to stretch what little food they already had. Failure to do so, women were informed, would translate into starvation conditions at home and at the front. The campaign also revealed the high level of civic organization characteristic of this stage of the war. Advertisements appeared in papers before the campaign began and reinforced its mission as women visited homes in the city. Women were now shuttling between the public and the private spheres to further enhance the capacity of Toronto and the nation to successfully prosecute the war.

Against this backdrop of dwindling food and labour resources, the details of the Military Service Act were explained in each of the daily papers. The Act outlined eight grounds for exemption:

1 The importance of continuing employment in habitual occupation.
2 Importance of continuing employment as ———, for which he is specially qualified.
3 Importance of continuing education or training.
4 Serious hardship owing to exceptional financial obligations.
5 Serious hardship owing to exceptional business obligations.
6 Serious hardship owing to exceptional domestic position.
7 Ill-health or in infirmity.
8 Adherence to religious denomination of which the articles of faith forbid combatant service.

The Act left ample opportunity for the men who sat on the exemption tribunals to use their own discretion in determining what constituted 'serious hardship,' 'exceptional' circumstances, 'specially qualified,' 'ill-health,' or a religious denomination that forbade active service. The tribunals were made up overwhelmingly of professional men, many of whom had relatives at the front. This fact was celebrated by Liberal and Conservative papers as something that augered 'well for the strict enforcement of the act.'[23]

Prior to the official calling up of conscripts, the Toronto Recruiting Depot announced on the morning of 15 September 1917 that it would inspect men without any obligation to enlist. Even as the city's women dedicated themselves to the thrift campaign, military officials were confronted with another massive rush to the Armouries as men took advantage of the opportunity to determine whether or not they were fit for active service. They were slotted into five categories: Class A for general service overseas; Class B for service abroad, but not for general service; Class C for service in Canada only; Class D for men temporarily unfit; Class E for men unfit for service.[24]

The busiest day in the history of the Recruiting Depot was 15 September. The rush continued into the following week, with more than five hundred men coming forward each day. Only one in ten men who faced the doctors was rejected outright, but only about 40 per cent of the men were fit for the trenches. On 6 October 1917, 775 men passed through the Mobilization Centre in Toronto, but only fifty-one were attested. The others had only been interested in securing their medical papers and determining their status for the upcoming call of Class One (or Class A) recruits. These free medical exams continued until 13 October 1917, with the quantity of those taking them increasing over time.

When voluntary enlistment finally reached its close on 13 October 1917, more than forty-five thousand local men had donned khaki uniforms in just over three years of war.[25] However, as the medical tests in the final days of volunteerism demonstrate, the percentage of those men fit for duty had dropped from about 60 per cent of those who presented themselves to closer to 40 per cent. Even taking the lower percentage as a guide for the number who volunteered but were rejected for medical reasons, approximately 75,000 Toronto men offered to serve their country. Compared with the 87,300 eligible, the numbers translate into an impressive percentage: 86 per cent of eligible local men had volunteered, more than four out of every five.

Even as these obligation-free medical exams were being conducted, the Canadian Corps was moving into place to take a more active part in the Passchendaele battle. Suffering along with their British counterparts in the mud and squalor common to the sector, the Canadians fought three major engagements, on 26 October, 30 October, and 6 November. When operations came to a close on 10 November, the Corps had sustained 16,041 casualties, including 3,042 killed.[26] These numbers gave new urgency to the need to successfully implement conscription at home.

In Canada, the first day for Class One men to report for duty was 15 October 1917, but they could wait as long as 10 November before coming forward, a total of twenty-seven days. In that time, Toronto had to conscript 6,750 men, and newspapers hoped that the calling of Class One men alone would be enough to fill the quota. As the registration period opened, however, nowhere near as many men showed up as had been hoped. Recruiting officials expected Military District No. 2 to register 82,000, with Toronto choosing 6,750 from among the 20,000 men assumed to be in Class One in its jurisdiction. These totals meant that just over 3,000 men would have come forward to register each day in District No. 2 with about 750 of that number registering in Toronto. However, at the end of the first day only 374 men in the *entire district* had put their names forward, and of these, only 15 had accepted service, the other 359 claiming exemption.[27] In other words, 25 men had had to register to secure one recruit, and there was a 60 per cent chance that this one recruit would not be fit for service in the trenches.

To assist military officials, Toronto residents flooded the Registrar for Ontario, Glyn Osler, with anonymous letters informing him of potential slackers. Although the names of the correspondents were often not included, most indicated that they had several relatives at the front. Osler promised that the letters would be put to good use after 10 November when officials began tracking down all Class One men who had failed to register. It appeared by 17 October that these letters might well be required, as only 3,000 registrants had reported, and a mere 264 of these accepted service; the rest filed for exemption. Registration carried on for the next few weeks, but many waited as long as possible before reporting. Two weeks before the deadline, only 20 per cent of the Class One men had come forward.[28]

Events overseas were conspiring to ensure that even greater demands would be placed on Canadian manpower. Not only did the Allies have to make good the casualties suffered at Passchendaele, but they had to prepare against renewed German attacks in the winter of 1917 and the spring of 1918. The Kerensky government in Russia had been overthrown by the Bolsheviks in the November Revolution, and a truce was signed between the Russians and Germans in late December 1917. As a result, tens of thousands of fresh German troops took up positions on the Western Front, hoping to exploit their new-found advantage before the Americans arrived in strength in 1918.[29]

Against this grim backdrop, conscription plans were followed rigidly. As the 10 November deadline approached, every attempt was made to ensure that as many men as possible would do their duty. Newspapers warned of the consequences of failing to register: five years imprisonment or immediate service in the ranks. Military Police roamed downtown Toronto on 7 November stopping every Class One man they encountered, asking him if he had been examined or made his report. If the likely recruit acknowledged that he had not yet registered, the penalties of failing to comply with the law were explained. Young men were warned to carry with them, at all times, the receipt attesting to the fact that they had registered, as failure to do so was 'apt to lead to great unpleasantness.'[30]

After the deadline passed, the scope of the attempts to locate those who had not complied increased. Registrar Osler, speaking through the press, announced that he would abide by the law and leave 'every so-called deserter, who has failed to register, to suffer the consequences.'[31] Half a dozen men then appealed to Osler directly to be allowed to register past the deadline, but he refused, saying he did not want to create a precedent. These efforts were directed at what military officials estimated to be the seventeen thousand men in Military District No. 2 who had failed to report.

Although there are no specific numbers for the city of Toronto, it must be emphasized that almost 80 per cent of the men in Military District No. 2 in Class One – a total of sixty-five thousand – had registered by the deadline. Military District No. 2 included the cities of Hamilton and Toronto, but also the surrounding rural areas where the pressure to report was less intense, and the willingness to report less pronounced due to the constant requirements of farm labour. It is entirely likely that Toronto supplied a greater percentage of registrants, given that it had consistently outpaced rural recruiting for the entire war. There were no reports of opposition to the draft. There were no organized efforts to oppose the registration scheme. Individual men made decisions not to register on their own, but many came forward in the days after the deadline and complied with the law.[32]

In the meantime, police drew up a list of eligible young men who, they believed, were attempting to avoid service, and supplied a copy to Osler. Given the number of men who had not registered, the Military Service Council in Ottawa announced that if those in Class One who were in default surrendered themselves to authorities without delay, they would not to be subject to civil proceedings. Employers assisted military officials in requiring men to report for service. Owners of businesses were required to submit names of all male employees who had evaded the Military Service Act by 17 November, but many did so earlier. Gradually, the issue of finding delinquent Class One men receded from the papers, as fewer and fewer were left to be found, and as attention focused on the progress of the next stage of conscription, the exemption tribunals.

These tribunals opened on 8 November 1917, two days before the deadline for all men from Class One to register. A pattern quickly developed; the tribunals became stricter over time. The *Star* reported that a large percentage of those men going before the tribunals on the first day were being granted exemption, at least temporarily. The procedures were tightened in the coming days, ensuring that borderline cases were 'being decided oftener against the applicant than was the rule during the first two days.' The case of Roy McCauley of 106 Gould Street is a good example. While two days earlier he might have been granted exemption on the grounds of having an exceptional domestic situation, his hearing on 10 November, before Tribunal 353 at 77 High Park Boulevard, was not sympathetic. McCauley claimed that his brother had been wounded at the front, leaving himself as the only support for their mother. 'What would become of your mother if you were to go out on the street and be killed by a motor car?' replied the tribunal chairman, Judge John Winchester. 'Don't look on the black side of things. Your brother is not dead, and instead of being killed you might come back with the Military Cross.' McCauley was drafted.[33]

By 12 November, several reports arguing that the tribunals were becoming tougher appeared in the papers. The *News* did a survey of the different tribunals that indicated a greater proportion of applicants were having their claims disallowed than had been the case the previous week. Requesting exemption on the basis of exceptional business obligations did not work for Thomas Aveling of 491 King Street East. Aveling managed a printing business, and informed the tribunal that if he left, the business would fail, as all attempts to get the owner to manage the business had come to nothing. The tribunal replied that the failure of the business would then be the responsibility of the owner, not Mr. Aveling, and the claim was denied. By 16 November, standards had been further tightened. One claimant appeared before the tribunal, accompanied by his wife. The man cited a wooden leg as grounds for his claim, and his application was accepted, but not before the tribunal had a look to confirm that the leg was in fact wooden.[34]

As the days went by, report after report in the papers cited the ever-tightening standards. Tribunals stated that given the emergency the nation now found itself in, 'no man is indispensable' with regards to business or financial obligations. In effect, the tribunals elected to selectively ignore the grounds for exemption on the basis of these two obligations contained in the Military Service Act. In addition, despite earlier allowances granted for men supporting infirm parents, by 19 November this consideration had also been largely dispensed with. Even claimants with two or more brothers at the front were often refused exemption, the tribunals citing the emergency confronting the country as grounds for refusal. The Military Service Act also allowed men to defer service to continue their education, but tribunals often disallowed this claim as well. A third year medical student, William Kennedy, claimed exemption until he graduated, but Tribunal 351 'thought this too long and disallowed the claim.'[35]

Claiming exemption because of religious beliefs was no guarantee to evade service either. Cecil H.G. Stovell of 290 Church Street cited his Christadelphian faith, specifically the fact that it was against his religion to take part in the army, as grounds for exemption. Judge Winchester, however, had no patience. 'What is the use of me sending my boy overseas and other people sending their sons to fight, and then leave you behind? Do you think that we have not as much faith in God as you have? In England they make Christadelphians serve in the army.' When Stovell replied that he believed he should not serve, Winchester replied, 'Well, I don't. Those are exhortations of our Lord to all mankind. Cowardice alone influences you people to take the stand you do. You will have to go overseas even if you go as a cook or a stretcher-bearer.'[36]

By 4 December 1917, the last day of the exemption tribunals, relatively few cases remained. On the same day, the Appeal Court began its proceedings. Appeals provided one final opportunity for men to plead their case, but few were allowed. Judge Winchester opened the first appeal tribunal in City Hall on 4 December, moving quickly through the cases. The first man called, Francis Moran of 5 Hambly Avenue, claimed exemption on the grounds of being the only support for his mother. One of the men sitting on the panel, Alexander Snow, asked if Moran was seeing a girl. When the reply was in the affirmative, Snow pressed, 'Is this girl keeping you back?' 'Maybe,' came the reply. The case was dismissed. Of the forty-seven men who appeared before Judge Winchester, only seven excused from service.[37]

When it became clear that most men were applying to have their cases dismissed, the tribunals sped up proceedings and granted fewer exemptions. Their activities were an extension of the recruiting pattern which had begun in August 1914. Recruiting officers had gradually expanded the scope of their appeals until it became necessary to conscript men for service. Given the overwhelming support of the population for the war, the only way conscription could have been avoided would have been for the fighting to end before 1917. When a man appeared before the tribunal, it quickly became apparent that he could not take much comfort in the grounds for exemption included in the Military Service Act. Making full use of the latitude contained in the Act, tribunal judges ensured that as many men were made to serve as possible. The burden of proof resided with the people, not the State. Being granted an exemption was as much a product of when the application was made, as why it was made, at least in Toronto.

There were few objections, however, to the way area tribunals were run. The fact that there was no outcry against the curt dismissals or treatment of potential soldiers indicates a general level of acceptance. The hearings themselves indicate that voluntary recruiting had been enormously successful. More than half the total eligible men had already left, with another third having offered themselves and been rejected on medical grounds. Even in this context, no one raised a hand against the process set in place to conscript even more men. The reasons that men still at home offered for applying for exemption reveal the extent to which the local population had already participated in recruiting. Families with two or more soldiers at the front were commonplace. Judging from the number of anonymous letters sent to Registrar Osler, many citizens wanted to make those who had avoided service join as soon as possible. They could read the reasons for which men wished to be exempt, and could imagine the hardships imposed on families and the sorrow of relatives left at home. However, as an election loomed in the fall of 1917, there was no sign of a significant anti-conscription sentiment.

While the tribunals were meeting, Toronto was also engaged in one of the largest financial support campaigns of the war. Along with the rest of the country, the city focused on the 1917 Victory Loan campaign. The issue dominated the papers for weeks, often pushing election coverage off the front page. Following what had become the pattern for loan campaigns, advertisements appeared in the papers for weeks prior to the drive emphasizing its importance. Papers offered extensive editorial support, aiming to secure $75 million from Toronto alone, half of the $150 million quota for Ontario. Campaign organizers arranged to have a tank available for a parade downtown. Citizens cheered as the 'great mechanical fabric which had instilled terror into German hearts at Courcelette and at other points on the Western Front, lumbered heavily through Toronto streets, its quick-firing guns peeping wickedly from the various embrasures and whirling around in response to the human touch within its armoured interior.'[38] Other Victory Loan parades involving thousands of civilians wound through the downtown area in the following days.

Despite this enthusiasm, by the end of November 1917, just before the close of the campaign, Toronto was in danger of failing to meet its target. The honorary chairman of the Toronto Committee published an open letter in the papers. He informed citizens that as of midnight on 30 November, $63 million had been donated to the Victory Loan, the culmination of subscriptions by 101,467 residents. As the totals for the final few days were tallied, many worried whether or not the quota would be achieved, but by 3 December, it was clear that it had been. Once again the city had oversubscribed, donating $76 million to the fund: an average of $5.4 million each day over the two-week period.[39]

As the Victory Loan campaign demonstrates, the war effort continued to draw broad support. However, it was becoming increasingly clear that even well-organized patriotic drives had their limits. Just as the elaborate crusades to secure voluntary recruits had ultimately proven unable to obtain the volume of men demanded, the 1917 Victory Loan campaign suggested that voluntary financial contributions were also nearing their limit. Still, the 1917 campaign was remarkable in its level of participation, averaging more than one donation per household, demonstrating that the *patriotism* of Torontonians was *not* reaching its limit. The level at which citizens participated in this drive indicates that they still fervently supported the war effort. The difficulty was not in securing the patriotic support of citizens, but in struggling to keep voluntary contributions up to the ever-increasing demands of the war.

Nationally, the 1917 election was a de facto plebiscite on conscription. A vote for Borden's Union platform was a vote for conscription and winning the war – every other issue was accorded secondary importance. This emphasis was necessary to hold together the otherwise fragile Union coalition. Laurier, on the other hand, chose to focus on conscription even though the support of his party did not require it. Laurier become 'a martyr to conscription' in order to secure French-Canadian and immigrant support for the Liberal party in the future. Borden ensured the potential opposition in English-speaking Canada would be at a minimum by promising in early December 1917 to exempt agricultural workers from conscription. Voting patterns were, therefore, drawn largely along linguistic lines, with most English Canadians supporting conscription, and most French Canadians opposing it.[40]

In Toronto, the most ardent supporters of the conscriptionist cause were the members of the Great War Veterans' Association. Beginning early in the campaign at nomination meetings, soldiers made their presence felt. At one preliminary meeting, a Laurier supporter called for three cheers for his leader. In response, several soldiers 'seized the demonstrative one and dragged him down the aisle. He uttered a loud piercing shriek as somebody administered a kick to part of his anatomy. Finally he was released, but not before he had been pretty well pummeled.' In another incident, another Laurier supporter was chased by soldiers up a lane. Unfortunately for him, he ran up a dead end. The soldiers dragged him the length of the lane and administered 'some punishment' before they let him go.[41] Veterans would go to any lengths to ensure that their comrades overseas were reinforced.

Conscription set the context for the election in Toronto, but most local campaigns were not waged between anti-conscriptionists and conscriptionists because four out of the six ridings did not even offer a candidate for the former cause. In North Toronto, long-time Conservative MP and Minister of Trade and Commerce Sir George Foster was selected as the Union candidate. Descended from United Empire Loyalists, Foster had a distinguished career at the University of New Brunswick and was eventually appointed as a professor of Classics and Ancient Literature. He was first elected to Sir John A. Macdonald's Conservative government in 1885, and returned several times before war began in 1914. In addition to parliamentary duties, Foster served on the boards of several mining and development companies, among them the Union Trust Company of Toronto.[42] Foster's opponent, A.J. Young, was an Independent Liberal, which meant that he was no longer able to support Laurier. Young had three sons at the front, and pledged to support aggressively all measures that would reinforce the soldiers overseas and help bring about the successful conclusion of the war. His reasons for opposing the Unionists, he maintained, had nothing to do with its policy of conscription, and everything to do with the scandals which had plagued the Borden government since the outbreak of hostilities. Young continued to emphasize this theme throughout the campaign, arguing that 'The Military Service Act must be supported. That is my position, and it is the position of a true Canadian, who is bound to support our boys overseas, and kill graft at home.'[43]

South Toronto was contested by two candidates, former Toronto Mayor Dr Charles Sheard, Unionist, and prominent labour organizer D.A. Carey. Sheard was born, raised, and educated in Toronto. He practiced medicine in the city throughout his life, while at the same time serving on the City Council and on the boards of numerous medical associations, such as the Toronto League for the Prevention of Tuberculosis. As the Unionist candidate, Sheard supported conscription, but so did Carey. In his youth, this Labour candidate had trained as a machinist, but later served as a reporter with the *Telegram*. He began his long-time association with the labour movement in 1880. He served as president to the Trades and Labour Congress of Canada in 1896–7, and later became the president of the Toronto Labour Temple.[44] Carey challenged 'anyone to say that organized labour has not done its share, and more than its share, in this war.' To avoid being labelled a Laurier supporter, Carey sent Laurier a telegram which was reprinted, suitably enough, in the *Telegram*: 'I am the candidate of the Greater Toronto Labour party in South Toronto – not the candidate of any political party – and do not desire your endorsation of my candidature for the House of Commons, especially as I am most emphatically opposed to the war

policy of the Opposition as declared in Parliament and in your mani-
festo.' The issue for Carey was not conscription, but securing a voice for
Labour in the upcoming Union government.[45]

East Toronto also witnessed a contest between a Unionist and a Labour
candidate. Former Minister of Militia Sir Edward Kemp ran against
G.T. Vick, the business manager of the Bricklayers' Union. Kemp's high
profile bolstered his re-election bid. He was a noted manufacturer, but he
devoted much of his energy to public life, serving as president of the Toronto Board of Trade 1899–1900, in addition to which he was a member
in good standing of many prominent social and philanthropic societies.
First elected to the House of Commons in 1911, he served as Minister
without Portfolio before becoming Minister of Militia on 23 November
1916 after Sam Hughes was fired. He transferred to the Ministry of Overseas Military Forces in October 1917.[46] Conscription was an issue in this
riding, but only its form, not its substance, as Vick argued that wealth
should be conscripted along with manpower.[47] Thus, East Toronto elec-
tors could vote for the nature and breadth of conscription, but they could
not cast an anti-conscription vote.

There was no anti-conscriptionist candidate in Centre Toronto (also
called Toronto Centre) either. Unionist candidate and local businessman Edmund Bristol had been elected three times on a Conservative
platform, in 1905, 1908, and 1911.[48] One of his opponents was a Liberal
endorsed by Laurier, J.G. Ramsden, and the other was an Independent
candidate, A. Draimin. The latter withdrew from the campaign, but did
so after the deadline to remove his name from the ballot had passed.
Despite being backed by Laurier, Ramsden differed from the Unionists
only on the form conscription should take, not its necessity. He believed
that not only men should be made to serve the Empire, but wealth
also. Thus, the campaign in Centre Toronto was between two pro-
conscriptionists candidates. As a result, the election there revolved
around support either for the Military Service Act, or for a broader form
of conscription which would include wealth.[49]

Unionist organizers decided that one of the six Toronto ridings
should be contested by a Unionist Liberal candidate and chose for this
the traditionally Conservative riding of Parkdale. The result was not without controversy. Upset that Toronto would have anything to do with the
Liberal party, many returned soldiers did not support Herbert Macdonald Mowat. Even Mowat's status as a prominent member of the
Queen's Own Rifles, including serving as the brigade major at Camp
Borden in 1916,[50] was not enough of a guarantee to some constituents

that the needs of the men at the front would be met. Rather, these ultra pro-war supporters threw their support behind returned soldier Major Carmon McCormack. The result was a contest between two men who both claimed to be win-the-war candidates. Speaking to a rally at his headquarters at Dundas and Lansdowne Streets, McCormack argued: 'I recognize the Union Government whether they recognize me or not. It is time that we cut out politics, and it is time that we mobilize this country as it should be mobilized for the winning of the war. I would not go to Ottawa if I did not think that I could not do more for the soldiers than men who do not understand their needs.'[51] McCormack was pro-Union government, and the election in Parkdale revolved around representation for soldiers in that government. Gordon Waldron ran in Parkdale as a Liberal, but his campaign was virtually buried in coverage accorded to the fight between Mowat and McCormack for the Union vote.

There is no conclusive evidence in the Toronto papers about Waldron's position on conscription. However, it is possible that he ran as a Laurier Liberal, along with his colleague in West Toronto, C.W. Kerr. In a campaign rally, Kerr made it plain that he was a Laurier supporter; he believed 'that the policies of Sir Wilfrid Laurier should be decided by the people.' However, Kerr's campaign had a different tone to it than did Laurier's campaign in Quebec, probably because Kerr had no illusions about winning if he did not openly support conscription: 'I ... look upon it [the chances of winning] as forlorn hope.'[52]

While Laurier emphasized the choice that French Canadians would have in supporting or rejecting conscription, Kerr presented the election choice as being between Borden's Military Service Act and another option which would be a more broadly based conscription of manpower and wealth. Running against former Toronto Mayor and Unionist candidate H.C. Hocken, and Labour candidate John Bruce, Kerr made sure that Torontonians understood that he was as pro-conscription as his opponents, but would listen to the voice of the people. In a letter to Laurier about his nomination meeting, Kerr noted, 'I declared myself a candidate on behalf of the people, a Liberal Win-the-War man.' He was firmly committed to the war effort; his business partner was serving at the front, along with 'some twenty relatives on my wife's side and my side of the family.'[53]

Kerr's platform was different from Laurier's policy. Kerr made it plain that he was himself a supporter of conscription, and if elected would push for an even more broadly based measure than would the Borden government. This strategy was necessary because both of his opponents were supporters of conscription, and most Torontonians endorsed compulsory service. As the Unionist candidate, Hocken supported the Borden government, and Labour nominee John Bruce sought representation for workers in the Union government.[54]

Toronto's population was not afforded the luxury, however, of indulging in a minute following of the details of various local campaigns. Two thousand kilometres away, Halifax exploded onto the front pages just over a week before the 17 December 1917 vote. In Halifax harbour on 6 December 1917, the Belgian ship *Imo* and the French munition vessel *Mont Blanc* collided, resulting in the detonation of over 2,750 tons of TNT. Out of Halifax's total population of 50,000, almost 1,600 died, and over 9,000 were injured in the largest human-made explosion until that time. The blast destroyed or damaged 13,500 buildings and left 6,000 homeless. For days, newspaper headlines bluntly informed Torontonians of the disaster: 'Halifax City Is Wrecked'; and 'Halifax Dead May Be 2000.' Over 150 former Toronto soldiers, returning wounded from the front, had left Halifax just before the explosion.

Halifax residents who survived the blast began the process of rebuilding their shattered homes in the face of a new enemy: the Canadian winter. Thousands were homeless as a blizzard blanketed the city. Torontonians responded to the call for help and sent nurses and city planners along with medical supplies and clothing. Two hundred carpenters and glaziers were sent to help construct temporary shelters. A depot was set up at 45 Richmond Street West to collect donations of clothing and blankets. As the scale of the disaster was discovered, Toronto counted its cost, again in terms of dead and wounded. Torontonians killed in Halifax numbered five, with one other missing: one petty officer; a seven-year-old girl named Elizabeth Hendry; one woman who had been working with the Salvation Army, Mrs Ensign Cornwell; a telegraph operator; and one other man. Three other cadets were injured, along with one other woman.[55]

It was against the backdrop of continued aid for Halifax residents that Torontonians went to the polls on 17 December 1917. Although there were a variety of issues before them, only a minority of citizens even had the opportunity to cast a vote against conscription. Throughout the campaign, locals read in the papers the ardent support of conscription offered by ex-soldiers returned from the front. Any who had doubts may have been persuaded to support conscription at this point since the men returned from the front were campaigning so fervently for its implementation. Opposition candidates ran on a variety of platforms, but whether they were displeased with the corruption associated with the Borden government, desirous of a voice for labour in the Union Government cabinet, upset that soldiers' needs were not being given sufficient priority, or annoyed at a conscription policy which conscripted men but not wealth, candidates who ran against Unionists in four ridings all supported conscription.

The other two ridings present something of an enigma. Nationally, Laurier-Liberals argued that citizens would be given the opportunity to vote in a referendum on conscription. However, the two Laurier-Liberal candidates in Toronto were confronted with a local population which required no such vote. As a result, they presented the referendum as a forum in which citizens could decide the form conscription could take, not its necessity. Both expressed their support for conscription, arguing that it must be more broadly based than the Military Service Act. Thus, it is difficult to gauge what citizens who cast ballots for Laurier Liberals in Toronto believed they were voting for.

It would be difficult to imagine a more complete level of support than that offered by all of the Toronto papers, Liberal and Conservative, secular and religious, for the Union government. Editorials in the daily press drew attention to the fact that there were several candidates in each riding who supported conscription. However, they were unanimous in supporting the Union government, reminding voters that despite high levels of conscriptionist sentiment, 'There is only one Union Government candidate in your riding.'[56]

Editorials in religious papers were also unanimous in their support for Borden's coalition. An editorial in *The Presbyterian* was typical of the major churches' reaction: 'Never in the history of the Dominion has there been an election in which the clergy and the courts of the Protestant Churches have taken sides so unabashedly as now. We have been used to hear of the Roman Catholic priests telling their flock how they ought to vote, but this time we have Presbyteries and district meetings and ministerial associations passing resolutions in favour of the Union Government and urging the members of their respective denominations to vote for its candidates. And they are right.' Papers also reported on the actions of Toronto's religious leaders, which in turn reinforced the attitudes expressed on the editorial pages of religious journals. At St George's Church on 6 December 1917, before a meeting of the British Unity League, ministers from the Anglican, Methodist, Presbyterian, and Baptist churches endorsed the Union government. Just over a week later, the day before voters went to the polls, Toronto pulpits 'spoke with one clear voice ... in a direct appeal to the people to carry their consciences to the polls and vote for the Union Government.'[57]

Women also organized to publicly proclaim their support of the Union campaign. At a meeting at Margaret Eaton Hall on 12 November 1917, the Club for the Study of Social Science met to endorse Union government and conscription. The following day, the Local Council of Women, representing seventy-two local women's organizations, and the Presidents of Federated Societies met to discuss Union government. The result was a resolution that argued that it was the 'duty of every patriotic woman to support the Union Government and the win-the-war movement.' Support for Borden's coalition continued to build, and a massive rally of women was held on 24 November 1917. The Royal Alexandra Theatre was the site for this bipartisan rally of Liberal and Conservative women which promised that the 'women of Toronto pledge ... anew to do everything in our power to support our men overseas, and to send to them at once the necessary reinforcements.' Two weeks later, women met again at the Young Women's Christian Association Guild Hall to emphasize the need to vote for Union government, informing both men and women that they must support the party that would help to win the war.[58]

On election day, newspapers informed voters that it was their duty to go out and vote for Union. After the polling booths closed, citizens again took to the streets to take part in the collective process of learning the results of the election. The King Street offices of the *Star* were surrounded by more than ten thousand citizens who stood and watched as the tallies were flashed on giant screens. Every time another big majority was announced for Unionist candidates, the crowd burst into spontaneous applause. Nationally, the Union government won a majority in the House of Commons, taking 152 of 234 seats. The results were fairly evenly divided, with most of French Canada rejecting conscription, and most of English Canada embracing it. By nine o'clock it was clear that Toronto was solid for the Union government, having returned Union candidates in all six ridings. Local election results are listed in Table 5.1.

There were 90,985 votes cast in the six Toronto ridings. Fully 92.6 per cent were cast for candidates who, regardless of political affiliation, supported conscription. The other 7.4 per cent were for candidates who supported Laurier, but interpreted Laurier's no-conscription-without-referendum policy differently than did their leader. Therefore, votes cast for the Laurier-Liberal candidates in Parkdale and in West Toronto may have been cast in the name of a referendum for the public to

Table 5.1
Toronto 1917 Federal Election Results[59]

Riding	Candidate	Party affiliation	Number of votes	Percentage of total votes in riding
North Toronto	Foster	Union-Conservative	17,384	86.3
	Young	Independent-Liberal	2,763	13.7
South Toronto	Sheard	Union-Conservative	4,966	68.1
	Carey	Labour	2,322	31.7
East Toronto	Kemp	Union-Conservative	11,813	73.8
	Vick	Labour	4,204	26.2
Centre Toronto	Bristol	Union-Conservative	8,600	68.2
	Draimin	Laurier-Liberal	216	1.7
	Ramsden	Independent-Liberal	3,802	30.1
Parkdale	Mowat	Union-Liberal	9,454	45.8
	McCormack	Soldier (Pro-Union)	7,605	36.9
	Waldron	Laurier-Liberal	3,567	17.3
West Toronto	Hocken	Union-Conservative	9,385	65.6
	Bruce	Labour	1,995	14
	Kerr	Laurier-Liberal	2,909	20.4

decide on a more broadly based conscription policy, not for the chance to oppose it. Even assuming that every Laurier-Liberal vote was anti-conscription, more than 90 per cent of Toronto voters, after more than three years of war and tens of thousands of casualties, supported conscription.

The results indicate a city almost unanimous in its commitment to the policy.[60] Only Parkdale witnessed a margin of victory for the Unionist candidate that was less than 10 per cent. However, the gap between the Unionist Mowat and the Soldier candidate McCormack had nothing to do with conscription. A ballot cast for either man, totaling 82.7 per cent of the ballots cast in the riding, was a vote for Union government. In a traditionally Conservative riding, Parkdale residents and soldiers were upset that the Unionists nominated a former Liberal to run on the Union government ticket. As a result, McCormack drew many votes that would otherwise have gone to a Conservative-Unionist candidate.

The behaviour of women voters sparked the interest of many contemporaries. C.W. Kerr, Liberal candidate in West Toronto, wrote to Laurier shortly after the campaign was over. A scrutineer on election night,

Kerr noted that organizers 'did not anticipate that women would poll their full registered strength.' In West Toronto, Kerr observed, 95 per cent of the women voted for Unionist candidate Hocken. If these results could be generalized to the other ridings, it would suggest that women voted much more strongly for Unionist candidates than their male counterparts who divided their pro-conscription votes between Unionist, Win-the-War Liberals, one Soldier candidate, and Labour representatives. The behaviour of women was also noted by Borden supporter J.M. Godfrey. Women had featured so prominently in the local campaign that Godfrey was moved to write to Borden, 'The two outstanding features of the campaign are the British Canadian solidarity for the war and the splendid work of the Women.'[61]

Toronto's soldiers at the front also cast their ballots overwhelmingly for Unionist candidates. Although the results of their voting were not known in the city until the end of February, soldiers supported conscription almost unanimously. Even without taking into consideration their votes for non-Unionist candidates who supported conscription, the results were impressively for Union: North Toronto, 96.6 per cent; South Toronto, 98.3 per cent; East Toronto, 95.3 per cent; Toronto Centre, 96.7 per cent; Parkdale, 93.6 per cent; and West Toronto, 94.8 per cent. Across all six ridings, 21,570 out of a total of 21,822 soldier votes were cast for candidates who officially endorsed conscription: 98.8 per cent.[62]

This support, however, was not uninformed. Endorsement of conscription was made in Toronto in the context of food shortages, labour shortages, and ever-increasing casualty lists. People understood what conscription meant: the best way to prosecute the war. They recognized that voluntary efforts were not enough to keep pace with the demands of the fighting, and they voted to increase the level of sacrifice. A vote for conscription was as much as anything else a formal declaration that the demands of the war had increased to such a degree that it was necessary to put the authority of the state behind war measures.

Torontonians learned about the election results in the same way they had learned about the declaration of war in August 1914. Gathering outside newspaper offices, they cheered announcements that Unionist candidates had carried the day. Collectively, citizens had voted overwhelmingly for a new stage in the war effort. Voluntarism had reached its limits in terms of efficiency, finances, and recruiting. The collective decision of thousands of individual Toronto residents ushered in a new phase of the struggle: total war.

6

Total War: Total Victory

When the federal election votes were counted in December 1917, no one could doubt the strength of Toronto's commitment to a total war effort. Its unanimity of purpose, however, was not based on any belief that the end of the war was in sight. The German-Russian armistice of 3 December 1917 meant that the enemy would soon be able to transfer additional divisions to the west, while the build-up of American forces in France was going much slower than expected. The war might last two or three more years and Torontonians would have to see their great crusade through to a distant conclusion. It is fortunate that war ended in 1918 since as the year unfolded it became apparent that the people of Toronto were strained to the limit. Fault lines began to show and conflict replaced community consensus.

The first crisis was a serious coal shortage which struck the city, province, and much of the country during one of the coldest winters of the century. Wartime industry had demanded enormous amounts of the coal that normally would have been used for home heating. Problems of distribution compounded those of supply. On 4 January 1918 a storm ripped through the city, delaying trains filled with coal, slowing down the delivery of the fuel. Two other blizzards buried residents in snow and ice before the end of January. At several points during January and February, the thermometer plunged to more than twenty degrees Fahrenheit below zero.

A wide array of measures were implemented to help save coal and electricity. Power Controller Sir Henry Drayton proclaimed the necessity of practicing 'the strictest economy in the use of electrical energy.' Drayton was another prominent pro-war supporter. One of his first public acts during the conflict was to supervise the removal of British men and women from enemy territory.[1] In the name of the war effort, every man, woman, and child was directed to economize wherever possible so that the manufacture of war essentials could continue. Using electrical energy to advertise was prohibited. Street lighting was reduced. Churches merged congregations for Sunday services. Residents urged that pool rooms and places of recreation be closed. Public schools temporarily shut their doors. Government regulation declared that Mondays would be 'heatless' until 18 March 1918.

These efforts, however, failed to solve the crisis and the federal government was forced to impose a three-day shutdown of industry. A Saturday, Sunday, and Monday, 9–11 February 1918, were chosen. On these days, businesses could use only enough coal to prevent damage to property from freezing, but could not manufacture. There were only three exceptions: plants that had to run continuously to prevent damage to their structure; plants manufacturing perishable foods necessary for immediate consumption; and 'plants devoted to the printing and publication of daily newspapers.'[2] This was a profound testament to the importance of daily newspapers, as they were considered more important than war industry.

Toronto adhered strictly to the guidelines, virtually shutting itself down for three days. A walk through the downtown streets would have revealed closed department stores, office buildings, banks, candy stores, jewelers, and florists. Very few people were outside. At noon hour the grocery stores and butcher shops closed, leaving open only the theatres, news-stands, restaurants, and newspaper offices. In all, 7,500 stores were closed while another 2,500 businesses closed at noon hour. Six thousand office buildings were closed, along with 900 factories, leaving 95,000 workers idle. Schoolchildren, university students, and teachers remained at home. On Monday, courtrooms opened, but heat was kept to a minimum, causing overcoat-clad judges and lawyers to shiver as they worked. The few City Hall workers also kept their coats on. Employees working in the detective office were so cold that the entire staff of thirty-six men transferred themselves to No. 1 Police Station, announcing that they would work out of that office until Tuesday. The only place where business was increased was in the local theatres, where operators did a brisk trade catering to citizens with time on their hands.[3]

Against this backdrop of a two-month struggle against the elements, citizens went about their business and the war effort continued. On 3 January 1918, the most visible result of total war became a reality:

draftees reported for military service. On the first day five hundred Toronto men reported at Exhibition Camp, followed by another five hundred over the next two days. As the new conscripts went through early training, visited the Dental Officer, and were outfitted for uniforms, the city undertook a campaign to catch defaulters. Police officers searched pool rooms for idle young men. Rewards of ten dollars were promised to anyone who turned in a 'shirker'; the defaulter was made responsible for paying the fine. Lists of absentee soldiers were drawn up and printed in the papers. Civil and military police visited the homes of men who had not reported, demanding an explanation: 'As no explanation will be accepted all men caught by the police will be taken at once to camp and will be put into uniform.' As the weeks went by, police began seeking defaulters while dressed in civilian clothes. These undercover officers patrolled the streets and pool halls looking to catch idlers off guard.[4]

By the middle of February 1918, all Class One men not already in uniform were required to carry their papers at all times. Failure to do so would result in immediate conscription. Under the authority of the Department of Justice, Dominion Police could arrest those who could not provide satisfactory proof for why they were not in khaki. Putting these powers to immediate use, five hundred men were examined at the Pavlova Dance Academy on the evening of 16 February 1918. At 10:15 p.m., a force headed by Inspector Tom Flanagan of the Dominion Police entered the dance hall and required all young men in attendance to produce identification. Over the next two hours, fifteen failed to do so, and were required to report to Dominion Police headquarters on 18 February.[5]

Supplying troops was considered a civic responsibility. Citizens were asked to participate in the process of rounding up defaulters as approximately one out of every five men who were ordered by law to report had not done so. The public facilitated this process by supplying information on draft evaders. Between fifty and sixty letters a day were received by military officials from citizens offering such details. Other residents helped by telephoning in their contribution.[6]

Even as they coped with a harsh winter, endured inadequate heating, and participated in the process of securing more recruits for the Canadian Expeditionary Force, Torontonians were called upon to support another round of fund-raising for the Toronto and York County Patriotic Fund. Scheduled for 22–4 January 1918, the campaign was to raise $3 million in three days. As in the past, secular and religious papers printed editorials which extolled the virtues of the fund. Particularly striking, however, were the full-page advertisements used in these papers to encourage citizens to contribute. Even in the context of total war, images that conveyed or implied horrible front-line experiences were used. One picture showed a young khaki-clad soldier kneeling in no man's land, surrounded by the wreckage and destruction of war. As shells burst around him, the soldier holds out his arms in an appeal to the people of Toronto. Beneath this picture of blood and destruction were the words from John MacCrae's 'In Flanders Fields': 'If ye break faith with us who die, We shall not sleep.'

Another advertisement showed returned veterans standing in line to thank a businessman who donated to the Patriotic Fund. All the veterans bear some visible signs of the cost of war. One man stands at the front missing an arm, dependent upon a cane to walk. Behind him are men on crutches, while others require the support of their comrades. Another advertisement carried the message: 'When the Story Is Written and Told.' Above the caption, an elderly man and woman are pictured thinking back to the war as they read about it in a book. The image in the book shows three men carrying a wounded and unconscious comrade on a stretcher across no man's land. All around them shells explode, destroying men and the landscape with equal ferocity. The advertisement asks each citizen: 'How you would like to change places with that man who has just crawled over the parapet to repair some wire, and whose presence has been revealed to the enemy by a "starlight." Think it over, and then picture what it would be like to be wounded and lack attention because of a shortage of Red Cross supplies.'

The Patriotic Fund campaign was launched with a large rally at Massey Hall. Among the local dignitaries who gave speeches was Sir Sam Hughes, the former Minister of Militia. The assembled crowd gave an ovation to Sir Sam and to the returned veterans who paraded into the hall. In the days after big rally, twenty-five hundred women began the painstaking process of house-to-house canvassing to secure donations. Accustomed by this point in the war to elaborate planning, the organizers divided, the city into twenty districts to ensure total coverage. The goal was to collect half a million dollars in direct donations to add into the $3 million campaign. Mrs H.P. Plumptre,[7] president of the Women's Committee of the Patriotic Fund, assured workers, 'We have never been so completely organized so long ahead.' In addition to the districts, women canvassed railway stations, and civic and veterans hospitals. Every resident of Toronto was a potential donor. Women were specifically targeted for donations, which reflects, possibly, that a greater percentage of women were working for a wage than ever before. One advertisement showed women serving the war effort in a variety of occupations. Images of women as factory operative, canvasser, stenographer, and nurse were mingled with images of women as nurturer and caregiver to children. The message was clearly that everyone could contribute.[8]

Veterans were also supportive. A representative of the Great War Veterans' Association, Major Sampson, declared, 'We are heart and soul behind this movement!' Returned soldiers promised to assist workers to ensure the success of the drive. At every major rally, and at every related public gathering, veterans occupied a prominent place. Many of their number gave speeches to support the fund, calling attention to the need to continue the war, and to support the families of departed soldiers.[9]

Nevertheless, for the first time in the war, the Patriotic Fund did not meet its target within three days. An extra day of campaigning was undertaken, after which the fund was again oversubscribed. The failure to raise $3 million dollars in three days, however, had little to do with a lack of patriotism. Total war had increased the cost of fighting without increasing the capacity of residents to pay for it. Still, the rallies at Massey Hall were filled to capacity. In the dead of winter thousands of volunteers worked to see to the success of the campaign. After recognizing that more time would be needed, organizers succeeded in reaching their goal!

Torontonians worried about the build-up of German forces on the Western Front. Throughout February and into March 1918 analysts discussed not whether the Germans would attack, but when and where. They knew that Russia had withdrawn from the conflict and were aware that Germany was transferring thousands of men west. Early in February, a *World* headline declared: 'German Offensive against British Army Is Imminent.' Citing the improvement in weather conditions, and the fact that 'German troops and guns keep pouring into the Western Front,' the article concluded that the 'Great offensive' would take place within the next several weeks. The following day, the *World* declared: 'German Drive on West Front Is Scheduled for March.' In the days that followed, speculation continued on when and where the Germans would attack. On the second anniversary of the opening of the German assault at Verdun on 16 February 1916, the *News* reported that the Allies were 'ready to meet the widely-advertised enemy offensive.'[10]

In the midst of waiting to hear of the attack, Torontonians received some welcome good news. Married men who had left with the First Contingent of 'Old Originals' in August 1914 had been granted furlough. On 18 March 1918, newspapers reported that a ship carrying 395 'Old Originals' home for a three-month leave of absence had arrived in Halifax harbour. The numbers told a grim story of the cost of war. The Princess Patricia's Canadian Light Infantry, for example, had sent over a thousand men with that First Contingent: of the married men, only 15 were left. In total, Military District No. 2 had 113 men returning, 80 of whom were from Toronto. Citizens waited anxiously for their arrival.

While they waited, newspapers cabled stories taken from interviewed soldiers as they travelled home. Pte. Frank Fallows of 90 Main Street related that 'The worst experience I ever had was when I was buried in a falling dugout, with not only the earth, but two of my comrades on top of me.' He and his comrades were dug out of their tomb, but it was necessary to remove a piece of bone from each of Fallows' knees.[11]

The men were scheduled to arrive in the evening of 19 March 1918, with two trains pulling in at North Toronto and one at Union Station. Each train carried over 200 veterans, most of whom were returning wounded from the front. Only a small percentage of the occupants of each train were 'Old Originals.' Given the staggered arrival of the heroes, Mayor Tommy Church decided not to have a formal civic reception. He declared that flags should fly at full mast, and citizens should be free to demonstrate their appreciation, but that every effort should be made to allow the men to return home with their families as soon as possible. A formal welcome would be arranged at a later date, involving a half-holiday and a great public gathering. Unfortunately, the veteran soldiers did not appear on 19 March 1918. Scheduling conflicts changed their arrival to early in the morning of 20 March, prolonging an already agonizingly long wait by friends and relatives.[12]

The trains finally pulled in on 21 March 1918. This homecoming was unlike the now-familiar arrival of broken soldiers. 'Everyone who has had anything to do with the welcoming of wounded veterans has become pretty familiar with the scenes of scores or hundreds of wounded heroes limping home on crutches, or being carried from the trains, or walking out with a coat-sleeve dangling helpless, or with the scars or bruises of war written plainly upon their features, and they have witnessed the pathetic cheerfulness with which the relatives have tried to hide all consciousness of that in the joy of their welcome, but yesterday's scene was quite different from all that.'[13] As the train pulled into North Toronto station just after three-thirty, a military band attempted to play 'Where Do We Go from Here?' The size and crush of a crowd of two thousand made it impossible.

Before the men detrained, however, a strange scene was played out. While on one track the cargo was over a hundred Old Originals and another hundred convalescents discharged from the army, the other track carried a very different load. The second train was headed for the front, carrying five hundred draftees who had just taken leave of their families. For a moment the two trains stood opposite one another, the soldiers exchanging cheers and best wishes. The moment passed, the conscripts proceeded to war, and the returned men turned to waiting families.

Reports spoke of the hearty look of those who had been to the front and survived the experience intact. After the order was given to dismiss, the veterans rushed to embrace loved ones. Tears of joy dotted faces. Words were few. Desperate hugging and cries of joy filled the air. Those who had no relatives 'gave vent to their feelings in cheers and handclappings, frequently turning their heads rather than witness scenes that seemed too sacred for mere spectators.' Husbands were reunited with their wives. Fathers greeted their children, some for the first time. Quietly, smiles beaming from their faces, reunited families proceeded home.[14]

Unfortunately, the homecoming did not last as long as promised. On the very day that the Old Originals arrived in Toronto, the German army launched its long-awaited spring offensive. Among the casualties of that action was the furlough for the newly returned fighting men. In desperate need of manpower to stop the German drive, officials cancelled leaves, and many of the men who had boarded troop trains in August 1914 did so again on 6 April 1918 to return to the front. Scenes of leave-taking were particularly poignant as men stood surrounded by their families, awaiting the train. Women smiled at their husbands through eyes filled with tears. As they boarded the coaches, just as they had done almost four years earlier, the men waved goodbye.[15]

In the first three weeks of March 1918, war continued to pervade life in Toronto. Citizens emerged from a harsh winter of poor food and sporadic heating to confront a spring that promised new fighting – and more casualties. If there remained any questions about the horrible cost of war, the return of the Old Originals put them to rest. Even allowing for the unmarried 'Originals' who had not been granted furlough, the number returning told the story. Of the thousands who had left amidst cheers in August 1914, only dozens returned in the spring of 1918. In addition, those who arrived either unhurt or recovered from wounds were heavily outnumbered by convalescents wounded so badly that they could no longer be of service. Although reports spoke of the wonderful change it was for trains to arrive carrying men who could step off the platform under their own power, Torontonians had become accustomed to the arrival of hundreds of men shattered by the war. And the Old Originals brought with them stories of the grizzly nature of frontline fighting. The war reclaimed these veterans earlier than had been promised, clearly reminding citizens that the demands of the conflict continued to escalate.

Germany had to take advantage of its temporary superiority to achieve victory before the Americans arrived in strength. British forces bore the brunt of an attack designed to separate them from the French, and drive them into the sea. Between 21 March and 5 April 1918, the situation was desperate. The news of the offensive was transmitted quickly. Headlines trumpeted: 'Germans Open Offensive,' 'Germany's Greatest Offensive,' and 'Enemy Onrush Furious.' The ensuing articles did not hide the fact that the Allies were driven back. The official British statement reported: 'Heavy fighting continued until late hours last night on the whole battle front. During the afternoon powerful hostile attacks, delivered with great weight of infantry and artillery, broke through our defensive system West of St. Quentin.' Newspaper reports put the action in context, informing readers that for the 'first time since the war began on the Western Front, since the opposing armies established themselves in their trench systems, the defensive zone has been broken through.' Analysts predicted that unless the British were able to re-establish the line, they would be forced to conduct their retreat while fighting an open field battle against onrushing German forces. Reports confirmed that the Germans used poison gas and high velocity shells to spearhead their attack, and the resulting artillery duel 'rocked the countryside for hours.'[16]

For days, headlines reported that severe fighting continued. Torontonians read and worried. An editorial in the *Christian Guardian* was typical of those printed in the press, clearly presenting the reasons for the German action, and the consequences of failing to stem the tide: 'To wait until United States troops become a decisive factor in the fighting would be to insure defeat, and so Germany has determined to make one tremendous effort to smash through the British lines. If Britain can be beaten, Germany wins the war. And so these two great adversaries are now locked in the greatest death-grapple of all time.'[17] Not since 1914 when the enemy approached Paris had Toronto experienced such anxiety. As citizens went to their beds on Saturday 23 March 1918, they did so knowing that the German offensive had punctured the Allied line. All day Sunday, residents again besieged newspaper offices looking for the latest. At the behest of Mayor Tommy Church, clergy from all denominations led prayers. Torontonians prayed that the preparations that had been made against the attack would be sufficient.

The initial German advance was halted, but other offensive actions were initiated in the coming months. Before the end of June 1918, Germany launched two more sustained offensives, the first in Flanders from 9 to 29 April, and the second at the Marne River from 27 May to 6 June 1918. The British once again bore the brunt of the fighting, slowing and finally halting the German advance, at incredible cost. Stopping the offensive cost the British 163,500 casualties and the French 77,000, while the Germans suffered 239,000, all of this in thirteen days. Included within the British figure were 796 Canadians, mostly from the three cavalry regiments.[18] The Canadian Corps had been spared the brunt of the German assault.

Replacing casualties was paramount. For the time being, soldiers were required to hold the line and work towards conducting what military planners believed would be winning offensives in 1919 or even 1920.[19] Prime Minister Robert Borden based his actions in the early spring and summer of 1918 on the basis of those dire predictions. He told his cabinet on 12 April that cancellations of all exemptions to the Military Service Act were necessary to reinforce troops at the front. An Order in Council was passed on 19 April 1918, cancelling exemptions for those between twenty and twenty-two years of age.

Farmers were quick to register their discontent. At the beginning of May 1918, a delegation of two hundred farmers proceeded to Ottawa to explain their case to Prime Minister Borden. The call was sent out from Toronto by a former MP for Durham, Charles Jonas Thornton, who chaired the farmers' meeting while travelling by train to the capital. Thornton told reporters that farmers supported the war effort: 'While farmers' sons have no more right to get off than others, the need of food production was great, he said. He expressed the fear that in a year and a half the situation might be worse from the lack of food than the lack of men.'[20]

Members of the delegation hoped that Borden would consider modifications to the Order in Council of 19 April. They were not successful. Covered extensively in the papers, Borden's response was unequivocal: 'I want you to understand there is a side of the situation which you do not seem fully to realize. I have been twice in France and I cannot bring myself to stop short of any measure to give our soldiers all the support they deserve ... Production is absolutely essential and the duty of the

Government is to see that it is carried on. But if we wait for longer consideration of exemption, if we have long delays and our men are destroyed or decimated, what answer can we make to them? To them who have suffered tortures in a German prison will it be any answer to say that we have increased production mightily?'[21]

Unwilling to give up, farmers organized a larger march on Ottawa. On 4 May 1918, over five hundred York County farmers gathered, reaffirming their belief that they should not be subject to military service. 'We want only fair treatment,' one man declared, 'We are no slackers; we want to win the war.' They decided to send a delegation of over fifteen hundred Ontario farmers to meet with the government on 14 May 1918. The chair of the meeting, R.L. Stiver, emphasized that farmers were not attempting to shirk their duty. He believed that the war effort would be better served if the government shut non-essential industries to free up more men for duty overseas. He implored Borden at the very least to leave the farm workers in place until the end of October so they could bring in the harvest. Failure to do so, he argued, would leave aged fathers to look after acres of arable land.[22]

The United Farmers of Ontario grew as a political force out of this opposition to the treatment of farmers during the war. Its president, R.W.E. Burnaby, stressed that the protest was being made by old men, not young men subject to the draft. He declared that the young farmers were prepared to do their duty, to do what was best for the country. The hardship, however, would fall on the older men left behind. Burnaby echoed the pleas made by other speakers, calling for the shutdown of non-essential industry before farmers' sons were taken. Reducing the available manpower on the farms this year, he believed, would translate into fewer crops being produced in the coming years and fields that would have to be reclaimed when the men returned.

Prime Minister Borden attempted to ground this new rally of Ontario farmers before it took flight, using the papers to send another message. He re-emphasized the demands of the day, and continued to maintain that farmers' sons would be required to serve. He reminded farmers that he had already met with the delegation of two hundred, and promised them that a delegation of two thousand would receive the same answer.

Undaunted, the largest delegation of Ontario farmers ever to attend a conference at Ottawa proceeded with its plans. Over two thousand farmers crowded into the Russell Theatre to plead their case. The first speaker, J.I. Haycock of Lennox, reminded the government of its election pledge: 'We are not coming here with our hat in hands to ask the Government for something to which we are not entitled. We simply ask them to keep a solemn pledge.' Another speaker, John I. Suggett, maintained that the farmers supported the war effort: 'We want to produce, we want to win the war, but the Government won't let us.' W.A. Amos of Palmerston carefully pointed out that he had no son in danger of being conscripted, and that he had campaigned to help elect the Union government. He objected to criticisms that the farmers were not willing to do what was necessary to win the war: 'Nobody has been any more loyal than the farmers. Our young men enlisted voluntarily. They went to the munition plants to help, and the farmers have strained every muscle to produce the last possible pound of food. We are willing to assume our share of sacrifice.'[23]

Despite the impressive number of attendees and the eloquent speeches, Borden remained immovable. He reaffirmed the demands for manpower and reminded farmers that if Germany succeeded in taking the channel ports, shipping food would be difficult. Such a military triumph, Borden argued, would allow Germany to escalate the submarine campaign to a point that would endanger the entire Allied war effort.

Agriculturalists did not accept this flat refusal as the end of the debate. At the behest of the United Farmers of Ontario, three weeks later a further delegation of over two thousand farmers gathered in Toronto. They filled the Labour Temple to capacity, prompting organizers to secure Massey Hall for the afternoon session. The mood was boisterous. From the middle of the floor, one delegate shouted, 'We are fighting against a military autocracy.' The delegate had been referring to the Borden government, not Germany, and the resulting roar of applause shook the building. Farmers maintained that their case was not presented in a fair way in the press – either Liberal or Conservative. They called for the formation of a newspaper that would reflect agricultural interests. They resented the fact that every Toronto paper had argued in the editorials that the farmers should accept the decision of the Borden government and realize that the need for manpower came first.[24]

The only exception came from the farmer's publication, *The Weekly Sun*. Its editorials, however, did not question the need for men, nor the requirement to reinforce the front, but whether sending farmers was in the best interests of the war effort. Citing the difficulties the Americans were having in securing enough ships to transport their men overseas, one editorialist wondered how the war effort would be improved by taking farmers off the land only to have them sit idly while awaiting transport to France. Another editorial suggested that an effective compromise might be found. Since any farmers drafted in the spring of 1918 would not arrive at the front until too late to participate in stopping the German drive, the writer suggested that the men be allowed to remain at home until the harvest was over. Failure to see to the needs of production, another writer argued, 'would be a calamity obliging a relaxation of our war effort.'[25]

Despite the heightened rhetoric by farmers in Ottawa, however, the Toronto meeting opened and closed with affirmations of loyalty to the war effort and the Empire. Delegate after delegate reaffirmed that they were there 'in the interests of the British Empire.' Earlier appeals which had called for the dissolution of Parliament were rejected by the convention. It was decided that such an appeal during wartime was inappropriate. Farmers defended themselves against charges that they were not being patriotic, and they 'also stoutly repudiated the charges that the farmers of Ontario had not been staunch supporters of the Union Government at the last election.' Their slogan, after all, had been 'Farm or Fight.' In keeping with a convention which supported the war effort, each night's business closed with a rousing singing of 'God Save the King.'[26]

The demands of the war caught the Union government between two solemn pledges: to reinforce the men at the front, and to allow exemptions for young men working on the farms. Faced with a grim decision, Borden decided that the needs of the army superseded those of the farmers. He argued that the people of Canada could not fail to reinforce the men overseas: doing so would jeopardize soldiers' lives. Both Borden and the farmers were squaring off over a war that would continue well into the foreseeable future – not just over one growing season. They debated the consequences of two or three years without adequate labour to work the land and the best way to achieve victory.

Desperate fighting continued at the front throughout late June and July 1918. Germany launched what would be its last offensive of the First World War on 15 July, which was brought to a halt on 6 August. Once again, the German army failed to seize Paris. They had suffered enormous casualties in the attempt; one million German soldiers had been killed or wounded since 21 March 1918. The exhausted remnants of the German army were about to face their sternest test.[27]

Prime Minister Borden continued to plan to improve the efficiency of the Canadian war effort for the campaign of 1919. To this end, another National Registration Day was held on 22 June 1918. Every resident of

Canada, British or alien, and over sixteen years of age had to provide vital information. Much of it was basic, such as name, address, and date of birth, but some parts were potentially more inflammatory. The Canadian government wanted to know whether or not the citizen in question was a British subject, and if so, by birth or by naturalization? To what country did the resident owe allegiance? What was the candidate's marital status? Did the individual have any physical disabilities? What was the present occupation, and what other work could the respondent do well? Would he or she be willing to serve the present national crisis by working in some other occupation? Did the candidate have any farm experience? Where? For how long? The campaign proceeded uneventfully in Toronto's Military District No. 2, with fully 93 per cent of residents completing the form prior to the last official day of the campaign on 22 June 1918.[28]

The Canadian government needed help in critical areas. Farm labour continued to pose a problem to the well-being of the country and to the Allies who needed Canadian foodstuffs. The questionnaire solicited information from people who could work on a farm and would be willing to do so for the length of the crisis. The registration scheme was also designed to locate potential enemy aliens, although the intentions behind this are unclear. It may have been that the government wanted to locate potential dissidents, but it was more likely an attempt to locate residents who had avoided military service. These individuals would put up the least resistance, and be missed the least, if they were moved around the country to help on farms or in factories. Questions about marital status had a direct influence on the implementation of the Military Service Act, since it told the government how many potential recruits were in each class.

These measures were increasingly necessary to deal with the growing demands of total war. As industrial, agricultural, and human resources were stretched to the limit, other unrest followed on the heels of the farmers' demonstrations. Strikes increased throughout 1918, with a great deal of attention focused on the Toronto city workers' job action that summer. Previous accounts of strikes in 1918 have emphasized worker militancy to bolster arguments about the antagonism between labour and capital. Toronto's experience with labour unrest had little to do with such ideological battles. Labour was caught up in the war effort and workers had seen their real wages drop by as much as 80 per cent since war began. Worker demands for a 20 per cent wage increase had nothing to do with what labour historian Bryan Palmer has interpreted as the ability of workers to 'extract concessions from employers.' Nor did it reflect what Gregory S. Kealey has termed the 'first significant nationwide working-class challenge to bourgeois rule.'[29] Accepting a wage increase of only 20 per cent was a sacrifice made by union members to ensure as little disruption to the war effort as possible, while allowing them a marginal cost of living increase.

Rather, the members of the Civic Employees' Union were angry that the Toronto City Council refused to backdate their wage increase to the first of the year, or even to grant the principle of conciliation. Workers had received a two dollar increase in weekly wages beginning on 1 April 1918, and they wanted it applied retroactively back to 1 January 1918. Union representatives, speaking on behalf of their thirty-five hundred members, warned that the entire workforce would strike, and that a large number of City Hall employees would join in sympathy. Mayor Church tried to de-escalate the rhetoric: 'The city wants to be just and fair to its employees, and set an example to private ownership. I hope the men will be patient, and not precipitate a strike.' He promised that the City Council would recognize the union, but requested that everything be done to avoid a strike. City Controller McBride was not as sympathetic, challenging the patriotism of the men, arguing that the threatened strike action 'is a mean, concerted attempt of the men to take advantage of war conditions and cause the civic administration to crawl.' Over the next several days, the papers reported discussions between the City and its employees. Opposing positions became entrenched, and it looked increasingly likely that there would be a strike. The civic workers met at the Labour Temple 3 July 1918 to discuss whether or not to walk off the job. The fundamental issue remained back pay from 1 January through to the end of March 1918.[30]

The *Industrial Banner* published an article in early July 1918 explaining why strikes were on the increase. It related that there had been fewer strikes in Canada since the beginning of the Great War than at any other similar period in its history, 'not because of lack of provocation but because the workers in order to help the Empire and the Dominion in the stress and strain of a colossal conflict were prepared to sink their differences in order, if possible, to ensure the greatest cooperation in the service of the state.' The article went on to lament that while workers had made sacrifices and volunteered to serve in the army, their real wages continued to decline. The government was blamed for failing to protect workers' wages, and it charged that wages could 'no longer compete with the even more rapidly increasing cost of living, [since] the bottom has entirely dropped out of the dollar bill ... That was why the civic employees in Toronto asked for a square deal.'[31]

The members of the Civic Employees' Union voted 98 per cent in favour of a strike, and union members walked out on 5 July 1918. About twelve hundred employees did not report for work on the first day, but many more threatened to walk out in the coming days. Virtually every aspect of 'City Works' was affected: 'street cleaning, parks, waterworks, including pumping station, sewer department, septic tanks, roadways and the filtration plant.' Secretary T.A. Stevenson of the Trades and Labour Council sent a telegram to the Minister of Labour, the Hon. Thomas Crothers: 'Civic Employees' Union on strike. Would advise endeavor be made immediately to bring about settlement or serious situation may develop, which would involve thousands of other workers.' Stevenson was referring to the more than twenty-five thousand local trade unionists whose representatives were meeting on the evening of 5 July 1918 to discuss striking in sympathy with city workers. The Labour Temple was a hive of activity the entire day as a long line of strikers registered. Outside, workers crowded Church Street, overflowing onto nearby church grounds.[32]

Over the next two days, there was little negotiation. The City continued to claim that it would not consider arbitration and that it could not afford to pay the strikers a backdated war bonus; the men refused to return to work without these concessions. The stakes were raised, however, when other trade unionists began to move towards sympathy strikes with civic employees. On 7 July 1918, over fifteen hundred machinists and specialists from Toronto met in the Labour Temple and elected to 'take any action which the District Trade and Labour Council might advise on behalf of the striking civic employees.'[33]

City officials were suddenly confronted with the prospect of a general strike. Other unions expressed their intention to support the civic employees. The Builders' Trades League with its eighteen unions and between five thousand and seven thousand men 'decided to vote in sympathy with the aims of the civic strikers.'[34] The Toronto locals of the Gloveworkers' Union took similar action. These votes did not necessarily mean that these unions would also go out on strike, but that at a minimum they would help the members of the Civic Employees' Union to be able to remain on strike until a settlement was secured. The *News* asked: 'Is Toronto hastening towards a great industrial upheaval, which, starting in the strike of the civic employees, will ultimately include all the great branches of organized labour?' The *World* summarized the situation succinctly: 'the labour situation in Toronto has rarely been more serious.'[35]

Into the breach stepped Toronto Mayor Tommy Church. While the city had previously objected to the idea of arbitration, Church was now willing to discuss it, telling reporters that the strike 'is purely a question of wages, and my own personal opinion is that the men should be offered the $2 a week dated back to January 1, and that if they return to work they should choose a representative who would meet with the representative chosen by the city and these two would choose a third. They would then be able to settle any other matter that might be in dispute.' Church was offering the two key terms that the union demanded: wage increases and arbitration. The civic employees grasped the olive branch, putting forward a counter proposal on the form of arbitration. Their union would agree to arbitration provided both it and the City supplied two delegates each.[36]

The final hurdle remained the approval of two-thirds of the Toronto City Council. During a three-hour debate, Mayor Church pleaded with the council: 'I cannot too strongly urge you that the existing strike should be settled forthwith. Conciliation should be met with conciliation. I cannot too strongly urge on Council that action should be taken to-day, so that the men may return to work.'[37] Church secured the two-thirds majority needed, receiving eighteen out of twenty-six votes. Arbitration was agreed to with each side choosing two representatives, who would in turn agree to a fifth member of the board. Workers went back to their jobs and the rhetoric about widening the strike disappeared.

It is evident here, as with other labour disputes in wartime Toronto, that workers organized into unions were part of the broad community of citizens anxious to avoid conflict that might damage the war effort. Given the ravages of inflation, the motivation of labour spokespersons and workers alike is a remarkable testament to the social cohesion that characterized the city during the Great War.

The city workers' strike also provides a glimpse of the considerable power the unions reserved during wartime. Production and labour were paramount, and threatened general strike action received the prompt attention of the City Council. The Union got the concessions it wanted quickly. It is truly remarkable that organized labour did *not* use this power earlier or more often. Workers' unwillingness to disrupt production or services until absolutely necessary is a strong testament to the commitment of labour to the war effort. As had been the case with the farmers the previous month, workers vehemently objected to claims that they were not patriotic. The debate was never about whether or not they should stop the war with a general strike. The timing of the strike was simply used as leverage to ensure that workers secured enough money to meet the demands of family – not to mention Victory Loans, Patriotic Funds, and Red Cross drives.

It was with relief that workers returned to their jobs. While they had been in conflict with the City Council, the demands of the war had not lessened. Another chapter had been written into the annals of its horrors, and once again Toronto felt the tragedy directly. Headlines on 2 July 1918 told the story: 'Canadian Doctors and Nurses Murdered, Hospital Ship Llandovery Castle Sunk.' Just seventy miles off the Irish coast, on the evening of 27 June, a German submarine torpedoed the Canadian hospital ship *Llandovery Castle*. There were 258 people on board, including fourteen nurses. The ship sank quickly, and survivors drifted in rescue boats for thirty-six hours before help arrived. Twelve of the fourteen nursing sisters had made their way to a lifeboat, only to be drowned when their boat capsized in the whirlpool created by the sinking ship. The only survivor of the life boat accident was an unnamed Canadian sergeant who managed to crawl onto the keel. In all, only twenty-four persons reached port safely.[38]

In the days that followed, Toronto once again counted the cost. Thirteen local residents were drowned, two made it back safely to port. Residents gathered on 14 July 1918 in St Andrew's Presbyterian Church on King Street to hold a memorial service for the dead. The service was attended by relatives of the deceased, representatives of the medical and nursing communities, and local citizens. The first three rows were occupied by nursing sisters from Toronto, who came to give tribute to their fallen comrades. The Rev. Dr J.W. McMillan presided, telling listeners that the lesson learned from the tragedy was to 'stick it through.' He argued that 'We are the true pacifists, because we will have peace at any price. They will not pay the price of war.'[39]

Now women were at the forefront of the ceremony to commemorate the sacrifice of more citizens to the cause. The nursing sisters who sat in the first pews of St Andrew's Presbyterian Church gathered just as soldiers did to honour comrades lost in the line of duty. Every passing day, women were involving themselves in greater numbers in activities which took them closer and closer to the front. In early July 1918, young Canadian women were given a chance to qualify as transport drivers for the Royal Air Force. At ten dollars per week these women were required to work from 8:00 a.m. until 5:30 p.m. with an hour and fifteen minutes for lunch, and half-days on Saturday and Sunday.[40]

Other women moved into factories to help build aircraft. In one plant alone, over one hundred women were employed. Major Newman, in charge of the unit, told a reporter from the *World*, 'during the last four or five weeks we have expanded considerably, and it is within this time that most of the women have come on, and they are all doing well.' Women had not been hired to do clerical work, but took part in every aspect of the factory's production. They dismantled machines in for repairs, sorted and cleaned parts, sorted belts and nuts, assisted in the tinsmith shops, made sails, and knotted wires as well as helping with myriad other tasks.[41]

The demand of total war continued to escalate. Toronto citizens continued to pay the unpredictable costs involved in fighting an enemy that used unrestricted submarine warfare. Women continued to step into places either vacated by men drafted for overseas service or newly created as a result of the exigencies of war. The dedication of the population to fighting and winning showed no signs of slackening. This resolve would be necessary to see the city and the country through the next four critical months.

Even as the Allies fought the last of the great German offensives to a standstill in the first week of August 1918, Torontonians fought their own battles – with the police. Just as the farmers and labourers had taken it upon themselves to act to defend their interests, it was now the turn of returned soldiers. These men constantly decried what they considered the 'soft' treatment of enemy aliens and what they saw as the failure of non-British subjects to give returned men priority job placement. The frustration of returned soldiers escalated into a crisis on 1 August 1918. A Private Cluderay argued with patrons and waiters in the White City Cafe at 433 Yonge Street. By the time police arrived, the veteran had a large gash in his head as a result of a fight with a Greek employee. Cluderay was charged with public drunkenness and fined fifteen dollars.

His comrades sought revenge the following day. A couple of hundred former soldiers and civilian sympathizers arrived at the cafe around six in the evening and ransacked the business. Plate glass windows were smashed. Mirrors were destroyed. Marble tabletops were removed. Food was scattered. As the destruction proceeded, the mob was reinforced by other soldiers and civilians, swelling its ranks to over four hundred. The leaders were in khaki, their crutches and missing limbs silent testimony to their service in France. The group went on a rampage, targeting branches of the White City Cafe and other Greek restaurants. The next incident occurred at the cafe located at 985 West Bloor Street, where police stood by out of fear of causing an unmitigated riot. They did, however, send word to close other White City Cafe locations. Finished at 985 West Bloor, the mob boarded cars and proceeded to the Star Lunch at 441 Yonge Street. Even though police had closed the location, the men forced their way in and demolished the business. Crowds gathered to watch the destruction, stopping traffic in both directions. Food, furniture, and boxes were thrown through broken windows. The police did nothing.

The mob then headed to 822 Yonge Street, the Marathon Lunch. After the lunch counter was routed, the crowd marched down Yonge Street, finally clashing with police. One constable was struck as he attempted to arrest a soldier, but he succeeded in dragging the offender to a waiting wagon. This action infuriated the crowd, and shouts of 'To the station! To the station!' filled the air. Just then two truck loads of police reinforcements arrived, setting up a picket.

Irate, the mob continued down Yonge Street, avoiding the assembled police. Several non-British restaurant owners were dragged into the street and made to salute the Union Jack. Soldiers chanted, 'We took our chance in France and we'll take it here!' Others yelled, 'This is the night we will get justice!' Military officials dispatched two truck loads of serving soldiers under the command of Maj. G.R. Rodgers, and stationed them on the edge of the crowd. Rodgers spoke to the mob from a window ledge of the Colonial Restaurant at 349 Yonge Street. He advised the men that taking part in such disturbances would accomplish nothing. He was interrupted, however, when a brick was launched through a window above him, scattering glass in all directions. Blocked from raiding this restaurant, the mob resumed its progress down Yonge.

The veterans were about to ransack the Superior Lunch at 257 Yonge Street when they discovered that some returned soldiers were employed there. Accordingly, they bypassed it and continued downtown, confronting a police line at the corner of Queen and Yonge Streets. No one was allowed to proceed further south. The crowd headed off in different directions in an attempt to bypass the line, but police and military officials had finally secured the upper hand, and spent the next few hours marching up and down Yonge Street, preventing further incidents.

When order was finally restored after 2:00 a.m., officials began to count the cost. Fifteen local restaurants had been broken into and looted. The damage to the first White City Cafe restaurant was $7,000 alone; the total bill exceeded $40,000. Scores of people had been hurt by flying objects and broken glass. One police officer was beaten by a returned soldier wielding his crutch. Another was struck in the head by a flying bottle. A soldier claimed that he was struck with the handle of a policeman's service revolver. Fifteen men were arrested; six had actually served in the Canadian Expeditionary Force. They were released pending the posting of $100 bail.[42]

Bitterness and recrimination were felt on all sides, as each blamed the other for precipitating the conflict. Unfortunately, the violence was only just beginning. On 3 August 1918, a Saturday night, returned soldiers again took to the streets demanding the outright release of the men arrested on Friday. About two hundred veterans paraded up Yonge until they reached Albert Street. At this point, the men began marching in fours, the crutch cases up front. By the time the procession reached Court Street it numbered some two thousand, made up of returned men and sympathetic civilians. Their objective was No. 1 Police Station. Anticipating trouble, the police were ready and used their batons freely. When the crowd would not disperse, about twenty police charged on horseback. Veterans were armed with sticks, but the police did not restrict their targets to men in uniform. After a brief skirmish, the crowd scattered. No arrests were made.

The crowd reformed and shifted its attention to No. 2 Police Station on Agnes Street, in the heart of Toronto's ethnic district, the Ward. The police were lined up at the corner of Terauley and Dundas Streets, barring access. Denied a second time, the crowd withdrew slightly, and pelted the police line with rocks and bottles. Once again the police charged, dispersing the agitators and making several arrests. The mob made two more rushes, one at 9:30 p.m. and another at 10:20 p.m., but each time the police forcibly dispersed it. After one charge involving police on foot and on horseback, over a hundred rioters were left stretched senseless on the pavement. A detachment of military personnel was kept on standby at City Hall, but no call was made on them. The final tally for the evening was ten arrests, twenty-six taken to hospital with injuries, and countless others tending wounds at home.

Tensions remained high through 7 August 1918, with repeated clashes between police and civilians. A rally at Queen's Park passed declarations condemning police activity and recommending 'drastic resolutions' regarding aliens: 'That licenses hitherto granted to all aliens, unnaturalized, or otherwise, be canceled for not less than two years after the war. That all aliens be returned to their several countries or drafted in the Canadian Expeditionary Force, and that enemy aliens be interned or put to work on the land. That all unmarried men of the

Toronto police force who participated in the outrage on Saturday night be drafted into the C.E.F.'[43] Each time a resolution was read, the crowd cheered.

City and military officials took steps to ensure there was no further trouble. Five hundred troops arrived from Niagara Camp for use in an emergency. Morning papers declared that Mayor Tommy Church would read the Riot Act from the steps of City Hall at noon. By the appointed hour, however, he changed his mind. The crowd of over five thousand shouted at Church as he squeezed his way through the crush gathered at the entrance to City Hall. The assembled citizens appeared unwilling to listen until the mayor managed to communicate to them that he would not read the Riot Act. The crowd cheered. The throng was in an antagonistic mood and would not have been likely to disperse quietly had Church so ordered them. He did, however, issue a proclamation demanding that citizens refrain from rioting. He banned public meetings and loitering around city streets and police stations, declaring that violators would be subject to imprisonment. Should any more rioting take place, he concluded, the Riot Act would be read, and police and military officials would have the authority to fire. He did, however, promise an inquiry into the alien situation. The meeting ended with a rousing singing of 'God Save the King.'[44]

There were no further disturbances. A heavy police presence, and the threat of the Riot Act and the military, kept mobs from forming. For added deterrent value, a troop of mounted dragoons, trained soldiers waiting to proceed overseas, carrying heavy ash pick handles instead of sabres, rode through the streets. Returned soldiers and civilians alike were intimidated by their very presence, and most people stayed in their homes or went about their business quietly. Calm returned to the streets of Toronto after almost a week of unrest.

There were repercussions. Many men arrested during the disturbances were given jail time ranging from three months to a year. Returned soldiers demanded new trials, or that the charges be dismissed. They won. Fifteen cases were dismissed in one morning alone. In addition, they demanded and received an inquiry into police behaviour, particularly on 2 and 3 August 1918. The Board of Police Commissioners formally investigated. Police officers and rioters were interviewed over twelve days; the final report, tabled by 19 October 1918, totalled 1,427 typewritten pages.[45] It determined that police were guilty 'in a sense' for failing to protect property. Several constables were retired at once, and others were advised to secure other forms of employment, but the 'responsibility for the succeeding too vigorous suppression was not directly placed.' Still other officers, however, were promoted for their leadership and success in protecting property on following nights.[46]

Community interest in the riots, however, did not extend much beyond 7 August 1918 when Mayor Church effectively ended the disturbances. In peacetime, citizens would have had the luxury to carefully digest what had happened. This luxury was not afforded in August 1918, as the focus shifted to the Canadian Corps spearheading a major advance on the Western Front. The riots and their causes, however, provide an avenue to understand the climate of Toronto in early August 1918. Under strain of total war, animosity towards enemy aliens expanded to include all subjects who were not of British stock. The Greek restaurant owners targeted on the opening night of the riots, after all, were from a nation allied with Britain. But in the eyes of angry returned soldiers, they were aliens, and did not belong in a 'British city.' Veterans continued to exert an enormous influence. Consistently numbering in the hundreds, with thousands of sympathetic citizens following their lead, they were at the vanguard of anti-alien activity. Drawn together by the stresses of total war, British citizens took deliberate action to marginalize others. Total war demanded total commitment, and the British population refused to accept anything less.

The sacrifices of four years of conflict finally bore fruit in the line on 8 August 1918. After months of relative rest, training, and reinforcement, the Canadian Corps spearheaded a new British offensive near Amiens. The first day's successes surpassed the wildest expectations of military planners, prompting the German chief of staff, Maj.Gen. Erich von Ludendorff, to write that 8 August was 'the black day of the German Army in the history of this war. Everything I had feared, and of which I had so often given warning, had here, in one place, become a reality.'[47] Toronto rejoiced in the news. Headlines relayed the successes: 'Canadians Played Part in Great Victory.' Finally, after months of waiting for the pendulum to swing back in favour of the Allies, Torontonians read about the Germans reaping the whirlwind.

The offensive slowed and halted on 11 August to allow supplies and artillery to be brought up. The lull lasted for eight days before the Allies, once again led by the Canadians, continued their advance. By 20 August, Canadians had liberated more than sixty-seven square miles, including twenty-seven villages, at a cost of 11,822 casualties. By the standards of trench warfare, it was an enormous victory. The Canadian Corps was then transferred to the Arras sector, a mile west of Fampoux, and fought the Battle of the Scarpe from 26 to 30 August 1918, advancing on an ever-widening front.[48]

As the Canadian Corps ground steadily forward, the Canadian National Exhibition again hosted over a million visitors. One of the most well attended events was Women's Day. Among the displays was a reproduction of tent field hospitals with nurses tending the wounded as other women delivered their human cargo in field ambulances. Women gave demonstrations using lathes, handling tractors, and working industrial machinery. Press reports recognized something different and noble about the behaviour of these women. The report in the *News* was typical: 'They [the women] seemed to typify the spirit of the new age, the age of strong, noble womanhood, the age of self-sacrifice and of service to the common cause of humanity. They did not seem like the same women of a year or so ago. They seemed inspired with a quiet, inmovable resolve, as those who have a great mission to perform, and who, feeling the all-importance of that mission are determined to carry it through to the finish. To many a man in the audience it was a new phase of womanly character which might never have been seen had it not been for the war.'[49]

Despite a heavy downpour, thousands of women paraded in front of the grandstand before the assembled crowd. Organizers had suggested postponing this event in the hopes that the weather would improve, but the women would have none of it: '"Our men stand far worse in the trenches so I guess we can do it too," said one mother whose three sons are all in France.' Several hundred nurses marched first, followed by Red Cross workers, and then women with relatives at the front. In their wake came the Woman's Christian Temperance Union, the Daughters of England, the Daughters of Scotland, and the Imperial Order Daughters of the Empire, followed by women volunteers. Next marched a steady stream of munition 'girls,' commanding a roar of applause from the stands, and fifty women from an aeroplane factory pulling an aeroplane with them. The passage of so many feet churned the field into mud, but each detachment of women waited patiently as their colleagues filed onto the field. Finally, when all eight thousand were assembled, the women joined with the crowd in the stands in singing, 'God Save the King.'[50]

How different this Women's Day at the Exhibition was from previous ones at the turn of the century! In *Becoming Modern in Toronto: The Industrial Exhibition and the Shaping of a Late Victorian Culture*, Keith Walden argues that as late as 1900 both men and women accepted that 'women's distinctive work involved pre-modern cottage skills.' He suggests that most male visitors to the fair greeted the Ladies' Department with 'almost complete indifference.' Whatever the attitude of its male visitors, one thing was certain, 'the building was a hive of middle-class maternal feminism ... Organizers were willing to acknowledge the importance of women's social contributions, but not to threaten the cult of domesticity. According to the official program, traditional gender distinctions remained safely intact.'[51]

Total war fundamentally altered the public image of 'modern' woman. The main exhibits in 1918 did not portray women performing domestic duties. The war had demanded that they move out into the public sphere. Female industrial workers, farm hands, and ambulance drivers marched literally hand in hand with women who marked their patriotism by having given their men to the war effort. Women in these new positions were not only accepted, they were cheered. Interestingly, the order of women within the procession changed from that used for the Empire Day parade of 1 July 1916. On that day, those who had given men to the army marched first. In August 1918, however, these women marched behind nurses and Red Cross workers. The ranks of female workers in July 1916 were small, but had grown enormously over the ensuing two years. Clearly, the status of these workers had risen in the eyes of the organizers, and a new hierarchy was presented to the crowds in the stands at the Exhibition. Women were praised for having met and triumphed over the demands of weather and disbelief. 'Modern' woman was just as comfortable wielding a lathe or machining an artillery shell as she was caring for her family.

The importance of artillery shells was proving itself again and again at the front. Throughout September and October 1918 the Canadian Corps was involved in continued offensive operations on the Western Front. Names like the Drocourt-Queant Line, the Canal du Nord, Bourlon Wood, the Marcoing Line, and Cambrai filled the pages of Canadian newspapers. Success after success was achieved by the Canadian Corps, but always at the price of high casualties. Between 22 August and 11 October, the Corps suffered the loss of 1,544 officers and 29,262 other ranks killed and wounded.[52] The Allied advance created instability within Germany. As early as 29 September 1918, Ludendorff and supreme commander von Hindenburg declared to party leaders that Germany could not win the war. However, they would not permit unconditional surrender – something their opponents insisted upon. The war continued throughout October 1918 with the Allies pressing their advantage.

Toronto suffered enormous losses as a result of the actions of Canadian soldiery on the battlefields of Europe. Day after day, casualty lists appeared in the papers, usually accompanied by small pictures of each man, often filling entire pages. Throughout the last three weeks of August and into September, the numbers were so high that it was a cause for relief that 'only 19 local men' were on the list for 3 September 1918. Since the opening of the Amiens offensive on 8 August to the beginning of September over one thousand Toronto men became casualties: 218 killed, 932 wounded, 34 gassed, 9 presumed dead, 15 missing, 11 ill, 3 prisoners, and 1 repatriated. The losses continued to grow at a phenomenal rate with daily totals hovering between 40 and 100 names. Total Toronto casualties reached 2,127 by 17 September: an average of just over 51 men killed, wounded, or missing each and every day.[53]

Torontonians were also facing another winter of coal shortages. In September, citizens learned that the coal they had ordered in the spring would not be supplied in full. Even those who had paid for their orders in advance by the end of April would be lucky to see more than a fraction of what they needed. Those who had not yet placed orders were even more desperate since coal dealers would not take new ones. The situation was serious, and plans to ration coal were discussed to ensure that everyone would have a minimum amount of heat over the coming winter.[54]

Towards the end of September a few newspaper articles appeared about a new threat: Spanish influenza. This particularly virulent strain killed 20 million people worldwide within the year. Two million Canadians got sick, and fifty thousand died. Ironically, the virus originated in the United States. It received its name because Spain was the first country to publicize its existence. Researchers traced the first case to Fort Riley, Kansas in March 1918. New recruits were exposed to it there and carried it to France. Front-line conditions ensured its spread.[55] Soldiers contracted the virus in the mud, squalor, and cramped conditions of the trenches, and those wounded and sent home carried it to Canada. In a matter of months the flu had killed roughly the same number of people as had been destroyed in over four years at the front.

Spanish influenza worked its way inland, and on 19 September the *World* reported that a few cases were discovered at an unnamed military camp in Ontario.[56] There was no cause for alarm, officials promised, as the patients had been quarantined. Nevertheless, the Board of Health warned those infected to remain in bed and consult a physician as soon as possible. The symptoms were related in detail to readers: 'sudden onset of chills, severe headache and pain in the back and limbs. The face becomes flushed and the fever runs from 99 degrees to 102 and occasionally from 103 to 104. The highest point is reached on the second day when there is a sudden drop and by the fourth day the patient is well. The disease is spread by germs carried in the nose and throat and the infection is usually passed from one person to another by direct contact, drinking, utensils, common towels, etc.'[57]

Despite the efforts at containment, on the last day of September 1918 Toronto learned that it was not immune. In the last three days of that month several hundred cases developed, but city officials decided not to take any special precautions besides the usual bulletins provided in the press. Provincial Medical Health Officer Lt.-Col. J.W. McCulloch declared it unlikely that special regulations would be required to stop the spread of the disease. He advised patients to 'Go to bed and secure the services of a physician.' Civilians apparently had little to be concerned about anyway as 200 of the 213 reported cases in the city affected military personnel. The first fatality, however, was a small girl referred to simply as 'Robertson' of 166 Inglewood Crescent. She died in Toronto General Hospital on 29 September. As a precaution, the child's school, Jesse Ketchum, was quarantined.[58]

The flu situation deteriorated dramatically within days. At the beginning of October, doctors continued to downplay the severity of the outbreak, suggesting only that school nurses send home any children who showed symptoms. Toronto Medical Officer of Health, Dr. C.J. Hastings, refused to consider closing schools, thinking that the consequences would be too heavy. Within a week, over 10,000 staff and students out of a total population of 66,000 pupils and 1,630 teachers were sick. Inevitably, severe cases ended up in hospital, resulting in over 600 new patients in civilian hospitals within a week, taking up all available beds. The problem was further compounded as doctors and nurses began to experience symptoms themselves. The crisis had a spiralling impact on the city. Almost 15 per cent of the women in the local branch of the Bell Telephone Company, for example, were unable to work because they were sick or caring for family members. Citizens were asked to use the telephone only for emergencies.

Dire predictions were made about the plague's eventual cost. Officials believed it would affect 'more than half of our population in all probability.' Dr. Hastings, speaking through the press, informed citizens that they must 'face the stern fact that this city will have tens of thousands of cases of Spanish influenza before the disease can be stamped out here, and must understand that they, themselves, must be the chief agents in preventing the spread of the malady. The experience of the cities of Europe and America shows that 40 per cent of the inhabitants have been affected by the epidemic, and there is no reason for Toronto's citizens to believe that the city will be the one exception in this respect.'[59] Hospitals were stretched beyond the breaking point, with staff turning away more patients than they were able to accept. By the end of the first week of October, eighty-three local residents were dead.

Drastic measures were put in place. Hospitals were closed to visitors. Officials strongly suggested private funerals to avoid multiplying tragedies. Conventions were banned. Arrangements were made to take over the old Mossop Hotel on Yonge Street to serve as a temporary hospital for two hundred patients even as city workers searched for other locations. Appeals were made to citizens employing two private nurses to release one to look after other patients. It was made a violation of the Public Health Act to cough or sneeze in public places. Schools were closed. Dance halls were shut. Churches, theatres, and picture halls were similarly affected. All civic automobiles were requisitioned by the Medical Officer of Health. The Young Men's Christian Association membership campaign was postponed. And still the death toll climbed.[60]

A general call was placed for citizens willing to learn the basics of caring for the sick. The Imperial Order Daughters of the Empire, the Women's Canadian Club, the Graduate Nurses' Association, the Women's Conservative Club, the Women's Liberal Club, and the Young Women's Christian Association all came forward immediately, with the result that eighty-one 'Sisters of Service' registered the first morning. By the afternoon, volunteers had swelled beyond the expectations of medical health officers; a larger room was requisitioned. Volunteers first sat through one of three lectures on caring for influenza victims. Even in the larger room, some women had to listen from the hallway.[61]

Even in the wake of all these special precautions, the death toll mounted. By the middle of October an average of fifty people died each day. More closures were ordered, including bowling alleys, pool rooms, and places of amusement. All public gatherings, luncheons, and dinners were banned. Professional sporting events were cancelled. The medical and nursing schools at the University of Toronto were shut down to allow students to serve the public. Even the circulation of library books was stopped. Calls went out for donations of bedding, night clothing, and towels, along with volunteers willing to deliver soups and other foods. Sundays passed in eerie silence since few churches called their congregations to worship. Over thirteen hundred Torontonians died of influenza in October, contributing to the highest mortality total of any month since records were kept.[62]

Industrial Toronto struggled to cope. Every aspect of the economy suffered. Department stores scrambled to secure enough employees to run shops. Munitions plants tried to adapt to missing hundreds of workers each day. The Bell Telephone Company was short over one-quarter of its workforce. The situation was so desperate that Bell published advertisements in the papers appealing to consumers to use telephones only when urgent, and to show special consideration for those operators who were able to report for work. Bank staffs were similarly hard hit, requiring those healthy enough to work to put in many overtime hours.[63]

The 'Sisters of Service' were deployed immediately. In one afternoon, twenty-five out of the total of four hundred volunteers worked at the Arlington Hotel to ready it to accept influenza patients. Hallways and rooms were disinfected, furniture was prepared for the influx of sick, and several hundred gauze masks were constructed to protect workers. Other women took over church kitchens and cooking classes in the schools to produce food.[64]

It was not until the end of October that the worst of the 1918 epidemic passed, and medical officers began to relax some of the precautions.[65] Churches resumed regular services and theatres opened. Schools were set to open on Monday, 5 November, provided that the outbreak continued to decline, and professional sports teams would again be allowed to play. For the first time in over a month, hospitals reported vacant beds.[66]

While the number of dead is alarming, the impact of the epidemic is best measured by the number of people who were sick but did not die. The experience of American cities suggested that the number of fatalities represented around 0.5 per cent of those who came down with the virus. The best case scenario was a 0.25 per cent death rate, although some cities reported death rates as high as 1.0 per cent of the total infected.[67] Using these numbers as a guide, Toronto's thirteen hundred dead suggests that approximately 260,000 residents were incapacitated for four to five days in October. More than half the population was sick at some point during the month. The impact on the city was incredible.

The influenza epidemic compounded the suffering from an already desperate coal shortage. The ranks of miners, train employees, coal yard operators, delivery personnel, shipping clerks, and desk clerks were decimated by the epidemic, resulting in thousands of lost working days. Officials estimated the loss in production from the flu to be about 50,000 tons daily, amounting to enough coal to have supplied at least twenty-five thousand families a week for the winter.[68] The long, cold winter ahead promised to be even more trying than the one just past.

The casualty toll from the front did not lessen because citizens at home were coping with the deadly flu. Day after day, as the Canadian Corps continued its advance on the Western Front, accounts of heavy losses filtered back to Toronto. By the end of October 1918, Toronto men had suffered just over 4,000 casualties since the Amiens offensive opened: 783 dead, 94 missing, 8 presumed dead, 2,766 wounded, 245 gassed, 77 ill, 20 prisoners, and 10 repatriated.[69] Casualty lists left no doubt about the human toll of war. The faces of young, uniformed men filled entire newspaper pages, accompanied by lists of killed and wounded. Citizens absorbed the bad news even as they worried about finding enough fuel to see them through winter.

Women formed the bulk of the reserve labour force used to combat the epidemic. Toronto's economy was booming, unemployment was virtually non-existent, and those workers already employed, both men and women, had to continue in that capacity to produce the war material so desperately needed at the front. Patriotic workers, mothers, daughters, students, and sisters stepped into the breach. Hundreds volunteered for the taxing and dangerous labour of attending to the sick. As at every other critical point in the war, when confronted with a crisis, the city mobilized its entire available resources to cope.

The influenza epidemic, the coal shortage, and the casualties from the front continued to draw Torontonians together. Faced with a common foe, a common dilemma, and a common grief, citizens accepted limitations on their everyday lives that would have been inconceivable outside of total war. Business owners closed their doors without question, nurses accepted reassignment without protest, customers greeted poor service with a smile, and employers managed with fewer employees. The limits of human endurance were pushed to the breaking point, but the city endured, hoping against hope that the war was almost over.

Dr. Hastings elected not to reopen the schools until the morning of 11 November. His decision was made easy, however, not for medical but for conservation reasons. In addition to containing the influenza, Hastings felt that coal resources could be saved by keeping the schools closed. The Board of Education distributed the conserved coal among the most desperate. The situation was so critical that the City Council allotted $3,000 to pay workers to cut down dead trees for fuel. Churches were directed to meet to find ways to reduce their usage of coal. By amalgamating congregations throughout the winter, by using oil burners, and by keeping heat at minimum levels, officials felt that a significant amount of fuel could be saved.[70]

Although they did not know it at the time, citizens would be relieved from the awful task of scanning papers for casualties in less than two weeks. The Canadian Corps continued to participate in offensive operations until the very end of the war. In the last week of fighting, there were no major engagements, but the Corps advanced at least two miles a day on all but two days, crossing into Belgium on 7 November. Their final objective was the city of Mons, the same place from which the small British Expeditionary Force had been driven in the early days of fighting in August 1914. The Canadians marched into the city on the morning of 11 November 1918, just hours before the Armistice took effect. The previous two days of fighting had cost them 18 officers and 262 men, with one death and 15 other casualties on 11 November.[71] During that final week and a half of war, Toronto suffered another 163 casualties for a total of 4,165 since 8 August 1918. An average of 43 Toronto homes were told each day that a loved one had been killed or wounded.

The end to all this striving, this grieving, and this anxiety, came in the middle of the night on 11 November 1918. At 2:30 a.m., wire services flashed the news in Toronto of war's end. In response, church bells peeled, factory whistles wailed, and Extras were printed. Fire trucks drove through the streets sounding their sirens. Awakened from sleep, tens of thousands of Torontonians headed downtown. Many traveled in nightclothes and slippers: propriety demanded only that a winter coat be thrown overtop. Hanging off streetcars, or piling on the running boards of automobiles, people flooded to the core. Groaning under the weight, vehicles carried their screaming and singing cargo to the celebration. Yonge Street was packed with revellers. The crowds were so thick that dozens of people walked over roofs to get to the party. Coal scuttles, tin cans, and garbage lids were grabbed – anything to add to the din. Bonfires were set to ward off the predawn chill. Cheering, patriotic songs, and skirling bagpipes filled the air. Fireworks lit up the night sky. Conversation was impossible – and unnecessary. A twenty-four-hour victory party, 1,567 days in the making, had begun.

Among the first on the scene was a group of women finishing the night shift at a munitions factory. These capped and overalled 'munitionettes' paraded up Bay Street singing as thousands filtered onto Yonge Street. Impromptu bands played patriotic favourites like 'Rule Britannia,' and 'It's a Long Way to Tipperary.' Veterans hoisted young women waving flags onto their shoulders. One woman, newly arrived to the scene, was picked up and raised on the shoulders of a group of khaki clad soldiers. She protested at first, but in her excitement grabbed a Union Jack, and sang with the crowd.

At dawn, headlines screamed 'Victory!' and 'Kaiser a Fugitive: Germany Vanquished and in Throes of Revolution: So Ends World War.' 'Victory Day' had finally arrived. The workday opened, but Torontonians paid it little heed. Office staffs, munitions workers, bank clerks, telegraph operators, virtually everyone missed work to join in the euphoric celebration. 'Work on the most momentous day in the history of the world was unthinkable.' Even pickpockets took the day off. Hungry for something to eat, but unwilling to miss the party, crowds descended like locusts on downtown restaurants. Joyous owners reported that not since the arrival of temperance had they sold so many bottles of 2 per cent beer.

At noon, before assembled thousands, Mayor Tommy Church read the official proclamation from the steps of City Hall. 'The citizens of Toronto may well be proud,' he declared, 'of the noble, glorious, and inspiring record it has made in this war. The memory of its war service will never fade.' In the afternoon, two hundred thousand people watched a victory parade. Proudly wearing their khaki uniforms, young soldiers, wounded earlier in the war, 'were cheered to the echo.' Marching four abreast, the procession of veterans extended for a quarter of a mile. Behind them in a fleet of automobiles followed the many young soldiers who could not march. Overhead, a fleet of aeroplanes wove around church steeples, delighting onlookers as the planes 'bombed' them with pamphlets, filling the sky with tiny sheets of white paper beseeching people to buy Victory Bonds. The parade began at the base of University Avenue. Spectators crowded twenty deep along the entire route to catch a glimpse of the heroes. Others stood on the South African monument or waved out of Osgoode Hall's windows. A tank, parked at the corner of Queen Street and University Avenue, provided another vantage point. The procession swung west on Queen to Simcoe, then east on King. Passing St James's Cathedral, the men marched north on Jarvis, before turning west again along Carlton and College to Queen's Park.

Queen's Park was the scene for an enormous service of thanksgiving. One hundred thousand citizens gathered to mark the occasion, filling to capacity the ten acres surrounding the Parliament Buildings. Speeches were given by local dignitaries, but few could hear their words over the vast throng. It did not matter. Citizens were there as a part of the community, to pay homage to the thousands of men who had

served. Besides, everyone heard the thousands of voices joined in song:
'Onward Christian Soldiers,' 'Oh God, Our Help in Ages Past,' 'Praise
God from Whom All Blessings Flow,' and 'God Save the King.' The service ended with a moment of silence for those who had lost their lives in
the great struggle. Gradually, the crowd dispersed, heading back to the
downtown core to absorb the joy of victory. The party continued well
into the night.[72]

Conclusion

The conflict that began on 4 August 1914 would eventually change the way Torontonians viewed war. However, they entered into it on the basis of lessons learned from the pre-war years. They expected the struggle to be short and victorious. This assumption determined their behaviour at the start of what was then considered 'a great adventure.' Citizens gathered around newspaper offices by the thousand to read the latest headlines posted in the windows. Newsboys did a brisk trade in Extras. Impromptu parades worked their way through the streets. Young men flocked to the Recruiting Depot. The city was enthusiastic about its upcoming part in the great struggle.

This grand undertaking, however, was not without its poignant moments. Citizens were not so wrapped up in the enthusiasm for war that they did not recognize its potential for grief. Dailies described heart-wrenching scenes at train stations, which revealed that citizens understood men would die. Even as they passed good luck charms and trinkets to the outstretched hands of soldiers, citizens stored up images to sustain them in the months and years ahead. The trains departed to the sound of patriotic music and cheering. After a final wave, a last glance, loved ones turned and began to make their way silently and solemnly to homes that felt empty.

Determined to 'do their bit,' citizens then dedicated themselves to supporting the war effort. It being considered a 'privilege' to serve, efforts at home and at the front were voluntary. There was no need to manipulate people or to drum up patriotic enthusiasm for the war. The challenge was to try to channel the already existing spirit into useful directions. Women organized a campaign to raise money for a hospital ship. Young men tried their best to qualify for overseas service. Civic leaders started the Toronto and York County Patriotic Fund to see to the needs of the families of departed soldiers.

The image of the enemy at this early stage centred on the figure of Kaiser Wilhelm II. It was he, the papers reported, who had led a toast 'To the Day.' The Kaiser, along with his advisers and generals, had been planning an attack for years. The German people were innocent dupes of an autocratic leader. The struggle in Toronto, then, was as much for the German people as against the Kaiser.

Information from the front changed the behaviour of Torontonians. In April 1915, papers carried the news from Second Ypres. 'Canadians Won Great Glory' vied with other headlines that spoke of the cost: 'Canadian Casualties Nearly 6,000.' The resulting glory and grief, celebrated and mourned by the local people, changed the conflict into 'a great crusade.' Tens of thousands gathered for the funeral of just one of the city's fallen, Captain Robert Clifton Darling. As his funeral cortège marched up Yonge Street to Mount Pleasant Cemetery, citizens participated in collectively mourning for all the local men killed or wounded in action.

In the coming days, they had the chance to read the letters written by soldiers who had survived the attack. Papers carried dozens of these private letters, launching them into the public domain. Residents read of the terrible conditions and the grizzly cost of modern machine guns, artillery, and poison gas. They could imagine the experiences that made men write of the horror of being 'raked ... with machine gun and rifle fire,' and seeing comrades 'dropping before [they] got properly started.' They could visualize the scene depicted by another soldier who reported that 'the dead are piled in heaps and the groans of the wounded and dying will never leave me.'[1] This information did not undercut popular support for war. It reinforced the people's commitment. Efforts at home were increased, patriotic donations rose, and more men volunteered to take the place of the dead and wounded.

The enlistment experience mirrored the city's war effort. Citizens rushed to enlist in the opening days, desperately seeking a place in the Canadian Expeditionary Force. Only the most qualified were chosen, resulting in relatively few Canadian-born men in the First Contingent. As the Second and Third Contingents were mobilized, the focus remained on the privilege of serving; one in three volunteers were rejected. But as the demands of the war grew and more men were needed, voluntary enlistment gave way to active recruiting. Military officers created a climate in which men would continue to come forward, relying on the participation of the community to prompt volunteers. Enlistment boomed.

The war was no longer against the German Kaiser and his generals. Horrified citizens read about atrocities committed by the German army in France and Belgium. The sinking of the *Lusitania*, the use of poison gas, and the submarine campaign made citizens alter their image of the enemy. Editorialists related the outrage felt by Torontonians that Berliners could take to the streets to celebrate acts of international piracy and terror. The language used to refer to the enemy changed. The 'noble' foe went down with the victims of the *Lusitania*. Adjectives such as 'diabolical,' 'fiendish,' and 'barbarous' were used instead. Torontonians were no longer fighting exclusively against distant militarism and tyranny abroad. They were fighting for their way of life.

As the conflict continued, newspapers carried reports that provided a detailed and comprehensive understanding of the nature and duration of trench warfare. Torontonians understood that attritional warfare would only gradually wear down German defences, and that the struggle would go on for years. Against the backdrop of increased casualties, citizens dedicated themselves to continuing the war effort. They would consider none of the early armistice offers, rejecting the late 1916 and early 1917 peace proposals by Germany and President Woodrow Wilson of the United States. This was not the decision of an uninformed, disengaged populace, but of one committed to a purposeful war.

Throughout the months and years of fighting, community leaders continued to work together to enroll the men necessary to maintain the Canadian Corps in the trenches. Daily reports related, in detail, the progress of local recruiting. The process of ensuring that the city provided its share of recruits struck a chord with residents, prompting hundreds of thousands of citizens to take part in patriotic rallies to promote enlistment. Riverdale Park was the scene of one such rally. Two hundred thousand arrived to show their support for recruiting. Over five hundred men volunteered in that one night. A year later, prominent citizens were authorized to raise their own local battalions. Men were drawn by the promise of camaraderie and the chance to serve with friends: thousands volunteered. Recruiters moved physically into the private lives of potential recruits, confronting prospective soldiers in their homes and on the streets. There were limits, however, to the number of men that could be secured in this way.

Recruiting gradually exhausted the supply of willing volunteers, and Torontonians, their organizations, and leading citizens appealed to Prime Minister Borden to impose conscription. The dedication of the local population is even more remarkable when one considers the number of men who had already volunteered. Out of a total of 87,300 eligible young men, more than 45,000 were in khaki and at least another 22,500 had volunteered but were rejected on medical grounds: approximately three out of every four Toronto men had offered to serve by 1918. And still the community demanded greater participation.

Potential soldiers could no longer keep their reasons for not enlisting private. Military officials and citizens alike demanded that men be able to publicly defend their choice to remain at home. Accordingly, the city welcomed the prime minister's May 1917 declaration that compulsory military service would become law. The December 1917 election was a de facto plebiscite on conscription. Citizens voted overwhelmingly for Borden's Unionist candidates, who polled more than 90 per cent of the vote. Voters behaved in this way knowing that the fighting would continue for months – possibly years. They knew the costs and consequences of further involvement. They had experienced the war's demands for coal, food, and soldiers. They had attended sombre ceremonies at train stations when soldiers departed for overseas. They had seen the human wreckage of war in the form of thousands of wounded, crutch-carrying veterans. They had read graphic accounts of front-line life and death in the papers. And yet, they voted to continue the struggle, ushering in a new phase: 'total war.'

Torontonians grimly faced another year of war in January 1918. Headlines relayed the desperate situation at the front, and editorialists announced the inevitability of a German assault in the spring. As the Allies struggled to regain lost territory, the consensus that had hitherto dominated Toronto's response to the war began to show its first cracks. Outraged that the Borden government had cancelled conscription exemptions, farmers marched on Ottawa, and Torontonians showed sympathy. Workers fought for wage increases to keep pace with inflation. Veterans targeted enemy aliens for harsh treatment, upset that non-British Canadians had not been made to play a greater role in the struggle. At no point, however, was the necessity of continuing the war questioned. Farmers, workers, and veterans all supported the great crusade. Their actions in the spring and summer of 1918 were designed to secure a more efficient war effort, not to halt its prosecution. As the Canadian Corps fought on to victory between August and November 1918, Toronto struggled against the deadly influenza virus, but citizens worked together to meet this challenge, just as they had met others over the previous four years.

Total war ended – overnight – after four and a half years of sacrificing lives, limbs, health, time, money, and youth. The unremitting tension was suddenly released in the largest party Toronto had ever known. Headlines captured the spirit of the day: 'Toronto Hails Peace in Delirium of Joy,' 'No Sleep for City When News Arrived That War Was Over,' and 'City Celebrated in Orgy of Joy.' The enormous tasks of the future were placed to one side. Entire nations had ceased to exist; new ones would have to be created. Armies had to return home; soldiers had to be reintegrated into civilian life. Citizens had to acclimatize themselves to something not experienced since 1815: a post-war world. Enormous tasks lay ahead, not the least of which was to impose order and meaning on the experience of the Great War. People would develop different memories of the conflict. Soldiers, civilians, men, women, young and old, would all remember things differently. But in the early morning of 11 November 1918, Torontonians joined together in marking an astonishing achievement: victory.

Their war effort had been a collective, community enterprise. From the first days when citizens gathered downtown by the thousands around newspaper offices to hear the latest news from the front, they drew strength from one another. This communal effort saw the city through recruiting campaigns, patriotic drives, casualty lists, and the influenza epidemic. The city supplied recruits for the front, money for Victory Loans, and support for the Empire. The community took precedence over the individual. The pride and integrity associated with belonging to something larger than oneself helped sustain citizens confronted daily with the demands of the war.

There were vital efforts made by distinct groups within Toronto. One of the most powerful of these was the local Great War Veterans' Association. A visible and numerous part of the community, veterans publicly and adamantly supported measures to increase the effectiveness of the war effort. They had been to the front, seen its horrors, and remained ardent supporters of continued participation. An integral part of every local patriotic rally after they first began to return to the city in the summer of 1915, veterans demanded greater exertions on the part of those at home. They exerted enormous influence, and would not tolerate anything which they considered a threat to the war effort or to the sacrifices they had made on its behalf.

Women's experience with the war effort also reveals a stunning record of achievement. Initially, they responded to the declaration of hostilities by giving their sons, husbands, and brothers. Their activities were reported in the dailies, expecially on the women's page of each paper. This section reported women's efforts in nurturing and caring for the Empire's soldiers. Newspapers also noted when women moved out of the private sphere to work tirelessly in a variety of public areas. Women supplied a reserve force of labour to allow local men to enlist. They worked long hours in munitions factories. They paraded in support of recruiting. They raised funds to care for the families of departed soldiers, and to supply the nation with the economic resources to win the war. When their efforts seemed at their peak, they found another reserve of strength to serve the city as voluntary nurses during the 1918 influenza epidemic.

Wartime Toronto: glory and grief. When the first troops left for the front in August 1914, prospects had ricocheted between glory and the potential for grief. Poignant scenes of leave-taking at the train stations spoke of concern for men who might not return. Throughout the war, citizens were proud of the accomplishments of the Canadian Corps, but were sobered by the cost of battle. In November 1918, they exulted in a hard-won victory. Torontonians took to the streets to mark the glory of that victory while grieving collectively for those lost in the struggle.

There is a wealth of information available for those looking for a window on Toronto during the First World War. Newspapers record not just opinions, editorials and otherwise, but the behaviour, the actions, and the values of citizens from all walks of life. When supplemented through the use of archival sources, newspapers permit the creation of a vivid, accurate portrait of a city and its citizens, permitting the historian to describe what the people believed. The link between knowledge and action answers why Torontonians behaved in the way that they did.

Archival sources such as personal correspondence serve as a check on the portrait drawn by the papers. Although they contain nothing like the wealth of information recorded daily in the news, personal letters allow us entry into the world outlined by the press. They tell individual stories of enlistment, of the desperate attempts by men like H. Anson Green to serve overseas, undergoing surgery in the hopes of qualifying. They relate the feelings of parents taking leave of sons, and the enormous pressure the community placed on its young men to put themselves forward. Archival sources also demonstrate that the civic leaders were not writing privately in a manner inconsistent with their public pronouncements. They were not, as some historians have argued, part of a massive conspiracy to manipulate the public into supporting a war they knew was wrong.[2] They believed in what they were doing, and expressed private hopes and fears similar to those offered in the papers. There was no difference between the public and private discourse of the time.

I have drawn upon different areas of historical inquiry to recreate wartime Toronto. National, political, women's, labour, military, social, and cultural studies have all been used. The resulting portrait demonstrates the utility of pulling together different strands of historical research. While national historians have been concerned with the relationship between French and English Canadians, Toronto's experience reveals little sensitivity to such cultural differences. Torontonians were devoted to supporting Britain, defending the Empire, and achieving victory.

The evidence presented here also challenges accounts of Canadian involvement in the war. Historian Jeffrey Keshen's *Propaganda and Censorship during Canada's Great War* argues that the war effort was underpinned by ignorance and carefully manipulated information. The specific example of Toronto, however, reveals something very different: Toronto's war effort was sustained by honest information and dedication. Torontonians understood the development of Allied and German strategy. Accounts of front-line life, ubiquitous casualty lists, exhausting victory and patriotic fund drives, coal shortages, and the loss of loved ones reinforced the dedication of Torontonians to winning the war. Throughout four and a half years of conflict, the response of citizens was both informed and committed. They knew the details of the campaigns fought on the Western Front and elsewhere. They understood the costs in men's lives. They read and talked about peace initiatives and continued to support a policy of total victory.

Post-war literature, and the history of the memory of the conflict, have been dominated by the grief associated with the losses incurred. People have gradually forgotten that both grief and glory were integral parts of the experience of the war. Both elements must be examined to create a foundation to comment on the years 1914–18. Jonathan Vance's *Death So Noble* has argued that Canadians created a 'myth' of the war which gave them a 'legacy, not of despair, aimlessness, and futility, but of promise, certainty, and goodness.'[3] Toronto's experience demonstrates that there was no need for Canadians to *create* such a myth. They were simply remembering their experience, memorializing glory and grief. They already believed, based on their experience, that the war had been purposeful and necessary. They did not need to take refuge in myths; they took comfort in their shared memory of sacrifice. Historians have assumed that the futility of the war was replaced with an artificial, constructed memory of purpose. The opposite occurred. The experience of shared sacrifice and a duty well done was supplanted by a constructed memory of futility.

Paul Fussell's *Great War and Modern Memory* presents post-war disillusionment as a product of the ignorance of people living at home regarding the costs involved. It was not until the late 1920s, he argues, that citizens learned the true nature of the fighting and the scale of the sacrifice; the sudden release of information in soldiers' memoirs accounted for the horror and outrage of people everywhere to the scale of the slaughter.

There is a different interpretation: post-war disillusionment grew despite an informed and dedicated population. In light of the evidence presented here, it is not possible to maintain that citizens were ignorant. The memoir literature published in the 1920s unquestionably caused a stir, but not for the reasons commonly ascribed to it. Given that people already knew the nature of the fighting, and the scale of the sacrifice, post-war literature must have been popular for another reason. The most likely conclusion is that it served as a catalyst to focus the disillusionment that had been growing out of the failure of the post-war world to realize the higher goals for which the war had been waged. People were disillusioned with the peace, not the war.

There were certainly important divisions of class, gender, and ethnicity within wartime Toronto, but the conflict proved to be a remarkably unifying force. Irish public opinion leaders were ardent supporters of a full roll for the Irish Catholic population. Irish Catholics volunteered in numbers as high as did British Protestants. Working-class men, union leaders, and unskilled labourers all demonstrated their faith in the war effort by volunteering, sacrificing, and caring for the families left behind. Society women directed an increasingly organized women's war effort with the support of most middle- and working-class women.

In 1918, people believed in what they had accomplished. During the time of the conflict, the very idea of war had changed, leaving behind the possibility of a 'great adventure.' What citizens knew about the international community affected their behaviour. Their ideas and assumptions about war were constantly challenged and updated on the basis of new information. It is inadequate to refer simply to the 'war years' as a block. For Toronto, August 1914 was thousands of casualties away from November 1918. The city and its people, however, had been consistent in their dedication to the war. They believed in its necessity, supported its prosecution, sacrificed in its name, and celebrated their achievement when victory finally arrived. They had endured.

Ethnic Composition of Toronto, 1911–1921

Ethnic origin*	Total 1911 census	Percentage of 1911 population	Total 1921 census	Percentage of 1921 population
English	181,315	48.1	260,860	50
Irish	81,804	21.7	97,361	18.7
Scotch	60,042	15.9	83,620	16
Other British	2,012	0.01	3,389	0.01
Total UK	325,173	85.71	445,230	85.3
Austro-Hungarian	553	0.1	not listed	
Belgian	46	0.01	215	0.04
Bulgarian and Romanian	104	0.03	256	0.05
Chinese	1,099	0.3	2,390	0.5
Dutch	1,639	0.4	3,961	0.8
Finnish	648	0.2	735	0.1
French	4,880	1.3	8,350	1.6
German	9,775	2.6	4,689	1.9
Greek	529	0.1	812	0.2
Hindu	6	0.002	not listed	
Indian	52	0.01	183	0.04
Italian	4,617	1.2	8,217	1.6
Japanese	12	0.003	42	0.008
Jewish	18,237	5	34,619	7
Negro	472	0.1	1,236	0.2
Polish	700	0.2	2,380	0.5
Russian	693	0.2	1,332	0.3
Swiss	324	0.09	583	0.1
Turkish	527	0.1	not listed	

*The ethnic categories reflect those used in the original censuses. 'Indian' refers to people of North American Aboriginal heritage.
Source: *Fifth Census of Canada, 1911*, 2:372; *Sixth Census of Canada, 1921*, 1:542.

Religious Composition of Toronto, 1911–1921

Religions (with more than 500 adherents)*	Total 1911 census	Percentage of 1911 population	Total 1921 census	Percentage of 1921 population
Anglican	120,405	31.9	173,522	33.2
Presbyterian	75,735	20.1	113,151	21.7
Methodist	73,281	20	84,895	16.3
Roman Catholic	46,368	12.3	64,773	12.4
Baptist	20,681	5.5	26,228	5
Jewish	18,143	4.8	34,377	6.6
Congregationalist	3,744	1	2,736	0.5
Lutheran	2,709	0.7	1,640	0.3
Salvation Army	2,583	0.7	2,977	0.6
Greek Church	1,384	0.4	3,632	0.7
Christian Science	902	0.2	2,192	0.4
Protestant	838	0.2	796	0.2
Christians	824	0.2	456	0.1
Disciple	757	0.2	498	0.1
Mormon	583	0.2	489	0.1

*The religious categories reflect those used in the original censuses.
Source: *Fifth Census of Canada, 1911*, 2:158; *Sixth Census of Canada, 1921*, 1:756.

Battalions Raised in Toronto

Name of unit	Organizing person/Militia unit	Month announced
First Contingent	Composite	August 1914
Second Contingent	Composite	October 1914
Third Contingent	Composite	January 1915
58th Battalion	Composite	May 1915
74th	Composite	June 1915
75th	Composite	June 1915
76th	Composite	June 1915
81st	Composite	July 1915
83rd	Composite	July 1915
84th	Composite	July 1915
92nd	48th Highlanders	July 1915
95th	Queen's Own Rifles	November 1915
123rd	Royal Grenadiers	December 1915
124th (Pals)	9th Mississauga Horse/Governor General's Body Guard	December 1915
134th	48th Highlanders	January 1916
166th	Queen's Own Rifles	January 1916
169th	109th Regiment	January 1916
170th	9th Mississauga Horse	January 1916
180th (Sportsmen's)	Crown Attorney R.H. Greer	January 1916
201st (Light Infantry)	E.W. Hagerty, high school principal	February 1916
204th (Beavers)	W.H. Price, MPP	March 1916
208th (Irish)	Herb Lennox, MPP	March 1916
216th (Bantam)	Lt.-Col. F.L. Burton	March 1916
255th	Queen's Own Rifles	November 1916

Note on Sources

Each Toronto newspaper had its own personality. J.F. Mackay directed the publication of one of the 'quality' Toronto dailies, the Liberal *Globe*, from its offices at 60–2 Yonge Street. Born in Toronto in 1868, Mackay gained experience as a reporter with the *Toronto Mail* and the *Montreal Herald*, eventually becoming managing editor of the *Globe* in 1903. His paper arrived on doorsteps in the morning, targeting a 'metropolitan audience of middle and upper income Canadians.' The front page shied away from bold, two or three word headlines, preferring instead to use something akin to a leader to spark interest. Throughout the war, a 'News of the Day' article appeared in the bottom left hand corner of the front page, usually dominated by recent war events. Only a few articles were published on the lead page, allowing long columns of text, and only rarely did a photograph or illustration appear. The editorial page included two to five lengthy editorials on the issues of the day, followed by a 'Notes and Comments' section for shorter observations: 'Your King and Country Need You – Now!' The Women's page related upcoming rallies and meetings, listed engagements, and often published a daily poem. Other pages were dedicated to local news, sports, stock market performance, and classified ads; most issues ended with a full-page advertisement from Eaton's.

The other 'quality' morning daily was the Conservative *Mail and Empire* based at 52–4 King Street West. Like the *Globe*, its general manager, W.J. Douglas, had an extensive background in journalism. Born in the United States and twenty-two years older than his counterpart at the *Globe*, Douglas emigrated to Canada in 1877 and had served as the manager of the *Mail and Empire* for years when the Great War began. Douglas' headlines were similar to Mackay's, usually consisting of a sentence rather than a one or two word bulletin. The rest of the front page, however, was more varied, printing some articles in large print, and other in a smaller font. There was no 'News of the Day' feature, but issues relating to the war filled the front page. Particular attention was paid to news events in the first pages of each issue, making room for reporting at the expense of space for advertisers. Occasionally, a photograph of a local event would appear, but this was usually the exception rather than the rule. The editorial page was well presented, with two to five lengthy commentaries on recent events each day. Advertisements were more prevalent in the women's and classified pages.

All but one of the remaining four dailies were published for the evening market. They were popular publications aimed at 'a local audience of middle and lower income readers.' The only broadly targeted morning paper was W.F. Maclean's Conservative *World*, based at 40 Richmond Street West. Maclean was a fixture in Toronto's journalism and political world in the years leading up to the Great War. Born in Wentworth County, Ontario, in 1854, he began his career as a reporter for the *Globe*. After receiving a Bachelor's degree from the University of Toronto in 1880, Maclean decided to strike out on his own, founding the *World*. Maclean ran unsuccessfully in the 1890 Ontario election as a Conservative candidate in North Wentworth. He was also defeated in his bid to win the East York riding in the 1891 federal election. His persistence paid off, however, and he won a federal by-election in East York in 1892, and was returned in 1896 and 1900. When the new constituency of South York was formed for the 1904 election, Maclean won it, and held the seat through elections in 1908, 1911, and 1917.

Unlike his morning competitors, Maclean made use of bold, large headlines. The front page was dotted with a variety of smaller articles, most requiring the reader to turn to the back pages to complete reading. Each issue printed a small box in the bottom left corner of page 1 under the heading 'War Summary.' As with every other daily, coverage of the war dominated its pages. The editorial page carried fewer editorials, allowing writers to develop their commentaries on local and national issues. Much of the paper was organized thematically, with weather, sports, stocks, and classified sections complementing local news coverage. Unlike other evening papers, the *World* only occasionally published photographs, electing to model its layout after the other morning papers which relied on text-based reporting.

The evening Liberal *Star* specialized in carrying many small news stories until a major story broke, when owner Joe Atkinson would unleash teams of reporters from the paper's offices at 18–20 King Street to cover the event extensively. Atkinson's style had been developed after years of working for a variety of papers. Born in Newcastle, Ontario, in 1865, he started his career with the *Weekly Times* (Port Hope) in 1884, before shifting to the *Globe* in 1889. A move to the *Montreal Herald* in 1896 brought with it a promotion to editor, but Atkinson returned to Toronto in 1899 to edit the *Star*. To grab reader attention, he began most issues with a short, sharp headline in boldface type. The entire front page was designed to catch a reader's eye, and pictures, boldface, and italicized articles competed for attention. Subsequent pages were similarly attractive – the second page, for example, regularly publishing a map of the fighting lines. Local and national news was reported, but was often pinched between claims of medical wonders and sales at clothing stores. The classified section was large, with news reports scattered throughout. The editorial page was similar to those in the other dailies, with half the page dedicated to lengthy commentaries, while a 'Note and Comment' section offered between ten and twenty pithy one-line remarks. The women's page accorded more space to announcing and reporting local women's activities than did the other dailies. Most issues ended with the ubiquitous Eaton's Department Store advertisement.

The Conservative *News*, based at 107 Bay Street, also used headlines and pictures to grab attention. Its owner, J.S. Willison, was one of the most 'admired journalists of his generation.' Born in Hills Green, Huron County, Ontario, in 1856, he received a law degree from Queen's University and worked for some years as a businessman. Eventually, he turned to journalism and was instrumental in rescuing the *Globe* from difficulty after George Brown's death. Willison, however, longed to work for an independent paper. He realized his dream in 1902 when he and industrialist Joseph Flavelle bought the *News*. During the war, small black-and-white photographs of local officers were commonplace on the front page. Articles were written in a variety of type sizes, with big, boldfaced headlines demanding attention, while others would only catch the eye of the more determined reader. As in the *Star*, photographs and maps were used throughout the paper to keep the reader involved. The editorial page was similar to those in the other dailies, but its editorials were more hard hitting, more opinionated. The women's page published a social calendar, fashion news, poems, and war news of particular interest to women. The sport section was larger than in other papers, as was the classified section.

The offices of the Conservative evening *Telegram* at 81 Bay Street produced a paper very different from the other five dailies. Its owner and founder, John Ross Robertson, was born in Toronto in 1841 and educated at Upper Canada College. He became the city editor of the *Globe* in 1864, and served as foreign correspondent and business reporter for that publication from London, England, for three years. He returned in 1876 to establish the *Telegram*. While all the other papers led with news items, the *Telegram* began each issue with six or seven pages of classified ads, by far the greatest number of any of its competitors. The front page published the *Telegram's* banner, followed by classifieds. During the war, small postage-size pictures of local men reported killed or wounded would appear alongside descriptions of their last civilian jobs and their addresses. The editorial page was different as well, dominated by short editorials which voiced more extreme, opinionated views on current events. Reporting was secondary to its importance as a vehicle for advertisements: these dominated it to a much greater degree than in any other local daily publication, virtually filling the women's, sports, and finance pages.

This study also draws on the influential weekly *Saturday Night*, the monthly *Maclean's*, the farmer's *Weekly Sun*, the labour publication the *Industrial Banner*, the women's monthly journal *Everywoman's World*, the government publication the *Labour Gazette*, and the religious periodicals of five major religious organizations, all published in Toronto: the *Christian Guardian* (Methodist), the *Canadian Churchman* (Anglican), the *Presbyterian*, the *Canadian Baptist*, and the *Catholic Register*. In conjunction with the daily papers, these sources allow an investigation of what people *knew* about the events at the front, and how they *behaved* during the war years.

Notes

Abbreviations

AO	Archives of Ontario
CB	*Canadian Baptist*
CC	*Canadian Churchman*
CG	*Christian Guardian*
CHR	*Canadian Historical Review*
CMH	*Canadian Military History*
CR	*Catholic Register*
CTA	City of Toronto Archives
DH	*Diplomatic History*
EW	*Everywoman's World*
Globe	*Toronto Globe*
IB	*Industrial Banner*
JCCHS	*Journal of the Canadian Church Historical Society*
JConH	*Journal of Contemporary History*
JCS	*Journal of Canadian Studies*
LLT	*Labour/Le Travail*
Mac	*Maclean's*
M&E	*Toronto Mail and Empire*
NAC	National Archives of Canada
News	*Toronto News*
OH	*Ontario History*
Pres	*Presbyterian*
SN	*Saturday Night*
Star	*Toronto Star*
Sun	*Weekly Sun*
Tel	*Toronto Telegram*
World	*Toronto World*

Introduction

1 'Toronto Praises Giver of Victory,' *World*, 12 Nov. 1919, 1, 3; 'Toronto Danced in Carnival Way,' *M&E*, 12 Nov. 1919, 4; 'Sobbed as They Sang; Tears Stained Faces,' *News*, 12 Nov. 1919, 4; 'Toronto Hushed Two Minutes in Reverie,' *Star*, 12 Nov. 1919, 2.
2 E. Remarque, *All Quiet on the Western Front*, trans. A.W. Wheen (Toronto: McClelland and Stewart, 1929). The best-known Canadian example is by an American writing about the Canadian Expeditionary Force, C.Y. Harrison's *Generals Die in Bed* (Hamilton: Potlatch Publications, 1928): it explores themes similar to Remarque's.
3 P. Fussell, *The Great War and Modern Memory* (Oxford: Oxford University Press, 1975), preface, 7–8.
4 S. Hynes, *A War Imagined: The First World War and English Culture* (New York: Maxwell Macmillan International, 1991), xii.
5 J. Terraine, *The Smoke and the Fire: Myths and Anti-Myths of War, 1861–1945* (London: Sidgwick and Jackson, 1980), 14.
6 M. Eksteins, *Rites of Spring: The Great War and the Birth of the Modern Age* (Toronto: Doubleday, 1989), 132; Hynes, *A War Imagined*.
7 G. Moorhouse, *Hell's Foundations: A Town, Its Myths and Gallipoli* (London: Hodder and Stoughton, 1992); M. Stephen, *The Price of Pity: Poetry, History and Myth in the Great War* (London: Leo Cooper, 1996).
8 J. Vance, *Death So Noble: Memory, Meaning and the First World War* (Vancouver: UBC Press, 1997), 266.
9 J. Keshen, *Propaganda and Censorship during Canada's Great War* (Edmonton: University of Alberta Press, 1996), x.
10 K. Walden, *Becoming Modern in Toronto: The Industrial Exhibition and the Shaping of a Late Victorian Culture* (Toronto: University of Toronto Press, 1997), 8–9.
11 J.E. Middleton, *Toronto's 100 Years* (Toronto: The Centennial Committee, 1934), 10, 92–102.
12 *Census of Canada, 1911*, Vol. 1 (Ottawa: C.H. Parmelee, 1912), 554; *Census of Canada, 1921*, Vol. 1 (Ottawa: F.A. Acland, 1924), 542; 'Recruiting Returns, Military District Number 2 Up To and Including Month Ending Aug., 1916,' Sept. 1916, NAC, RG 24, Vol. 4303, File 34–1–59, Military District No. 2, General Recruiting, Vol. 8.
13 M. Piva, *The Condition of the Working Class in Toronto, 1900–1921* (Ottawa: University of Ottawa Press, 1979), 8–9. For a detailed breakdown of the ethnic origins of the Toronto population in the 1911 and 1921 Census, see Appendix A.

14 That is, Anglican, Baptist, Methodist, or Presbyterian. For a detailed break-down of the religious affiliation of the Toronto population in 1911 and 1921, see Appendix B.

15 M.G. McGowan, 'Sharing the Burden of Empire: Toronto's Catholics and the Great War, 1914–1918,' in M.G. McGowan and B.P. Clarke, eds., *Catholics at the 'Gathering Place': Historical Essays on the Archdiocese of Toronto 1841–1991* (Toronto: Dundurn Press, 1993), 178.

16 E. Jarvis and M. Baker, 'Clio in Hogtown: A Brief Bibliography,' *OH* 76, no. 3 (1984): 290; Walden, *Becoming Modern in Toronto*, 27.

17 P. Rutherford, *The Making of the Canadian Media* (Toronto: McGraw-Hill Ryerson, 1978), x; *The Canadian Newspaper Directory*, 9th ed. (Montreal and Toronto: A. McKim, 1915); *The Canadian Newspaper Directory*, 11th ed. (Montreal and Toronto: A. McKim, 1918).

18 Rutherford, *Making of the Canadian Media*, 58.

19 R.C. Brown, *Robert Laird Borden, A Biography*, Vol. 1, *1854–1914* (Toronto: Macmillan, 1975), 148.

20 E.L. Woodward, *Great Britain and the German Navy* (Oxford: Clarendon Press, 1935), 308–322; A.J.P. Taylor, *The Struggle for Mastery in Europe, 1848–1918*, 2nd ed. (Oxford: Clarendon Press, 1960), 471–2; I.C. Barlow, *The Agadir Crisis* (North Carolina: Archon Books, 1971), 231–387.

21 'Germany and Morocco,' *M&E*, 4 July 1911, 6.

22 'Straining Diplomacy,' *News*, 16 Oct. 1912, 6.

23 'Declares Grey, Averted Crash; All Praise Him,' *News*, 31 May 1913, 1.

24 'Note and Comment,' *Star*, 3 July 1913, 6; editorial, *M&E*, 7 July 1913, 6.

1 A Great Adventure: Toronto Goes to War

1 'War Call Stirs Patriotic Toronto,' *Globe*, 5 Aug. 1914, 6; 'Last Song Always God Save the King,' *News*, 5 Aug. 1914, 3; 'How the News Was Received in Toronto,' *News*, 5 Aug. 1914, 4; 'War Call Stirs Patriotic Toronto,' *Globe*, 5 Aug. 1914, 6; 'City Rang with Cheers When War Was Declared,' *Tel*, 5 Aug. 1914, 13; 'Toronto Heard War Call with Quiet Dignity,' *Star*, 5 Aug. 1914, 3.

2 'Anxiously Awaited News,' *Tel*, 7 Aug. 1914, 17.

3 The most recent study is P. Maroney, '"The Great Adventure": The Context and Ideology of Recruiting in Ontario, 1914–1917,' *CHR* 77, no. 1 (1996): 62–98.

4 B.M. Greene, *Who's Who and Why, 1921* (Toronto: International Press Limited, 1921), 174.

5 'Toronto Soldiers Eager for Action,' *M&E*, 10 Aug. 1914, 4.

6 'Highlanders Recruits Four Hundred Men,' *Globe*, 11 Aug. 1914, 6.

7 '48th Highlanders to Be in Camp Monday,' *Star*, 15 Aug. 1914, 3; 'Local Infantry Regiments to Encamp at Long Branch Ranges,' *World*, 15 Aug. 1914, 2.

8 'Will Meet You In Berlin! Was Cry,' *News*, 20 Aug. 1914, 1, 3; 'Hundreds Stood in Rain to See 1000 Troops Off,' *Star*, 20 Aug. 1914, 1; 'Nine Hundred Men Left For Quebec,' *World*, 21 Aug. 1914, 3; 'Volunteers Leave for Valcartier,' *M&E*, 20 Aug. 1914, 4.

9 Hocken was in his second year as mayor, but he had also served for five years as a controller for the Council of Toronto. Ernest J. Chambers, ed., *Canadian Parliamentary Guide, 1918* (Ottawa: Mortimer, 1918), 146.

10 '1,522 Toronto Soldiers Leave; Highlanders Go in One Week,' *Star*, 22 Aug. 1914, 1; 'Seventeen Hundred Will Entrain Today,' *World*, 29 Aug. 1914, 8; 'Kilties Leave for War Cheered on by Thousands,' *Tel*, 31 Aug. 1914, 6; 'Volunteers Pass the Medical Test,' *M&E*, 31 Aug. 1914, 2.

11 Letter from Ian Sinclair to his sister, Dorothy Sinclair, 17 Aug. 1914, NAC, MG 30, E 432, File 1–16, Correspondence, Transcripts, Aug. 1914–Dec. 1914, 1; Letter from Ian Sinclair to his mother, Mrs Angus Sinclair, 24 Aug. 1914, from Long Branch Camp in Toronto, NAC, MG 30, E432, Vol. 1, File 1–16, Correspondence, Transcripts, Aug. 1914–Dec. 1914, 2.

12 Ian Sinclair, Diary Entry, 23 Aug. 1914, NAC, MG 30, E432, Vol. 1, File 1–2, 2; Ian Sinclair, Diary Entry, Aug. 1914 (precise date not listed, although likely 29 or 30 Aug.), NAC, MG 30, E432, Vol. 1, File 1–2, 3.

13 'Women Anxious to Serve as Volunteers,' *World*, 5 Aug. 1914, 2.

14 'I.O.D.E. Has Launched Campaign to Raise a Hospital Ship Fund; Regent Issues Personal Appeal,' *World*, 8 Aug. 1914, 8.

15 'Thousand Women Plan for Hospital Ship,' *Globe*, 12 Aug. 1914, 7; 'Enthusiasm Is Growing among Women Who Have Undertaken Ship Fund,' *World*, 12 Aug. 1914, 1; 'Women Enthusiastic about Hospital Ship,' *News*, 12 Aug. 1914, 4; 'Suffrage Campaign Dropped during War,' *Star*, 11 Aug. 1914, 10; 'Canadian Women to Outfit Men for Cold,' *Star*, 12 Aug. 1914, 4.

16 'Ladies Will Be Busy for Good Cause,' *Globe*, 14 Aug. 1914, 6; 'It Was Ladies' Day in Toronto,' *News*, 14 Aug. 1914, 4.

17 'Hospital Ship Fund Now Provided For,' *M&E*, 20 Aug. 1914, 4.

18 H.Groves, *Toronto Does Her 'Bit'* (Toronto: Municipal Intelligence Bureau, 1918), Thomas Fisher Rare Book Library, University of Toronto, flem0704, 49; 'Patriotic League Formed by Women,' *Globe*, 21 Aug. 1914, 5; 'Women to Present Concert Friday,' *World*, 22 Aug. 1914, 5; 'Nurses Sewing for Soldiers,' *Globe*, 1 Sep. 1914, 5.

19 Mrs F.M. Pauley, letter to the editor, *Star*, 21 Aug. 1914, 6; One More Patriotic Soul, letter to the editor, *Star*, 21 Aug. 1914, 6. Unfortunately, the papers do

not record why the members of the CWBC opposed the hospital ship, nor
why it changed its position to one of support. The CWBC, however, was a
consistent and vocal supporter of the war effort, suggesting that it only
opposed the specific plan to donate money for a hospital ship, possibly preferring that women devote their attention to another task.

20 'Prayer for Victory,' *CC*, 13 Aug. 1914, 519; 'In Time of War,' *Pres*, 13 Aug.
   1914, 123.
21 Katherine Rodpit, 'Biographical Sketch of Samuel Dwight Chown,' United
   Church of Canada Archives, Samuel Dwight Chown Fonds, Accession Number 86.008c, Finding Aid 23, i–ix, 1983.
22 S.D. Chown, 'A Call to Prayer in View of Present Conditions in Europe,' *CG*,
   12 Aug. 1914, 6.
23 'German Peril,' *CR*, 13 Aug. 1914, 4; 'Circular: To the Priests of the Archdiocese of Toronto,' *CR*, 20 Aug. 1914, 3.
24 'Ministers Ask Pulpit Support,' *World*, 22 Aug. 1914, 4.
25 'Canada Will Not Quail, Says Premier Whitney,' *Globe*, 5 Aug. 1914, 7; Toronto Board of Control, *Appendix 'A' to the Minutes of the City Council* (Toronto:
   Carswell, 1915), CTA, 1583; 'City Will Insure Lives of Soldiers,' *M&E*, 14
   Aug. 1914, 4; Toronto City Council, *Minutes of the Proceedings of the Council of
   the Corporation of Toronto for the Year 1914* (Toronto: Carswell, 1915), CTA, 363.
26 Chambers, ed., *Canadian Parliamentary Guide, 1918*, Greene, ed., *Who's Who
   and Why, 1921*, and Henry James Morgan, ed., *Canadian Men and Women of
   the Time*, 2nd ed. (Toronto: William Briggs, 1912).
27 'The Patriotic Fund,' *Star*, 17 Aug. 1914, 6.
28 'Let Your Patriotism Loose Your Purse Strings,' *Tel*, 24 Aug. 1914, 10; 'The
   Local Patriotic Fund,' *World*, 24 Aug. 1914, 6.
29 'Patriotic Fund Loyally Launched,' *M&E*, 25 Aug. 1914, 4; 'Loyalty to Britain
   and Knowledge of Duty Fills Massey Hall,' *World*, 25 Aug. 1914, 1.
30 *Appendix 'A' to the Minutes of the City Council 1914*, CTA, 1583.
31 Greene, ed., *Who's Who and Why, 1921*, 592.
32 I. Miller, '"Until the End": Brantford's Response to the First World War'
   (MA thesis, Wilfrid Laurier University, 1995), 27; 'Ladies Will Be Busy for
   Good Cause,' *Globe*, 14 Aug. 1914, 6; '$882,000 Raised for Patriotic Fund,'
   Globe, 29 Aug. 1914, 6; 'Ottawa Gives Half a Million to War Fund, Ottawa
   Learns,' *M&E*, 21 Aug. 1914, 1; 'Girl Guides Are Proving Their Mettle,'
   News, 10 Aug. 1914, 4.
33 'Hundreds of Workers Are Giving a Day's Pay,' *Star*, 26 Aug. 1914, 2.
34 'Canada Must Stand at Britain's Side,' *M&E*, 5 Aug. 1914, 5.
35 'City Rang with Cheers When War Was Declared,' *Tel*, 5 Aug. 1914, 13;
   'United for Security,' *News*, 7 Aug. 1914, 6.

36 'The Call to Canadians,' *News*, 25 Aug. 1914, 6.

37 'Why This War Is Inevitable,' *Globe*, 5 Aug. 1914, 4; 'For a Scrap of Paper,' *Globe*, 20 Aug. 1914, 4.

38 'Our Empire,' *CC*, 13 Aug. 1914, 520; Robert Bridges, 'The Call to the Nation,' *CC*, 20 Aug. 1914, 539.

39 A.D. Watson, 'Battle Hymn,' *CG*, 12 Aug. 1914, 16; 'A United Canada,' *CG*, 26 Aug. 1914, 5; 'In Time of War,' *Pres*, 13 Aug. 1914, 123; 'A Word of Caution,' *CB*, 13 Aug. 1914, 8; 'German Peril,' *CR*, 13 Aug. 1914, 4.

40 'A Right Perspective,' *Star*, 11 Aug. 1914, 6.

41 'Angry Mob Surrounds the Local Liederkranz Club,' *News*, 6 Aug. 1914, 1; 'Tore Down German Flag,' *Tel*, 6 Aug. 1914, 8.

42 'German Club May Fly British Flag,' *News*, 7 Aug. 1914, 4.

43 'The Great Day,' *News*, 5 Aug. 1914, 6.

44 'Foolish, Costly, Un-Christian,' *CG*, 19 Aug. 1914, 5–6.

2 A Great Crusade: Keeping Faith with Those Who Died

1 'The Just Claim of a Brave People,' *Tel*, 14 Oct. 1914, 8; Professional Villager, letter to the editor, *Globe*, 24 Oct. 1914, 4; 'The Front Page,' *SN*, 31 Oct. 1914, 1; Lashley W. Hall, 'Bring Belgians to Canada,' *CG*, 11 Nov. 1914, 28.

2 Toronto City Council, *Minutes of Proceedings of the Council of Corporation of the City of Toronto for the Year 1914* (Toronto: Carswell, 1915), CTA, 20 Oct. 1914, 447; Toronto Board of Control, *Appendix 'A' to the Minutes of the City Council 1914* (Toronto: Carswell, 1915), CTA, 3 Nov. 1914, 1859.

3 P.S., letter to the editor, *SN*, 14 Nov. 1914, 2; 'Twenty Thousand for the Belgians,' *World*, 7 Jan. 1915, 1; W.T. Herridge, 'The Belgian Relief Fund,' *Pres*, 21 Jan. 1915, 64.

4 Rudyard Kipling, 'For All We Have and Are,' *World*, 2 Sept. 1914, 1.

5 'Canada in the Battle of Ideas,' *Globe*, 18 Jan. 1915, 4.

6 'Is Britain Justified?' *CC*, 3 Sept. 1914, 568; 'The Desire for Peace,' *CC*, 13 Oct. 1914, 663; 'National Righteousness,' *CC*, 14 Jan. 1915, 21.

7 'International Obligations,' *World*, 2 Sept. 1914, 6; 'The Roll of Honour,' *World*, 3 Mar. 1915, 6; 'Good Out of Evil,' *M&E*, 8 Dec. 1914, 6.

8 'Editorial Comment,' *CB*, 22 Apr. 1915, 1.

9 See for instance, D. Morton and J.L. Granatstein, *Marching to Armageddon: Canadians and the Great War, 1914–1919* (Toronto: Lester and Orpen Dennys, 1989), 58–63, and G.W.L. Nicholson, *Canadian Expeditionary Force, 1914–1919: Official History of the Canadian Army in the First World War* (Ottawa: Queen's Printer and Controller of Stationery, 1962), 49–92.

10 'Canadians at Langemarck,' *Star*, 24 Apr. 1915 1; 'Canadians Won Great

Glory,' *Star*, 24 Apr. 1915, 1; 'London Is Aflame over Canada's Feat,' *Globe*, 26 Apr. 1915, 1.

11 'Await Further List with Much Anxiety,' *News*, 26 Apr. 1915, 1.

12 Morgan, ed., *Canadian Men and Women*, 232.

13 'Half of City Officers Fall in Fierce Fight,' *Globe*, 29 Apr. 1915, 3.

14 'Fear That Casualties May Number Into the Thousands,' *News*, 1 May 1915, 15.

15 'Canadian Loss to Reach 6,000,' *M&E*, 3 May 1915, 1; 'Those in Forward Trenches Killed Almost to a Man,' *News*, 4 May 1915, 3.

16 'Canadian Losses Over 6,000, Heroism Was Magnificent,' *Star*, 3 May 1915, 1; 'The Price of Glory,' *World*, 3 May 1915, 6.

17 The Warren correspondence appeared in 'Spartan Mother Speaks Message to the Bereaved,' *Star*, 1 May 1915, 1. The experience of the Sinclairs can be found in the following letters: Mrs Angus Sinclair to son Ian Sinclair, 27 Apr. 1915, NAC, MG 30, E432, Vol. 1, File 1-17, Correspondence – Transcripts – Jan. 1915–Apr. 1915; Bob Sinclair to brother Ian Sinclair, 4 May 1915, NAC, MG 30, E432, Vol. 1, File 1-17, Correspondence – Transcripts – Jan. 1915– Apr. 1915.

18 'Toronto Hit Heavily in List of Officers,' *Globe*, 26 Apr. 1915, 1; T.L. Church, qtd. in *Appendix 'C' to the Minutes of the City Council, 1915* (Toronto: Carswell, 1916), CTA, 49.

19 K. Beattie, *48th Highlanders of Canada, 1891–1928* (Toronto: 48th Highland-ers of Canada, 1932), 18–19, 46; Morgan, ed., *Canadian Men and Women*, 296, 520–1.

20 'Impressive Service Marks Captain Darling's Funeral,' *News*, 7 May 1915, 11.

21 'Last Tributes to War Hero; Capt. Darling Borne to Grave,' *Tel*, 6 May 1915, 8; 'Silent Crowd Lined Route,' *News*, 6 May 1915, 1; 'Toronto Pays Mighty Tribute to Captain Darling,' *Star*, 6 May 1915, 1; 'Grateful Tribute to Toronto Hero,' *M&E*, 7 May 1915, 5; 'Impressive Service Marks Captain Darling's Funeral,' *News*, 7 May 1915, 11; 'Sermon of Hope, Tender Comfort, Valiant Worldds,' *Star*, 7 May 1915, 10; 'Toronto Pays Tribute to Gallant Soldier,' *Globe*, 7 May 1915, 7. The inscription on his monument is from Mount Pleas-ant Cemetery, Internment Register No. 3, 21709-35339, 210, No. 33272.

22 'Known Survivors From Lusitania Total 703 – Lost Number 1,364,' *Tel*, 8 May 1915, 17.

23 'Awful Toll of Babes, 150 of Whom Died in the Water,' *News*, 10 May 1915, 3.

24 'Toronto Pulpits on Teutonic Savagery,' *Star*, 10 May 1915, 8. For a brief sur-vey of Cody's life, see W. White, *Canon Cody of St. Paul's Church* (Toronto: Ryerson Press, 1953).

25 'Survivors Tell of Their Escape,' *M&E*, 10 May 1915, 1.

26 Greene, ed., *Who's Who and Why, 1921*, 1450; 'Toronto Ladies Suffer from Shock,' *M&E*, 12 May 1915, 4.

27 'Paid Solemn Tribute to Murdered Dead,' *Globe*, 17 May 1915, 8.

28 *Minutes of Proceedings of the Council of the Corporation of the City of Toronto for the Year 1915*, 17 May 1915 (Toronto: Carswell, 1916), CTA, 176.

29 'French Retired While Canadians Battled against Terrific Odds,' *World*, 13 May 1915, 6.

30 'How Canadians Saved the Day Told by Tommy Atkins Himself,' *World*, 14 May 1915, 3.

31 'Only Twenty-Six Men of 4th Battalion Escaped Inferno,' *Star*, 19 May 1915, 2.

32 R. Service, 'The Red Harvest of the Trenches,' *Star*, 14 Dec. 1915, 2.

33 Nicholson, *Official History*, 160–3. Some historians have argued that the Somme offensive was successful, but most post-war literature has been very critical of Haig and the Somme battle. See J. Terrraine, *The Smoke and the Fire: Myths and Anti-Myths of the First World War, 1861–1945* (London: Sidgwick and Jackson, 1980).

34 'British Carry German Line; Twenty Mile Front is Taken in Assault,' *News*, 1 July 1916, 1.

35 The Allied Advance,' *Star*, 3 July 1916, 6.

36 'Dominion Day Will Long Be Remembered,' *Star*, 3 July 1916, 14.

37 'Big Progress by British: Conquer Whole First Line,' *Globe*, 12 July 1916, 1; 'War Summary,' *Globe*, 12 July 1916, 1.

38 A. Pateman, 'Keep the Home Fires Burning: Fuel Regulation in Toronto during the Great War' (MA thesis, University of Western Ontario, 1988).

39 Nicholson, *Official History*, 169–80.

40 'Feel High Cost of Living,' *Tel*, 20 Sept. 1916, 17.

41 'Canadian Troops Share in Big British Victory,' *Globe*, 16 Sept. 1916, 1.

42 'Canadians Add to Their Fame,' *Globe*, 19 Sept. 1916, 1; 'In Their First Big Offensive Canadians Went Right to the Mark,' *Tel*, 19 Sept. 1916, 15.

43 'Casualty List Is Increasing Daily,' *World*, 23 Sept. 1916, 4; 'Of 804 Toronto Men 170 Have Lost Their Lives,' *Star*, 27 Sept. 1916, 2; '125 Toronto Men in Latest Casualties,' *Star*, 29 Sept. 1916, 2; '101 Toronto Names in Casualty Lists,' *Star*, 30 Sept. 1916, 5.

44 Nicholson, *Official History*, 180–98.

45 'Bread May Take Two-Cent Jump Monday Next,' *Star*, 26 Oct. 1916, 1.

46 '164 Men in Latest Casualties,' *Star*, 2 Oct. 1916, 2; '103 Men, 2 Officers in the Latest Lists,' *Star*, 3 Oct. 1916, 2; 'Toronto Officers Killed in Action,' *World*, 5 Oct. 1916, 6; '229 Toronto Names in the Casualty Lists,' *Star*, 10 Oct. 1916, 3; 'War Has Taken a Toll of Over 2,000 Toronto Lives,' *Star*, 28 Oct. 1916, 5.

47 'The Price of Victory,' *CC*, 5 Oct. 1916, 631.
48 Letter from a soldier to Ven. Archdeacon Cody, 13 Oct. 1916, AO, MU 4970, Rev. H.J. Cody Papers, Series A-6: General Correspondence, 1889–1918, File 13, 2-4; 'Voices From the Firing Line and the Road to the Trenches,' *Tel*, 28 Oct. 1916, 12.
49 'The British Red Cross Needs Your Help,' *Globe*, 16 Oct. 1916, 1; 'Toronto Heeds Empire's Call,' *M&E*, 17 Oct. 1916, 1.
50 Advertisement, *World*, 18 Oct. 1916, 11; Editorial from the *Globe*, reprinted, 'Opinions on the Pictures of the Battle of the Somme,' *World*, 18 Oct. 1916, 6; 'New Record Is Made Every Day,' *World*, 21 Oct. 1916, 4.
51 H. Anson Green, to his father, 22 Oct. 1915, NAC, H. Anson Green Papers, MG 30, E440, File 10, Green Family Correspondence, 1914–1915, 4.
52 'Largest Toronto List Yet Issued,' *World*, 24 Oct. 1916, 3; 'Premier Borden Issues a Call,' *Globe*, 24 Oct. 1916, 1.
53 'Few Local Names in Casualty List,' World, 25 Nov. 1916, 6; B. Rawling, *Surviving Trench Warfare: Technology and the Canadian Corps, 1914–1918* (Toronto: University of Toronto Press, 1992), 81.
54 'Two Millions for Coal Yards,' *News*, 25 Jan. 1917, 1.
55 'Germany Proposes Peace,' *Star*, 13 Dec. 1916, 6.
56 'Germany's Peace Offer,' *World*, 13 Dec. 1916, 6; 'The Peace Proposals,' *Sun*, 20 Dec. 1916, 1.
57 A.S. Link, ed., *Woodrow Wilson Papers* (Princeton, N.J.: Princeton University Press, 1966), 40: 274.
58 'Toronto Condemns Wilson Peace Move,' *Star*, 21 Dec. 1916, 1; 'Amateur Diplomacy,' *World*, 23 Dec. 1916, 6; 'The Front Page,' *SN*, 30 Dec. 1916, 1.
59 Advertisement, *Globe*, 16 Jan. 1917, 5; Advertisement, *Globe*, 20 Jan. 1917, 12.
60 'Big Patriotic Fund Campaign Endorsed by Labour Council,' *News*, 19 Jan. 1917, 2; 'The Patriotic Fund Workers,' *Globe*, 20 Jan. 1917, 6; 'Serve by Giving,' *News*, 20 Jan. 1917, 6; 'To the Students,' *Varsity*, 22 Jan. 1917, 2; 'Every Minister Made an Appeal,' *World*, 22 Jan. 1917, 4.
61 '$3,258,972.14,' *World*, 27 Jan. 1917, 1.
62 Link, ed., *Woodrow Wilson Papers*, 40: 274.
63 '"Peace Without Victory" Talked a Shame to the U.S.A. and a Reproach to Woodrow Wilson,' *Tel*, 23 Jan. 1917, 8; 'President Wilson and the Senate,' *World*, 23 Jan. 1917, 6.
64 J. Swettenham, *To Seize the Victory: The Canadian Corps in World War I* (Toronto: Ryerson Press, 1965), 145–52.
65 Ibid., 161; Rawling, *Surviving Trench Warfare*, 131.
66 'Huns Cleared from Vimy Ridge; Counter-Attacks Repulsed,' *Tel*, 10 Apr. 1917, 13.

67 'Flags Out for Vimy Ridge,' *World*, 14 Apr. 1917, 6.
68 'Waged at an Awful Price,' *CB*, 19 Apr. 1917, 2.
69 Greene, ed., *Who's Who and Why, 1921*, 894.
70 'Soldiers in Small Riot,' *Tel*, 13 Apr. 1917, 20; *Minutes of the Proceedings of the Council of the Corporation of the City of Toronto for the Year 1917*, 30 Apr. 1917 (Toronto: Industrial and Technical Press, 1918), CTA, 96–7.
71 *Appendix 'A' to the Minutes of the City Council, 1915*, 18 Oct. 1915 (Toronto: Carswell, 1916), CTA; ibid., 27 Oct. 1915, 1047; *Appendix 'A' to the Minutes of the City Council, 1916, 17 Apr. 1916* (Toronto: Industrial and Technical Press, 1917), CTA, 307.
72 'Honoured Men of St. Julien; Veterans' Parade and Service,' *Tel*, 23 Apr. 1917, 8; 'Thousands Honour Canada's Bravest,' *World*, 23 Apr. 1917, 3.
73 'Lull at Exhibition before Borden Opens,' *Globe*, 2 May 1917, 8.

3   Enlistment and Recruiting: Sending Citizens to War

1 *Fifth Census of Canada, 1911*, 2: 372.
2 *Sixth Census of Canada, 1921*, 1: 542.
3 'Recruiting Returns, Military District Number 2 Up to and Including Month Ending Aug., 1916,' Sept. 1916, NAC, RG 24, Vol. 4303, File 34-1-59, Military District Number 2, General Recruiting, Vol. 8.
4 The 1921 Census lists the total number of men between 14 and 18 at 21,270 while those between 41 and 45 number 17,366, a difference of only 3,904. Divided equally over the war years, that means an increase of less than 1,000 new eligible recruits each year (*Sixth Census of Canada, 1921*, 2: 104–5).
5 'Second Call of Canada for Men Sends a Patriotic Thrill across the Dominion,' *News*, 7 Oct. 1914, 1.
6 The information on Irish Catholics, Italians, and Ukrainians was taken from: Mark G. McGowan, 'Sharing the Burden of Empire: Toronto's Catholics and the Great War, 1914–1918,' in McGowan and Clarke, eds., *Catholics at the 'Gathering Place': Historical Essays on the Archdiocese of Toronto, 1841–1991* (Toronto: Canadian Catholic Historical Association, 1993), 183; J. Zucchi, *Italians in Toronto: Development of a National Identity, 1875–1935* (Montreal: McGill-Queen's University Press, 1988), 164; Z.Y. Sokolsky, 'The Beginnings of Ukrainian Settlement in Toronto, 1891–1939,' in R.F. Harney, ed., *Gathering Place: Peoples and Neighbourhoods of Toronto, 1834–1945* (Toronto: Multicultural History Society of Ontario, 1985), 299–300.
7 'Keen Competition for Active Service,' *News*, 23 Oct. 1914, 2.
8 A recruit had to be at least 5 feet 3 inches tall, with a chest measurement of

33½ inches (D. Morton, *When Your Number's Up: The Canadian Soldier in the First World War* [Toronto: Random House, 1993], 9).

9 Nicholson, *Official History*, 32–9.

10 'Canadian Losses,' *CC*, 13 May 1915, 295; 'Church News,' *CC*, 13 May 1915, 302; 'Queen's Own Honour Their Heroic Dead,' *News*, 6 May 1915, 3; 'Solemn Memorial for Lost Q.O.R. Men,' *Globe*, 6 May 1915, 6.

11 'Volunteers Rally to Empire's Cause,' *Globe*, 11 June 1915, 6.

12 'Recruiting Sergeants and Appealing Posters,' *Globe*, 30 June 1915, 8.

13 'Recruiting Sergeants Got Poor Results,' *Globe*, 2 July 1915, 6.

14 'More Efforts Needed to Enlist Men Here,' *Globe*, 3 July 1915, 8; 'Open More Offices to Aid Recruiting,' *News*, 5 July 1915, 9; 'Military Men Meeting to Plan Recruiting,' *Star*, 5 July 1915, 3; 'Draw Top Schemes to Aid Recruiting,' *News*, 6 July 1915, 9.

15 An attempt has been made to locate the first names, or initials, of all people mentioned in this book. Unfortunately, such information is not always available.

16 'Success Follows Recruiting Call,' *World*, 7 July 1915, 1; 'Good Response to Call for Recruits,' *News*, 8 July 1915, 3; 'Pick Out Places Where Men Meet,' *World*, 8 July 1915, 7.

17 '1,000 Toronto Men Enlisted This Week,' *Globe*, 10 July 1915, 6; 'Badge for Those Who Are Rejected,' *World*, 12 July 1915, 4; 'Proved Good Day for Recruiting,' *Globe*, 13 July 1915, 6; 'Plans Formed after Parade to Secure Further Recruits,' *News*, 15 July 1915, 10; 'Queen's Own Parade Tracks Recruits,' *World*, 15 July 1915, 2.

18 'Cheer Clarion Call to Canada's Manhood,' *Globe*, 16 July 1916, 1, 6; 'Toronto Welcomes Home Colonel John A. Currie,' *World*, 16 July 1915, 1, 3; 'Ministers Asked to Assist Recruiting from the Pulpit,' *News*, 17 July 1915, 14; 'Officials Endorse Recruiting Action,' *Star* 18 July 1915, 4; 'Urges Its Members to Enlist at Once,' *Globe*, 19 July 1915, 7.

19 'Big Recruiting Meeting,' *Star*, 13 July 1915, 5.

20 'Enthusiasm Reached High Pitch at Monster Massey Hall Meeting,' *Star*, 21 July 1915, 3; '500 Men Enlisted; More Still Coming,' *Star*, 21 July 1915, 4; Fifteen Thousand Hear Speakers at City Hall,' *World*, 21 July 1915, 1; 'The Recruiting Drum,' *M&E*, 21 July 1915, 6; 'Flame of Patriotic Fervor to Stimulate Recruiting,' *Globe*, 21 July 1915, 1, 6; George Foster, Diary Entry, 20 July 1915, NAC, Sir George Foster Papers, MG 27 D7, Vol. 4.

21 'City Has Lately Recruited over 3,000 Men,' *News*, 22 July 1915, 7; 'Baby Battalion Sets Fast Pace,' *Globe*, 26 July 1915, 6; 'More Men! Is Call from Niagara Camp,' *World*, 24 July 1915, 6; 'Recruiting League Down to Business,' *World*, 24 July 1915, 6.

22 'Lt. Col. Stewart Will Command the New 84th,' *Globe*, 28 July 1915, 6.

23 H. Anson Green to his mother on 30 July 1915, 13 Aug. 1915, and 25 Nov. 1915. NAC, H. Anson Green Papers, MG 30, E440, File 10, Green Family Correspondence, 1914–1915; NAC, H. Anson Green Papers, MG 30, E440, File 12, Green Family WWI Correspondence, 1916–1917.

24 'Men Come Forward to Serve Country,' *Globe*, 5 Aug. 1915, 6.

25 'Labour Men Prove Their Patriotism by Enlisting,' *Star*, 7 Aug. 1915, 5.

26 Open Recruiting Campaign To-Night,' *News*, 7 Aug. 1915, 2.

27 'Hundred Thousand Witness Tattoo in Riverdale Park,' *World*, 10 Aug. 1915, 1.

28 'Toronto's Patriotic Heart Stirred by Martial Music,' *Star*, 10 Aug. 1915, 5.

29 'Sergeants Busy among the Crowd,' *World*, 10 Aug. 1915, 2; 'Tens of Thousands of Hearty Voices Joined in Singing "Rule Britannia" and "Tipperary,"' *News*, 10 Aug. 1915, 10; 'Riverdale Park Filled to Limit,' *M&E*, 10 Aug. 1915, 4; 'Greatest Throng City Ever Saw Reveled in Patriotic Concert,' *Tel*, 10 Aug. 1915, 7; 'Vast Singing Throng Sweeps Riverdale,' *Globe*, 10 Aug. 1915, 1, 6.

30 For a description of the structure of the depot, see 'Circular on the Structure of the Toronto Recruiting Depot,' NAC, RG 24, Vol. 4304, File 34-1-59, Military District No. 2, Recruiting Generally, Vol. 2. The daily operations of the depot were funded by donations from the militia regiments. ''Statement on the Toronto Recruiting Depot,' *Appendix 'A' to the Minutes of the City Council, 1915*, 20 Dec. 1915 (Toronto: Carswell, 1916), CTA, 1260.

31 'Civilians Storm Recruiting Depot,' *News*, 16 Aug. 1915, 1; 'Consent Required Say New Orders,' *World*, 16 Aug. 1915, 4; 'Recruiting Depot Has Busy Opening,' *Star*, 16 Aug. 1915, 2; 'Recruiting Depot Will Open To-Day,' *M&E*, 16 Aug. 1915, 4; 'All Day Busy Rush at Recruiting Depot,' *Globe*, 17 Aug. 1915, 6; 'Bad Teeth No Bar: Good Ones Supplied,' *Globe*, 17 Aug. 1915, 7.

32 'Wife's Consent Is Not Now Needed,' *World*, 21 Aug. 1915, 6; 'Men Come Forward for Overseas Service,' *Globe*, 18 Aug. 1915, 6.

33 The number of rejected volunteers was calculated assuming that between 30 and 40 per cent of volunteers were refused on medical grounds. This percentage was arrived at by comparing the total of both the number of men in the army and those rejected after having volunteered with the total number of men available in 1915.

34 'Labour Day Parade Liberally Besprinkled with Men Wearing Uniform of the King,' *News*, 7 Sept. 1915, 13; 'Crowds Cheer for Labour Day Parade,' *World*, 7 Sept. 1915, 5; 'War Themes Rampant in Labour Parade,' *Globe*, 7 Sept. 1915, 6; Le Grand Reed, to A.A.G. 2nd Division, Niagara Camp, 1 Sept. 1915, NAC, RG 24, Vol. 4301, Papers of Military District No. 2, File 34-1-59, Recruiting Generally, Vol. 2.

35 'Start New Plan to Get Recruits,' *World*, 5 Oct. 1915, 5; 'Thirty-Two Posts to

Take Recruits,' *News*, 5 Oct. 1915, 3; 'To Organize City for More Recruits,' *Globe*, 5 Oct. 1915, 6.

36 'Recruiting Depots at Picture Shows,' *News*, 26 Oct. 1915, 12.

37 'Colonel Kingsmill for Commander,' *World*, 2 Nov. 1915, 2; 'Artillery Arrives in Pelting Rainstorm,' *Globe*, 5 Nov. 1915, 6.

38 The troops that marched were from the following units: the 58th, 37th, 74th, 75th, 81st, 83rd, 92nd, and the newly authorized 95th Battalions.

39 'Monster Parade through City To-Day,' *Globe*, 9 Nov. 1915, 6; 'Ten Thousand Men on March,' *News*, 9 Nov. 1915, 1; '10,000 Men in Khaki Capture Toronto,' *Globe*, 10 Nov. 1915, 9; 'Ten Thousand Troops March in Big Parade,' *World*, 10 Nov. 1915, 1; 'Military Parade Inspiring Sight,' *M&E*, 10 Nov. 1915, 4.

40 'Largest Number Enlist in a Day,' *World*, 9 Nov. 1915, 2; 'Toronto Averages 100 Recruits a Day,' *Globe*, 11 Nov. 1915, 6; 'Over 500 Enlisted during Last Week,' *Globe*, 15 Nov. 1915, 6; 'Biggest Day in Depot's History,' *World*, 16 Nov. 1915, 6; 'Five Toronto Churches Assist in Campaign to Raise Recruits,' *World*, 22 Nov. 1915, 1.

41 'Go into Homes in Search of Recruits,' *News*, 2 Dec. 1915, 13; 'Need of Recruits to Be Accentuated,' *News*, 4 Dec. 1915, 10. The nature and scope of Kingsmill's campaign is confirmed by a letter he wrote to W.A. Logie, 2 Dec. 1915, NAC, RG 24, Vol. 3401, Papers of Military District No. 2, File 34-1-59, Recruiting Generally, Vol. 3, 3

42 'Toronto Recruiting Breaks All Records,' *Globe*, 7 Dec. 1915, 8; 'Grenadiers Make Recruiting Jump,' *News*, 7 Dec. 1915, 12; 'Recruiting Campaign Is Bringing Results,' *World*, 7 Dec. 1915, 2; W.A. Logie to Sir Sam Hughes, 8 Dec. 1916, NAC, RG 24, Vol. 3401, Papers of Military District No. 2, File 34-1-59, Recruiting Generally, Vol. 3.

43 'Men Called from Recruiting Work,' *News*, 14 Dec. 1915, 1.

44 'Census Necessary,' *News*, 15 Dec. 1915, 3; 'Holding Back Men for Their Regiment,' *News*, 16 Dec. 1915, 11; 'Ginger Up, Men! Don't Be Slackers,' *Globe*, 17 Dec. 1915, 8; 'Recruiting Shows Slight Increase,' *News*, 17 Dec. 1915, 13.

45 'Recruiting Sags Again, But Week Brought 483,' *Globe*, 20 Dec. 1915, 8.

46 'Recruits Pour in for New Battalion,' *News*, 29 Dec. 1915, 2.

47 C.P. Stacey, *Canada and the Age of Conflict: A History of Canadian External Policies*, Volume I, *1867–1921* (Toronto: Macmillan, 1977), 191–3.

48 S.D. Chown, Superintendent of the Methodist Church, to Robert Borden, 1 Jan. 1916, NAC, Borden Papers, MG 26, H1 a, Vol. 16, 36,295; George Foster to Robert Borden, 3 Jan. 1916, NAC, Borden Papers, MG 26, H1 a, Vol. 16, 36,325.

49 'Military Census Got Poor Encouragement,' *Star*, 3 Jan. 1916, 3; 'Military Census Meets Opposition,' *Star*, 5 Jan. 1916, 3; 'Military Census Is Going to

Be Difficult,' *World*, 4 Jan. 1916, 5; 'Idle Men Should First Be Enlisted,' *News*, 5 Jan. 1916, 13; 'Seek Loafers First, Says Sir John Eaton,' *Globe*, 5 Jan. 1916, 7.

50 'Pals' Battalion Has Rapid Growth,' *Globe*, 5 Jan. 1916, 7; 'City's Biggest Week: 1,200 Volunteered,' *Globe*, 10 Jan. 1916, 6; 'Battalion Complete,' *News*, 12 Jan. 1916, 15.

51 'Rush to the Colours Taxes Accommodation,' *Globe*, 12 Jan. 1916, 8.

52 'Brand New Barracks for the Grenadiers,' *Globe*, 15 Jan. 1916, 9.

53 'Records for Recruits Was Made Yesterday,' *World*, 18 Jan. 1916, 1.

54 'Appeals for Recruits in Toronto Churches,' *World*, 24 Jan. 1916, 3; 'Hundred Recruits Before Noon Hour,' *News*, 25 Jan. 1916, 1; 'Record for Recruiting in Toronto – 544 Offered,' *World*, 25 Jan. 1916, 1; 'Appeals at Sunday Meetings Bring Forth Many Recruits,' *News*, 31 Jan. 1916, 2; 'Halted the Dance to Hear Recruiter,' *Globe*, 31 Jan. 1916, 6.

55 'Toronto Recruiting Takes Another Leap,' *Globe*, 29 Jan. 1916, 8; Groves, *Toronto Does Her 'Bit'*, 24.

56 'New High Record Set in Recruiting,' *News*, 31 Jan. 1916, 5; 'Day's Recruiting Again Sets Record,' *M&E*, 1 Feb. 1916, 4; 'First Half of Week Recruiting Figures,' *World*, 3 Feb. 1916, 2.

57 'Battalions Will Be Recruited by Shifts,' *Globe*, 19 Feb. 1916, 8.

58 Ibid. Burton had already been overseas with the 75th Battalion and been wounded. While convalescing in England, he saw British Bantams training and upon his return to Toronto was one of the loudest and most colourful advocates of a Bantam Battalion. Several hundred recruits were secured in the opening hours, but eventually the battalion was granted the right to recruit from the entire Central Ontario District. By July 1916 they were up to over one thousand recruits, and these proceeded overseas in April 1917. The unit was broken up for reinforcements almost immediately upon its arrival, its members serving out the war in construction and labour units, as well as in front-line formations. See S. Allinson, *The Bantams: The Untold Story of World War I* (London: Howard Baker Press, 1981), especially chapter 9, 'The Canadians,' 175–201.

59 'Sir Sam Hughes Leads Parade of 18,000 Men,' *Star*, 1 Mar. 1916, 1; 'Toronto Troops Made Fine Showing,' *M&E*, 2 Mar. 1916, 8; 'Parade of 17,997 Soldiers,' *Tel*, 1 Mar. 1916, 13; 'Six Miles of Fighting Men Marched Through the City,' *News*, 1 Mar. 1916, 1; 'Spirited Recruiting Keeps Up in Toronto,' *Globe*, 1 Mar. 1916, 8; 'Toronto Views Greatest Parade Ever in Canada,' *News*, 1 Mar. 1916, 1; 'Toronto Sees Finest Parade in Its History,' *World*, 2 Mar. 1916, 1, 2.

60 J.E. Edmonds and G.C. Wynne, *History of the Great War Based on Official Documents: Military Operations, France and Belgium, 1915* (London: Macmillan, 1927), 51.

61 'Prize for a Recruit Extra Day's Leave,' *Globe*, 3 Mar. 1916, 6.

62 'Friends of Lieut. Col. Price Signed Pledge to Secure Recruits for 204th Battalion,' *News*, 15 Mar. 1916, 5.

63 'Adopt New Plan to Secure Recruits,' *News*, 6 April 1916, 8; 'Are Locating the Young Eligibles,' *News*, 10 April 1916, 9.

64 'Bantams Start on Personal Canvass,' *News*, 6 April 1916, 2.

65 Lieut. R.V. Jones to W.H. Price, Chief Recruiting Officer, 204th Battalion, 24 April 1916, NAC, Papers of Military District No. 2, RG 24, Vol. 4302, File 34-1-59, Recruiting Generally, Vol. 5, 1–2.

66 'H.R.H. Duchess of Connaught and Col. Septimus Denison at Toronto's Largest Open-Air Church Service Yesterday Morning in Queen's Park,' *Star*, 1 May 1916, 5; '18,000 Soldiers in Queen's Park,' *M&E*, 1 May 1916, 1, 7; 'Overseas and City Battalions Massed at Queen's Park Service on Sunday,' *Tel*, 1 May 1916, 13; 'Eighteen Thousand Soldiers at Service in Queen's Park,' *News*, 1 May 1916, 7; 'Great Gathering at Queen's Park,' *World*, 1 May 1916, 5.

67 'Highland Unit Is Bound for East,' *World*, 18 May 1916, 4; 'Will Ye No' Come Back Again, Kilties?' *Globe*, 18 May 1916, 8.

68 'Recruiting Drops Below Average,' *World*, 27 May 1916, 2.

69 '18,000 Men in Toronto Are of Military Age,' *Globe*, 20 May 1916, 8. Unfortunately, there are no further details on how the survey was conducted, or who was included.

70 'New Recruiting Ideas Discussed,' *World*, 6 June 1916, 2.

71 'Synod Willing to Favour Conscription,' *News*, 9 June 1916, 4; M. Robin, 'Registration, Conscription and Independent Labour Politics, 1916–1917,' *CHR* 67, no. 2 (1966): 101–18; 'Women of Toronto Demand a National Registration,' *Star*, 13 June 1916, 7; 'Manufacturers Talk Recruiting,' *Globe*, 15 June 1916, 7; 'Mobilization of Men and Resources,' *News*, 28 June 1916, 7; 'More Equitable Recruiting Plan,' *Globe*, 16 June 1916, 1.

72 Letter from T. Crawford Brown, chairman of the Clerical Patriotic Association, Toronto, to religious leaders in Toronto, Archives of the Roman Catholic Archdiocese of Toronto, Neil McNeil Papers, War Box, 1914, FWWEO1.09, 14 June 1916.

73 'A Call for Service from Brig.-General Logie,' *World*, 17 June 1916, 1; 'Big Recruiting Day: Over 100 Volunteers,' *Globe*, 20 June 1916, 8; 'Recruiting Workers at End of Their Rope,' *Globe*, 28 June 1916, 6.

74 Le Grand Reed to W.A. Logie, 26 June 1916, NAC, RG 24, Vol. 4302, File 34-1-59, Military District Number 2, Recruiting Generally, Vol. 6.

75 'Volunteer System Becoming Obsolete,' *World*, 3 July 1916, 4; 'Recruiting Picks Up at the Depot,' *World*, 4 July 1916, 2; 'Recruiting Was Quiet; 23

Obtained Yesterday,' *Globe*, 13 July 1916, 6; 'Nine Units Share Ten Recruits,' *Globe*, 14 July 1916, 6.

76 'Recruiting Faster as Campaign Opens,' *World*, 12 Sept. 1916, 4.

77 'French Canada and Recruiting,' *Globe*, 27 Sept. 1916, 6; 'Quebec and the War,' *CG*, 25 Oct. 1916, 5.

78 'In the Place of Conscription,' *Globe*, 10 Oct. 1916, 6.

79 J.M. Godfrey, writing in his capacity as president of the Canadian National Service League, to Robert Borden after National Registration was announced on 18 August 1916, NAC, Borden Papers, MG 26, H1 a, Vol. 16, 34695.

80 See S. Macintyre, *The Oxford History of Australia*, volume 4, *1901–1942* (Melbourne: Oxford University Press, 1986).

81 'Audience Approves Conscription Call,' *World*, 30 Oct. 1916, 2; 'Ask Compulsion to Get Recruits,' *Globe*, 9 Nov. 1916, 1; 'Get the 100,000 Recruits Even by Conscription,' *Globe*, 10 Nov. 1916, 1; Letter from S.D. Chown to Rev. Kenneth Kingston regarding conscription, United Church of Canada Archives, Samuel Dwight Chown Fonds, 86.008C, Box 1, File 13, Correspondents Regarding World War I, 1915–1916, 30 Nov. 1916, 1, 2.

82 R.G. Haycock, *Sam Hughes: The Public Career of a Controversial Canadian, 1885–1916* (Waterloo: Wilfrid Laurier University Press, 1986), 288–310.

83 Advertisement, *World*, 30 Nov. 1916, 3.

84 'National Service,' *M&E*, 23 Dec. 1916, 6; 'Premier Borden Brings Call for National Service Home to All,' *Tel*, 23 Dec. 1916, 10.

85 'Patriotic Duty to Fill Out Cards,' *Globe*, 3 Jan. 1917, 8; 'Fill Out the Cards, Says Labour Council to Unions,' *Star*, 5 Jan. 1917, 5; 'Let It Rest in Peace,' *Tel*, 13 Jan. 1917, 14; Nicholson, *Official History*, 220–1. An extensive search was conducted at the NAC for the National Service files for Toronto. Unfortunately, such files are not available.

86 'Militia Act Should Be Put into Force,' *Star*, 24 Jan. 1917, 1; 'Want Militia Act Enforced,' *News*, 24 Jan. 1917, 1; 'Enforce the Militia Act,' *Globe*, 25 Jan. 1917, 1.

87 *Minutes of the Proceedings of the Council of the Corporation of the City of Toronto for the Year 1917*, 14 May 1917 (Toronto: Industrial and Technical Press, 1918), CTA, 102. City Council was reiterating the position stated in a similar resolution passed three months earlier on 19 Feb. 1917 (Ibid., 47).

88 Groves, *Toronto Does Her 'Bit,'* 7.

4   Women and War: Public and Private Spheres

1 'Send Help to the Belgians,' *News*, 12 Oct. 1914, 4.

2 *The Canadian Newspaper Directory*, 11th ed. (Montreal and Toronto: A. McKim, 1918), 95.

3 L.S. Doyly, 'Canadian Women Help the Empire: "What Could Women Do in Time of War?"' *EW*, Nov. 1914, 8, 32; H. Groves, *Toronto Does Her 'Bit'* (Toronto: Municipal Intelligence Bureau, 1918), 70.

4 'Mightier Than the Sword,' *EW*, Sept. 1914, 5; Swanton, 'Canadian Women,' *EW*, Nov. 1914, 32.

5 H.J. Morgan, ed., *Canadian Men and Women of the Time: A Handbook of Canadian Biography of Living Characters*, 2nd ed. (Toronto: William Briggs, 1912), 287; Toronto Public Library, Biographies of People, Film T686.3, Vol. 16, 357.

6 Morgan, ed., *Canadian Men and Women*, 621; 'What Twelve Canadian Women Hope to See as the Outcome of the War,' *EW*, April 1915, 6–8.

7 'Canada's Sons Are Wounded: We Must Equip Hospital,' *News*, 26 April 1915, 4.

8 'Canadian Women and the "Peace" Congress,' *SN*, 1 May 1915, 21.

9 B. Roberts, 'Women's Peace Activism in Canada,' in L. Kealey and J. Sangster, eds., *Beyond the Vote: Canadian Women and Politics* (Toronto: University of Toronto Press, 1989), 279; L. Kealey, *Enlisting Women for the Cause: Women, Labour, and the Left in Canada, 1890–1920* (Toronto: University of Toronto Press, 1998), 279–81; B. Roberts, *'Why Do Women Do Nothing to End the War?': Canadian Feminist Pacifists and the Great War* (Ottawa: CRIAW, 1985).

10 'Canadian Women and the "Peace" Congress,' *SN*, 1 May 1915, 21.

11 'Women Will Care for the Wounded,' *World*, 6 May 1915, 4.

12 'Making Respirators for the Soldiers,' *Globe*, 11 May 1915, 8.

13 'When Bowed Head Is Proudly Held,' *Globe*, 8 May 1915, 10.

14 A search was conducted to determine whether similar arrangements were made in Britain. No mention could be found of a purple arm band, but there are examples of local traditions to mark the death of soldiers. In the home town of the Lancashire Fusiliers, Bury, local residents pulled the blinds in the homes of the deceased soldiers. At times whole streets were darkened as news filtered back from the front (Moorhouse, *Hell's Foundations*, 90–6). Thus, Toronto's experience with the purple arm band may have been an adaptation of the British tradition of local measures to mark the passing of young men.

15 'Offer Services to Help Recruiting,' *News*, 17 July 1915, 1.

16 'To Bid God-Speed to Canadian Boys,' *Globe*, 19 July 1915, 6.

17 Helen Ball, 'The Big Recruiting Meeting from Woman's Point of View,' *News*, 21 July 1915, 4.

18 'Massey Hall a Vast Sea of Women's Faces,' *Star*, 21 July 1915, 3.

19 Ibid.

20 The practice of bestowing a white feather on young civilian men originated in Britain in the early days of the war. The phenomenon began with a patri-

otic speech by Admiral Penrose Fitzgerald in a speech from a bandstand in Folkestone, England, in August 1914, in which he called upon women to mark shirkers with white feathers. Militant suffragists were among the first to act on his suggestion, but soon many other women joined in the process. See P. Simkins, *Kitchener's Army: The Raising of the New Armies, 1914–16* (Manchester: Manchester University Press, 1988).

21 'Riverdale Park Filled to Limit,' *M&E*, 10 Aug. 1915, 4; 'Toronto's Patriotic Heart Stirred by Martial Music,' *Star*, 10 Aug. 1915, 5.

22 'What Business Women May Do,' *Globe*, 15 Aug. 1915, 5; 'Business Women Are Organizing,' *Globe*, 24 Aug. 1915, 5.

23 'Crowds Cheer for Labour Day Parade,' *World*, 7 Sept. 1915, 5; 'Labour Day Parade Liberally Besprinkled with Men Wearing Uniform of the King,' *News*, 7 Sept. 1915, 13; 'War Themes Rampant in Labour Parade,' *Globe*, 7 Sept. 1915, 6; 'When Big Parade Reached Grounds,' *World*, 7 Sept. 1915, 4; 'Soldiers Swelled Parade,' *Tel*, 7 Sept. 1915, 11.

24 'Tag Day to Aid Recruiting Here,' *News*, 4 Nov. 1915, 3; '2,500 Women to Aid in Recruiting Tag Day,' *Globe*, 5 Nov. 1915, 7; 'Keep Toronto Ahead Is Tag Day Slogan,' *World*, 5 Nov. 1915, 4; 'Plans Completed for Big Tag Day,' *World*, 6 Nov. 1915, 7; 'Keep Toronto Ahead Is Tag Day Motto,' *Globe*, 8 Nov. 1915, 7; 'Must Buy Tag to Be Really Dressed,' *News*, 8 Nov. 1915, 10; 'Ran Out of Tags Before Noon, and Used Flags,' *News*, 9 Nov. 1915, 1; 'Army of Girls Will Tag Toronto,' *M&E*, 9 Nov. 1915, 10; 'Toronto Gives with Free Hand,' *M&E*, 10 Nov. 1915, 1, 7; 'Fair Taggers Do Job Well,' *Tel*, 9 Nov. 1915, 10.

25 Ontario Sessional Papers, Vol. 48, Part X, *Report of the Women's Institute of the Province of Ontario, 1915* (Toronto: A.T. Wilgress, 1916), 111, 155.

26 Groves, *Toronto Does Her 'Bit,'* 54, 68; K. Delhi, 'Love and Knowledge: Adult Education in the Toronto Home and School Council, 1916–1940,' *OH* 88, no. 3 (1996): 207–8.

27 'Women Enlist as Street Car Conductors,' *Globe*, 4 Dec. 1915, 10.

28 'Toronto Recruiting Breaks All Records,' *Globe*, 7 Dec. 1915, 8; 'An Appeal to Women to Make Men Enlist,' *World*, 8 Dec. 1915, 4; 'Day of Recruiting Meeting Is Over,' *News*, 13 Dec. 1915, 1.

29 'Huge Christmas Party for Soldiers' Kiddies,' *Globe*, 24 Dec. 1915, 8.

30 'Womanhood Will Work to Assist Enlistment,' *Globe*, 6 Jan. 1916, 6.

31 Groves, *Toronto Does Her 'Bit,'* 66; M. Kluckner, *Toronto the Way It Was* (Altona, Man.: Friesen Printers, 1988), 282; Toronto Public Library, Biographies of People, Film T686.3, Vol. 16, 357.

32 'Toronto Women Have Plan to Free 14,700 Men for War,' *Star*, 6 Jan. 1916, 2; 'How All Ontario Women Can Aid in Recruiting,' *News*, 8 Jan. 1916, 4.

33 'Emergency Corps to Register Women,' *Globe*, 12 Jan. 1916, 10.

34 'Women's Emergency Corps Outlines Recruiting Plans,' *News*, 15 Jan. 1916, 4.
35 'Will Release Men for Active Service,' *World*, 22 Jan. 1916, 4; 'Women Organize to Replace Enlister's,' *Globe*, 22 Jan. 1916, 8; 'Registration of Women for Service,' *News*, 22 Jan. 1916, 4.
36 'Monster Reception for Wives and Mothers of Soldiers,' *News*, 25 Jan. 1916, 8; 'Soldiers' Folks at Big Reception,' *M&E*, 25 Jan. 1916, 4; 'Great Crush at Reception,' *Tel*, 25 Jan. 1916, 6; 'Reception of 10,000 Soldiers' Dependants at City Hall,' *Star*, 25 Jan. 1916, 2.
37 'Plans to Mobilize Boys, Men and Women,' *Globe*, 11 Feb. 1916, 6; 'Women for Men's Positions Needed,' *News*, 12 Feb. 1916, 16.
38 'Emergency Corps Bans Shirkers' Relatives,' *Globe*, 10 April 1916, 4.
39 'Thousands Say Good-Bye to Departing Battalions,' *World*, 26 April 1916, 1.
40 'Whole City Tagged for Kitchener Day,' *News*, 4 May 1916, 8; 'Ablaze with Union Jacks for Kitchener's Day,' *Tel*, 4 May 1916, 20.
41 'Enlist Women to Get After City Young Men,' *Globe*, 6 June 1916, 8.
42 'Mass Meeting of Women Finds All Ready to Serve,' *News*, 13 June 1916, 8.
43 'Women's Mass Meeting at Massey Hall Monday,' *World*, 9 June 1916, 12; 'Issued Statement Regarding Meeting,' *World*, 12 June 1916, 2; 'Women to Honour the Fighting Men,' *Globe*, 12 June 1916, 10; 'National Registration for Canada Demanded by Women's Mass Meeting,' *Globe*, 13 June 1916, 1, 6; 'Women Plan to Fill Men's Places,' *World*, 13 June 1916, 7; 'Huge Mass Meeting of Women Ask National Registration,' *Tel*, 13 June 1916, 16; 'Women to Free Eligible Men,' *M&E*, 13 June 1916, 1, 10.
44 'Emergency Corps Meeting Yesterday,' *World*, 23 June 1916, 5.
45 'Crowds Line Route of Women's Parade,' *News*, 3 July 1916, 4; 'Inspiration Parade of 3,000 Women,' *Globe*, 3 July 1916, 9; 'Inspiring Site as Women Marched,' *World*, 3 July 1916, 5; 'Most Wonderful Procession in Toronto's History,' *Tel*, 3 July 1916, 18; 'Toronto Women Took Part in Grand Parade,' *M&E*, 3 July 1916, 5; 'Women's War Work in Inspiring Parade,' *Globe*, 3 July 1916, 10.
46 'Women's Section,' *SN*, 15 July 1916, 21.
47 'Shipped Comfort Valued At $429,379,' *Globe*, 12 Sept. 1916, 4.
48 'Demand for Women Workers Increasing,' *Globe*, 18 Oct. 1916, 10; 'Women Flocking to Banks and Perhaps to Stay,' *Globe*, 26 Oct. 1916, 9.
49 'Local Council Votes in Favour of Conscription,' *Globe*, 22 Nov. 1916, 10.
50 Groves, *Toronto Does Her 'Bit*,' 51; 'Women Munition Workers' Banquet,' *World*, 1 Jan. 1917, 4; 'Of 4,000 Women Workers on Munitions, City Has 2,500,' *Star*, 2 Jan. 1917, 10; 'Thrilling Sight When 1,500 Women Toast King,' *Tel*, 2 Jan. 1917, 18.
51 'Advertisement,' *Globe*, 17 Jan. 1917, 7.

5 Conscription: A Decided Commitment

1 'Editorial,' *CC*, 24 May 1917, 327; 'Pleased with Conscription,' *News*, 19 May 1917, 21; 'Audience Cheers for Conscription,' *World*, 28 May 1917, 4. Originally called the Returned Soldiers' Association when formed in May 1916, the local Great War Veterans' Association grew to 3,400 members by the end of 1916. See H. Groves, *Toronto Does Her 'Bit'* (Toronto: Municipal Intelligence Bureau, 1918) 35, 36, 51.

2 H.J. Morgan, ed., *Canadian Men and Women of the Time: A Handbook of Canadian Biography of Living Characters*, 2nd ed. (Toronto: William Briggs, 1912), 1025.

3 'How Toronto Labour Leaders Regard Conscription Policy,' *News*, 19 May 1917, 1. Simpson's attitude, which was quite typical of labour leaders in Toronto, contrasts sharply with the portrait of labour offered by C. Heron and M. Siemiatycki in their 1998 article, 'The Great War, The State, and Working-Class Canada,' in C. Heron, ed., *The Workers' Revolt in Canada, 1917–1925* (Toronto: University of Toronto Press, 1998), 11–42.

4 'Thousands Call for Conscription,' *World*, 4 June 1917, 4; 'Conscription Resolutions,' *News*, 2 June 1917, 1; 'Thousands of Torontonians Advocated Conscription Law,' *News*, 5 June 1917, 5; '10,000 Gather at Queen's Park to Endorse Conscription Act,' *Tel*, 4 June 1917, 6; 'Mass Meetings for Conscription,' *M&E*, 4 June 1917, 5; 'Women Unanimous at Conscription Meeting,' *Star*, 4 June 1917, 4; 'Toronto to Speak for Conscription,' *Globe*, 2 June 1917, 8.

5 'No More Conscription Talk at Labour Temple,' *Star*, 4 June 1917, 2; 'Anti-Conscription Meeting a Fizzle,' *M&E*, 4 June 1917, 10; 'Broke Up Socialist Meeting Enraged Returned Soldiers,' *Tel*, 4 June 1917, 11; 'Returned Men Spoil Meeting for Socialists,' *World*, 4 June 1917, 1, 3.

6 'Police Must Allow Indoor Meetings,' *News*, 4 June 1917, 1.

7 'Labour Men Endorse Conscription Policy,' *World*, 11 June 1917, 4.

8 J.L. Granatstein and J.M. Hitsman, *Broken Promises: A History of Conscription in Canada* (Toronto: Oxford University Press, 1977), 66–8.

9 'Toronto United for Compulsion,' *M&E*, 12 June 1917, 4.

10 'Police Arrest Eighty Aliens,' *World*, 11 June 1917, 5.

11 See J. English, *The Decline of Politics: The Conservatives and the Party System, 1901–1920* (Toronto: University of Toronto Press, 1977), 139; D. Morton and J.L. Granatstein, *Marching to Armageddon: Canadians and the Great War* (Toronto: Lester and Orpen Dennys, 1989), 146.

12 See Nicholson, *Official History*, 292–7.

13 'Win-tar League Plans Convention,' *World*, 25 July 1917, 6; 'Tense and Deep

Emotion in Win-the-War Audience,' *Star*, 3 Aug. 1917, 1; 'United Action Demanded of Canada's Statesmen,' *World*, 3 Aug. 1917, 1, 4.

14 Advertisement, *World*, 3 Aug. 1917, 5; 'Women Grimly Knitted as before French Guillotine,' *Star*, 4 Aug. 1917, 1, 6; 'Women United in Opposing Election Now,' *World*, 4 Aug. 1917, 1, 4; 'Women Pledged to Aid in War,' *News*, 4 Aug. 1917, 15; 'Women of Province Want Reinforcements to Support Heroes in the Trenches,' *Globe*, 4 Aug. 1917, 1.

15 'Will Get Men for Harvest,' *Globe*, 4 Aug. 1917, 7.

16 'Woman in Role of Man-Hunter,' *Globe*, 23 Aug. 1917, 7.

17 English, *The Decline of Politics*, 153–85.

18 Rawling, *Surviving Trench Warfare: Technology and the Canadian Corps, 1914–1918* (Toronto: University of Toronto Press, 1992), 143.

19 'Labour Bodies Accept the Conscription Law,' *Star*, 4 Sept. 1917, 6.

20 'Says "Substitute" Is Thrift War Cry,' *World*, 17 Sept. 1917, 2.

21 'Thirty-Two Thousand Women Have Signed the Food Pledge,' *News*, 19 Sept. 1917, 1.

22 These advertisements appeared in all the major daily papers.

23 'Exemption Tribunals Men Conscripted by County,' *Globe*, 7 Sept. 1917, 3. Twenty-eight local tribunals heard exemption claims. Organized into the same six wards used in municipal elections, and then further sub-divided, each tribunal was responsible for an area large enough to comprise approximately 3,000 registered voters. There were more Liberal members chairing tribunal hearings than Conservatives. Eighteen Liberals were appointed against only 10 Conservatives. Most chairs were Protestant, accounting for 24 of the 28 appointments, with 3 Catholics and 1 Jew ('Toronto: 28 Districts for Exemption Tribunals,' NAC, Sir Edward Kemp Papers, MG 27, II, D9, Vol. 76, File 'Tribunals – Toronto Area 1917').

24 'Medical Board Ready for Draftees,' *M&E*, 15 Sept. 1917, 4.

25 Groves, *Toronto Does Her 'Bit,'* 7.

26 Rawling, *Surviving Trench Warfare*, 146–66.

27 'Woefully Small Start towards Toronto's [District] 82,000,' *Star*, 16 Oct. 1917, 1.

28 'Registrar Is Being Warned of "Slackers,"' *News*, 18 Oct. 1917, 1; 'It Is Slow March With Class One,' *Globe*, 27 Oct. 1917, 8.

29 J. Swettenham, *To Seize the Victory: The Canadian Corps in World War I* (Toronto: Ryerson Press, 1965), 192.

30 'Military Police After Eligibles,' *M&E*, 8 Nov. 1917, 4.

31 'No More Eligibles Allowed to Register,' *Star*, 12 Nov. 1917, 2.

32 An extensive search was conducted at the NAC for the records of the Military Service Act, and the Tribunals proceedings. Unfortunately, these

records were intentionally burned after the war because they would have been 'a living menace to national unity.' E.L. Newcombe, chair of the Military Service Council, burned all records, and believed that 'he had acted in the national interest by denying future researchers the opportunity of ascertaining the truth.' See David Richards Williams, *Duff: A Life in the Law* (Vancouver: University of British Columbia Press, 1984), 95.

33 'Toronto Tribunals Begin Sitting; Most Applicants Get Exemptions,' *Star*, 8 Nov. 1917, 1; 'Local Tribunals Tightening Up Their Procedure,' *Star*, 10 Nov. 1917, 1; 'Tribunals Are Tightening Up on Exemptions,' *News*, 10 Nov. 1917, 1. Winchester was born in Elgin, Scotland in 1849, but emigrated with his family to Toronto and was educated at the Toronto Grammar School. A Presbyterian, he served on the board of the local church and was also a long-time supporter of the Liberal party. He trained as a lawyer and practiced in the city until becoming a judge for York County. He was repeatedly asked to investigate and report upon public matters (Morgan, ed., *Canadian Men and Women*, 1179).

34 'Fast Work Is Accomplished by Tribunals,' *News*, 12 Nov. 1917, 1; 'War Is Murder, Said Pennington, But He Must Go,' *Star*, 12 Nov. 1917, 10; 'New Record Set Up by the Tribunals,' *News*, 17 Nov. 1917, 7.

35 'Exemptions Now Harder to Get,' *World*, 19 Nov. 1917, 4; 'Crushing Blow for Mother Was Verdict of Tribunal,' *Tel*, 14 Nov. 1917, 13.

36 'This Man Wants to Fight; Quits Christadelphians,' *Tel*, 15 Nov. 1917, 15.

37 'Few Appeals Are Allowed by Tribunals,' *News*, 4 Dec. 1917, 1; 'Few Exemptions by Appeal Court,' *M&E*, 4 Dec. 1917, 4. Snow was another prominent Toronto lawyer who served on the exemption tribunals. Born in Hull, Quebec, in 1857, Snow was educated at Ottawa Collegiate Institute and by private tutor. He was called to the Ontario Bar in 1884 and served as a Crown prosecutor. During the war he acted as Registrar of Aliens in 1915. One of his two sons had been killed fighting at Courcelette in 1916. His other son was serving overseas, and was wounded during the attack on the Hindenburg Line in August 1918 (Greene, ed., *Who's Who and Why, 1921*, 1352).

38 'City Cheered as Huge Tank Rumbled Past,' *News*, 21 Nov. 1917, 10.

39 'Toronto Loan Total Was over $76,000,000,' *Star*, 4 Dec. 1917, 8.

40 English, *The Decline of Politics*, 189.

41 'War Is the Only Issue,' *Tel*, 20 Nov. 1917, 18.

42 Chambers, ed., *Canadian Parliamentary Guide, 1918*, 137–8.

43 'A.J. Young Promises Support to M.S. Act,' *Star*, 5 Dec. 1917, 13.

44 Morgan, ed., *Canadian Men and Women*, 199, 1015 ; 'Mr. Carey Opposes Dr. Charles Sheard,' *News*, 20 Nov. 1917, 11.

45 'Carey and Sheard Named,' *Tel*, 20 Nov. 1917, 18; 'Carey Is for Conscription;

Doesn't Want a Laurier Tag,' *Tel*, 20 Nov. 1917, 21. The telegram also appears in the NAC , Wilfrid Laurier Papers, 19 Nov. 1917, 198485.

46 Chambers, ed., *Canadian Parliamentary Guide, 1918*, 149.

47 'Two Run in East Toronto,' *Tel*, 20 Nov. 1917, 18.

48 Chambers, ed., *Canadian Parliamentary Guide, 1918*, 115–16.

49 'Former Member Answered Critics,' *News*, 20 Nov. 1917, 11.

50 Chambers, ed., *Canadian Parliamentary Guide, 1918*, 168–9.

51 'G.W. [Great War] Veterans Stand by Major Carson McCormack,' *Tel*, 3 Dec. 1917, 7.

52 'Three Candidates in Parkdale Field,' *News*, 20 Nov. 1917, 11; C.W. Kerr to Wilfrid Laurier, 31 Oct. 1917, NAC, Wilfrid Laurier Papers, 197915.

53 C.W. Kerr to Wilfrid Laurier, 19 Nov. 1917, NAC, Wilfrid Laurier Papers, 198-486, 198487.

54 'Rocky Road for H.C. Hocken; Nomination Was Stormy,' *Tel*, 20 Nov. 1917, 18.

55 '164 Veterans Left Halifax Just in Time,' *Star*, 6 Dec. 1917, 7; 'Explosion and Fire Devastate Large Section of Halifax,' *Tel*, 6 Dec. 1917, 15; 'Halifax City Is Wrecked,' *Star*, 6 Dec. 1917, 1; 'Halifax Dead May Be 2,000,' *Globe*, 7 Dec. 1917, 1; 'Over 2000 Killed at Halifax,' *World*, 7 Dec. 1917, 1; 'Toronto Sends Supplies, Money, Nurses and Men,' *Star*, 8 Dec. 1917, 1.

56 'The Name to Put Your Cross To,' *M&E*, 17 Dec. 1917, 6.

57 'The Church and the Elections,' *Pres*, 13 Dec. 1917, 557; 'Clear Note of the Pulpits,' *Globe*, 17 Dec. 1917, 1.

58 'Women Endorse Union Government,' *M&E*, 13 Nov. 1917, 10; 'Women Support the Government,' *Globe*, 14 Nov. 1917, 10; 'Women Stand by Union Government,' *Star*, 26 Nov. 1917, 14; 'Mass Meeting of Women Inspired by Addresses,' *News*, 4 Dec. 1917, 8.

59 This table was prepared using results listed in Chambers, ed., *Canadian Parliamentary Guide, 1918*, 205, 208, 209. These results are very similar to those published immediately after the election in the six Toronto papers. The total number of votes cast changed only by 185 (the papers reported 91,170 votes cast), and the number of conscription supporters by .1 per cent.

60 The results from Centre Toronto (called Toronto Centre in local papers but Centre Toronto is the official record of results) provide a glimpse into the votes of non-British Torontonians. Alan Gordon has argued that one third of its residents were not British. A majority of these were Jews, accounting for 23 per cent of Bristol's constituents according to the 1911 Census ('Edmund Bristol and Political Management,' *CHR*, 5). Despite the label of the most ethnically non-British of the Toronto ridings, the Laurier-Liberal candidate withdrew at the very beginning. The result was a contest between two conscriptionist candidates.

61 C.W. Kerr to Wilfrid Laurier, 24 Dec. 1917, NAC, Wilfrid Laurier Papers, 199121; J.M. Godfrey to Robert Borden, 19 Dec. 1917, NAC, Robert Borden Papers, MG 26, H1 a, Vol. 16, 4047.
62 Ibid.

6   Total War: Total Victory

1 Greene, ed., *Who's Who and Why, 1921*, 1–2.
2 'No Heat Saturday, Sunday or Monday and Heatless Mondays Till March 18,' *World*, 5 Feb. 1918, 1.
3 'To-day, Saturday, Is like a Sunday,' *M&E*, 9 Feb. 1918, 4; '3,500 Tons of Coal Saved during First Heatless Day,' *Tel*, 9 Feb. 1918, 13; 'Dearth of Trade on Heatless Day,' *M&E*, 11 Feb. 1918, 4; 'Toronto May Have to Work at Night Now,' *News*, 12 Feb. 1918, 10; 'Toronto Responds to Closing Order with Good Heart,' *World*, 12 Feb. 1918, 4; 'Quiet Days in Toronto,' *Globe*, 11 Feb. 1918, 1, 9.
4 'Police Are After the Defaulters,' *M&E*, 23 Jan. 1918, 5; 'Regular Raids on Young Men Playing Pool,' *News*, 8 Jan. 1918, 1; 'Reward Offered for Defaulters,' *M&E*, 8 Jan. 1918, 4; 'Awards Offered for Delinquents,' *World*, 8 Jan. 1918, 4; 'Search Begins for Defaulters,' *M&E*, 9 Jan. 1918, 4; 'Search Begun for Absentees,' *Globe*, 23 Jan. 1918, 6; 'Will Launch Drive for Draft Evaders,' *Star*, 12 Feb. 1918, 7.
5 'Five Hundred Dancers Forced to Show Papers,' *World*, 18 Feb. 1918, 1.
6 'Information on Draft Evaders,' *Globe*, 23 Feb. 1918, 8; 'Invite Public to Give Names of Defaulters,' *World*, 19 Feb. 1918, 1.
7 A biographical sketch of Plumptre is provided in Chapter 4.
8 'Women Ready for Campaign,' *Globe*, 19 Jan. 1918, 10; 'Women are Ready for Big Campaign,' *World*, 19 Jan. 1918, 5; 'Will the Toronto Women Bring in Half a Million?' *News*, 19 Jan. 1918, 8; 'Big Army of 2,500 Canvassers Will Sweep Over City,' *Star*, 21 Jan. 1918, 1; Advertisement, *News*, 23 Jan. 1918, 3.
9 'Patriotic Campaign Could Not Be Better Endorsed,' *Tel*, 19 Jan. 1918, 12.
10 'German Offensive Against British Army Is Imminent,' *World*, 12 Feb. 1918, 1; 'German Drive on West Front Is Scheduled for March,' *World*, 13 Feb. 1918, 1; 'Verdun Anniversary Finds Great Armies Tense and Expectant,' *News*, 16 Feb. 1918, 9.
11 'Buried in a Dugout with Others on Top,' *Star*, 19 Mar. 1918, 9.
12 'Many Veterans Arriving Home,' *Globe*, 19 Mar. 1918, 2; 'Three Contingents of Original Firsts Come This Morning,' *World*, 20 Mar. 1918, 1; 'All Honour to Furlough Men!' *Tel*, 20 Mar. 1918, 9; 'Welcomes for Furlough Men,' *Globe*, 20 Mar. 1918, 6.

13 'Original Firsts Are Home at Last,' *M&E*, 21 Mar. 1918, 4.

14 'Furlough Men Arrived Early Here for a Month's Vacation,' *Tel*, 21 Mar. 1918, 18; 'Home Coming Heroes of Firsts; Keep Red Patches on Shoulders,' *Star*, 21 Mar. 1918, 5; 'Scenes When the Original Firsts Got Home,' *Tel*, 21 Mar. 1918, 16; 'Originals Arrive Home on Furlough,' *World*, 21 Mar. 1918, 1; 'City Thrilled by Return of the Firsts,' *News*, 21 Mar. 1918, 9; 'Great Welcome for Veterans,' *Globe*, 21 Mar. 1918, 7.

15 'Heroes' Second Farewell,' *Tel*, 6 April 1918, 22; 'Original Firsts Take Departure,' *M&E*, 6 April 1918, 4; 'Dry-Eyed and Cheery Was Farewell Given Departing Fighting First,' *Star*, 6 April 1918, 5; 'Original Firsts Return to Front,' *World*, 6 April 1918, 5.

16 'Haig's Forces Near St. Quentin Fall Back on Prepared Positions Farther to West; Northern Line Firm and Battle Continues,' *News*, 23 Mar. 1918, 1; 'Country-Side Rocks With Artillery Duel,' *Globe*, 22 Mar. 1918, 1.

17 'Germany Takes the Plunge,' *CG*, 27 Mar. 1918, 3.

18 Nicholson, *Official History*, 362–8.

19 Nicholson, *Official History*, 369–76; C.P. Stacey, *Canada and the Age of Conflict: A History of Canadian External Policies*, vol. 1, *1867–1921* (Toronto: Macmillan, 1977), 223–4.

20 '200 Ontario Farmers Invade Ottawa To-Day,' *Star*, 3 May 1918, 11.

21 'Young Farmers Will Be Called,' *M&E*, 4 May 1918, 1. See also 'Farmers Told That Youths Must Serve,' *Star*, 4 May 1918, 9.

22 'Farmers No Slackers, But Want Square Deal,' *Star*, 6 May 1918, 5.

23 'Farmers More Eloquent in Numbers Than in Sentiment,' *Tel*, 14 May 1918, 13; 'Farmers' Demand Will Be Refused,' *M&E*, 14 May 1918, 1; 'Farmers Say Production Canada's Greatest Duty,' *Globe*, 14 May 1918, 1; 'Farmers Seek Chance to State Views in House,' *Star*, 14 May 1918, 1; 'Farmers Press Their Request for Exemption,' *News*, 14 May 1918, 1.

24 'With Backs to Wall, Farmers Show Fight,' *Star*, 7 June 1918, 6; 'Farmers of Ontario to Fight or Produce,' *World*, 8 June 1918, 1.

25 'The New Conscription Law,' *Sun*, 24 April 1918, 1; 'Conscription,' *Sun*, 1 May 1918, 1; 'The Farmers' Appeal,' *Sun*, 15 May 1918, 1.

26 'Thousand Farmers Meet to Discuss Drafting of Stalwarts from Country,' *News*, 7 June 1918, 7; 'Farmers Will Appeal Again,' *Globe*, 10 June 1918, 1; 'Farmers Are Organizing for Political Activity,' *Tel*, 7 June 1918, 15; 'New Military Act Angers Farmers,' *M&E*, 8 June 1918, 4; 'Farmers Massed in Toronto Score Union Government,' *Globe*, 8 June 1918, 8.

27 Nicholson, *Official History*, 378.

28 '422,000 Registered in Toronto District,' *Star*, 22 June 1918, 1.

29 B. Palmer, *Working Class Experience: Rethinking the History of Canadian Labour,*

1800–1991 (Toronto: McClelland and Stewart, 1992), 164; G.S. Kealey, 'State Repression of Labour and the Left in Canada, 1914–1920: The Impact of the First World War,' *CHR* 72, no. 3 (1992): 281.

30 'Call Special Meeting to Discuss Men's Case,' *Star*, 21 June 1918, 3; 'Conspiracy by City Employees Is Allegation,' *News*, 19 June 1918, 7; 'May Take Strike Vote at the Mass Meeting,' *Star*, 3 July 1918, 2.

31 'Why Strikes in Canada Are Everywhere on the Increase,' *IB*, 5 July 1918, 1.

32 'Civic Employees Decide to Go on Strike Today,' *World*, 5 July 1918, 1.' Labour Appeals to Government for Settlement,' *Star*, 5 July 1918, 1.

33 'Machinists Place Matter in Hands District Council,' *World*, 8 July 1918, 1.

34 'Many Unions Discuss Civic Strike,' *World*, 9 July 1918, 1.

35 'Both Parties Fear Outcome of Agitation,' *News*, 9 July 1918, 4; 'Many Unions Discuss Civic Strike,' *World*, 9 July 1918, 1.

36 'Mayor Has Plan to Settle Civic Strike,' *Star*, 9 July 1918, 2; 'The Men's Offer to the City,' *Star*, 10 July 1918, 1; 'Critical Stage of Civic Strike,' *M&E*, 10 July 1918, 4; 'Board of Five is Suggestion Made by Mayor,' *World*, 10 July 1918, 1; 'A Statement of Terms in Civic Strike,' *News*, 10 July 1918, 3.

37 *Appendix 'C' to the Minutes of the City Council, 1918* (Toronto: Industrial and Technical Press, 1919), CTA, 10 July 1918, 57.

38 'Boat Containing 12 Nurses Capsized and All the Women Were Drowned,' *M&E*, 2 July 1918, 1.

39 'Most Impressive Memorial Service,' *M&E*, 15 July 1918, 10; 'Stick It through Is Llandovery Message,' *Tel*, 15 July 1918, 10; 'Honour Nurses Lost on Hospital Ship,' *Star*, 15 July 1918, 13; 'Heroic Nurses Are Honoured,' *Globe*, 15 July 1918, 10.

40 'Women Drivers of Transports,' *Globe*, 3 July 1918, 8.

41 'Women Efficient in Flying Corps,' *World*, 10 July 1918, 5.

42 'Angry Crowd Wrecks Several Restaurants,' *World*, 3 Aug. 1918, 1, 4; ' Veterans Parade Destroys Many Restaurants,' *M&E*, 3 Aug. 1918, 4; 'Returned Soldiers Raid Many Greek Restaurants,' *Globe*, 3 Aug. 1918, 1, 3; 'End the Disorder,' *News*, 3 Aug. 1918, 1; 'Restaurants Wiped Out by an Angry Mob,' *News*, 3 Aug. 1918, 4; 'Angry Mob Wrecks Dozen Restaurants,' *Star*, 3 Aug. 1918, 10; 'Estimate Damage at Forty Thousand,' *World*, 5 Aug. 1918, 5.

43 '5,000 Citizens in Park Pass War Resolutions,' *Globe*, 7 Aug. 1918, 6.

44 'Troops Are Here to Stop Riot,' *World*, 7 Aug. 1918, 1; 'Riot Act Will Be Read; Troops Are Held Ready,' *World*, 7 Aug. 1918, 1, 2; 'Mayor Is to Read Riot Act on City Hall Steps To-Day,' *Globe*, 7 Aug. 1918, 1, 6; 'Mayor Read Proclamation,' *Tel*, 7 Aug. 1918, 13; 'Proclamation, Not Riot Act, Is Read by Mayor at Noon on Steps of the City Hall,' *News*, 7 Aug. 1918, 1; 'Mayor to Read the

Riot Act,' *M&E*, 7 Aug. 1918, 1; 'Troops Our Ready to Quell Riots,' *M&E*, 7 Aug. 1918, 4.

45 An extensive search has been conducted for this document. Unfortunately, inquiries at the CTA, AO, NAC, and the Toronto Police Museum have not been able to produce the document.

46 J. Castell Hopkins, *The Canadian Annual Review of Public Affairs* (Toronto: Canadian Annual Review, 1918), 588; 'Report of Police Board Respecting Toronto Riots,' *M&E*, 19 Oct. 1918, 1, 9.

47 General von Ludendorff, qtd. in Nicholson, *Official History*, 405–6.

48 Nicholson, *Official History*, 406–19, 427–32.

49 'Weaker Sex Opened Eyes of Mere Man,' *News*, 29 Aug. 1918, 7.

50 'Women Show a Fine Spirit in the Parade,' *News*, 29 Aug. 1918, 6; 'All Honour to Women Who Took Part in Pageant!' *News*, 29 Aug. 1918, 8; 'Woman Hold Great Parade Despite Deluge of Rain,' *Globe*, 29 Aug. 1918, 7; 'Women See It Thru in Spite of Rain at the Exhibition,' *World*, 29 Aug. 1918, 4; 'Women Carrying on in Spite of Downpour,' *Star*, 29 Aug. 1918, 5; 'Pluck of Women Saved Their Day,' *M&E*, 29 Aug. 1918, 1, 5.

51 K. Walden, *Becoming Modern in Toronto: The Industrial Exhibition and Shaping of a Late Victorian Culture* (Toronto: University of Toronto Press, 1997), 178, 181.

52 Nicholson, *Official History*, 432–60.

53 '53 Toronto Names in Casualty Lists,' *Star*, 18 Sept. 1918, 3; 'Casualty Lists Are Still Heavy,' *M&E*, 21 Sept. 1918, 4.

54 'Anxiously Glance at the Coal Bin,' *World*, 9 Sept. 1918, 5; 'Only Cold Comfort for Coalless Folk,' *Star*, 27 Sept. 1918, 5.

55 D.A. Herring, 'The 1918 Influenza Epidemic in the Central Canadian Subarctic,' in Ann Herring and L. Chan, eds., *Strength in Diversity: A Reader in Physical Anthropology* (Toronto: Canadian Scholars' Press, 1994), 367–9.

56 The camp was most likely Niagara Camp.

57 'Spanish Influenza Makes Appearance,' *World*, 19 Sept. 1918, 2.

58 'Spanish Flu like Measles; Get a Doctor,' *News*, 30 Sept. 1918, 7; 'Over 200 Cases of Flu and One Death Here,' *Star*, 30 Sept. 1918, 2.

59 'If You Have the Flu, Its Your Own Fault,' *Star*, 10 Oct. 1918, 2.

60 'Local Hospitals Shut to Visitors,' *M&E*, 7 Oct. 1918, 4; 'Dr. Hastings Forbids Conventions in City,' *Star*, 11 Oct. 1918, 2; 'To Use Hotel Mossop for Flu Patients,' *Star*, 12 Oct. 1918, 3; 'More Deaths Occur from Spanish Flu,' *World*, 16 Oct. 1918, 4; 'To Close Theatres Because of Flu,' *World*, 17 Oct. 1918, 5; 'Sunshine Aid to Combat Flu,' *Globe*, 10 Oct. 1918, 6; 'Churches Were Closed,' *Globe*, 14 Oct. 1918, 4.

61 'Epidemic Crisis Not Reached Yet,' *World*, 14 Oct. 1918, 6; 'Epidemic Is Not

Abating,' *Globe*, 14 Oct. 1918, 8; 'Lectures Given to Volunteers,' *Globe*, 16 Oct. 1918, 4; 'Women Volunteer to Fight Malady,' *News*, 15 Oct. 1918, 9.

62 'Deaths from Flu Are on Increase,' *World*, 18 Oct. 1918, 4; '31 Deaths in Toronto Ascribed to Influenza,' *Globe*, 17 Oct. 1918, 6; '87 Deaths the Day's Total,' *Globe*, 19 Oct. 1918, 8; 'Influenza Claims 35 More Victims,' *M&E*, 19 Oct. 1918, 4; 'Thirteen Hundred Epidemic Victims,' *News*, 26 Oct. 1918, 1; 'Flu Deaths Still Decrease,' *Globe*, 1 Nov. 1918, 10. The 1,300 who died in Toronto represented 26 per cent of the total fatalities in Ontario from the epidemic, which amounted to 5,000 dead. J. Castell Hopkins, *The Canadian Annual Review of Public Affairs, 1918* (Toronto: Canadian Review Co., 1919), 574.

63 'Holding Down the Epidemic,' *Globe*, 22 Oct. 1918, 9; 'Advertisement,' *World*, 19 Oct. 1918, 5; 'Phone Girls Hit Hard,' *Star*, 19 Oct. 1918, 2; 'Bank Staffs Hit by Influenza Epidemic,' *Star*, 12 Oct. 1918, 17.

64 'Hundreds of Masks Made for Patients,' *Star*, 18 Oct. 1918, 17; 'I.O.D.E. Start in Sick Relief,' *Globe*, 21 Oct. 1918, 8.

65 Another wave of sickness and death swept through the whole of North America in March 1919. See E. Pettigrew, *The Silent Enemy: Canada and the Deadly Flu of 1918* (Saskatoon: Western Producer Prairie Books, 1983).

66 'Lift Ban on Theatres Monday, Says M.O.H.,' *Star*, 28 Oct. 1918, 1; 'Hospital Reports To-Day on Epidemic,' *Star*, 30 Oct. 1918, 2; 'Death Rate Drops, Flu on Decline,' *World*, 30 Oct. 1918, 4; 'Schools Open Next Monday,' *Globe*, 29 Oct. 1918, 8; 'City Death Rate Falls Rapidly,' *Globe*, 30 Oct. 1918, 9; 'Spanish Malady on the Wane,' *M&E*, 28 Oct. 1918, 4; 'Epidemic Crest Is Passed; Theatres Reopen Monday Next,' *Tel*, 28 Oct. 1918, 13.

67 'Can Keep Down the Mortality,' *Globe*, 11 Oct. 1918, 6.

68 'Influenza Stopping the Output of Coal,' *World*, 18 Oct. 1918, 4.

69 '35 Toronto Names in Casualty List,' *Star*, 2 Nov. 1918, 2.

70 'Use Dead Trees of City as Fuel,' *Globe*, 5 Nov. 1918, 6.

71 Nicholson, *Official History*, 475–82.

72 'Toronto Hails Peace in Delirium of Joy,' *Star*, 12 Nov. 1918, 5; 'Fleet of Aeroplanes Take Part in Parade,' *Star*, 12 Nov. 1918, 14; 'No Sleep for City When News Arrived That War Was Over,' *News*, 11 Nov. 1918, 1, 2; 'Wonderful Service of Thanksgiving in Queen's Park Here,' *News*, 11 Nov. 1918, 2; 'Victory Parade Easily Shattered All City Records,' *News*, 11 Nov. 1918, 7; 'Day of Rejoicing Was the Greatest in Local History,' *News*, 12 Nov. 1918, 3; 'Toronto Outdoes Itself in Celebrating Victory,' *World*, 12 Nov. 1918, 4; 'Shrill Siren Sounds Sweet,' *Globe*, 12 Nov. 1918, 10; 'Women Show Way at Dawn,' *Globe*, 12 Nov. 1918, 10; 'How Toronto Got the News; Telegram Spread It First,' *Tel*, 11 Nov. 1918, 6; 'City Started to Celebrate as Soon as The News Spread,' *Tel*, 11 Nov. 1918, 13; 'City Celebrated in Orgy of Joy,' *M&E*, 12 Nov. 1918, 1, 4.

Conclusion

1 'Only Twenty-Six Men of 4th Battalion Escaped Inferno,' *Star*, 19 May 1915, 2.
2 Keshen, *Propaganda and Censorship.*
3 J.F. Vance, *Death So Noble,* 266.

Selected Bibliography

PRIMARY SOURCES

Archival Sources

National Archives of Canada

Personal Papers:
   Borden, Robert (MG 26)
   Denison, George Taylor (III) (MG 29)
   Devonshire, Victor Christian William (MG 27)
   Dewart, Herbert Hartley (MG 27)
   Foster, George (MG 27)
   Godfrey, John Milton (MG 30)
   Green, Anson (MG 30)
   Kemp, Edward (MG 27)
   Laurier, Wilfrid (MG 26)
   Lyon, Thomas Stewart (MG 30)
   Maclean, William Findley (MG 27)
   Massey, Chester (MG 32)
   Pearson, L.B. (MG 26)
   Rowell, N.R. (MG 27)
   Sinclair, Ian Macintosh Roe (MG 30)
   White, Thomas (MG 27)

Organizational/Departmental Records:
   Canadian Fraternal Association (MG 28)
   Canadian Patriotic Fund (MG 28)
   Canadian Press Association (MG 28)

Chief Censor Papers (RG 6)
Department of National Defence, Military District No. 2 (RG 24)
External Affairs (RG 25)
Imperial Order Daughters of the Empire (MG 28)
Mobilization Accounts of all Toronto Battalions (RG 24)
National Council of Women (MG 28)
Report of the Canada Registration Board (RG 2)
Sermons and Addresses by Presbyterian Ministers about Canada and the
    First World War (MG 55)
War Diaries of all Toronto Battalions (RG 9)

Provincial Archives of Ontario

Personal Papers:
  Arbuckle, Sadie
  Belcher, Alexander Emerson
  Bristol, Edmund
  Chown, Samuel Dwight
  Church, Thomas Langton
  Cody, Henry John
  Duncan, Lewis
  Fraser, A.
  Grier, Edmund Wyly
  Hearst, William
  Henry, George S.
  Hopkins, J. Castell
  Jennings, C.A.C.
  Long, Matthew
  Maclaren, George P.
  Madill, Ralph
  Mason, Harry
  Perley, George
  Robertson, Irvine G.
  Stevenson, Douglas A.
  Wallace Family
  Whitney, J.P.

Organizations/Department Records:
  Canadian Patriotic Fund Association
  Imperial Order Daughters of the Empire

Miscellaneous Military Records
Office of the Premier
Ontario Provincial Police
Ontario War Memorial Committee Papers
Toronto Local Council of Women, Minutes

City of Toronto Archives

Personal Papers:
  Geary, George R.

City Council Records:
  Appendices A, B, and C to the Minutes of the Toronto City Council
  Minutes of the Proceedings of the Council of the Corporation of Toronto

University of Toronto Archives

Personal Papers:
  Cassidy, Harry Morris
  Madill, Henry Harrison

Organizations/Department Records:
  University of Toronto Report of the Board of Governors
  University of Toronto, Office of the Registrar
  University of Toronto, Department of Graduate Records

Pamphlets:
  Canadian Hospitals in the War, 1915–17
  Coal Shortage During the War, 1915–18
  COTC, OTC and Flying Corps, Etc., 1914–18
  German Professors and the War, 1914–15
  Honour Roll – General, 1915–17
  Khaki University, 1917–19
  Lists, Enlisting, Promotions, Honours, 1914–18
  Military Service, Recruiting, etc.
  University Base Hospital, 1915–19
  Varsity Veterans, 1915–22
  Victory Loans and the Red Cross, 1915, 1918
  War Memorial Tower, 1915–29
  Women and War Work at the University,1914–18

University of Toronto – Thomas Fisher Rare Book Room

Groves, H. *Toronto Does Her 'Bit'* (Toronto: Municipal Intelligence Bureau, 1918).
Mason, J. Collection, 'Notes from the Seat of War.' University of Toronto Manuscript Collection, MS 119, Box 47A, B.

Metro Reference Library

Toronto Public Library Scrapbook, Biographies of People.

Metro Reference Library – Baldwin Reading Room

Personal Papers:
  Carstairs, J.S.
  Cawthra Family
  Grange Family
  Harman Family
  Jarvis, Arthur
  Johnson, Main
  Keys, Erskine
  Keys, Jean
  Keys, Norman A.
  McDougall Family
  Murton, E.H.
  Neil Family
  Shanley Family

United Church of Canada / Victoria University Archives

Personal Papers:
  Burwash, Nathanael
  Chown, Samuel Dwight
  Cummings, Robert Bremner
  Hincks, William Henry
  Kilpatrick, George Gordon Dinwiddie
  Macdowell, Thane Wendell
  Oliver, Edmund Henry
  Smith, Harold Morrey
  Wallace, Francis Huston

Organizations/Department Records:
  Correspondence of World War I Alumni, 1915–18
  Department of Evangelism and Social Service (Methodist)
  Methodist Church Army and Navy Board
  Presbyterian Church in Canada, General Board
  Presbyterian Church in Canada, Synod of Toronto and Kingston
  Presbytery of Toronto, Minutes of Presbytery
  Victoria College (Toronto) Alumni Association

Pamphlets:
  Armageddon, or the World-Movement
  A Student in Arms
  Religion and the War
  The Call of the War
  The Message of the Canadian Chaplains, Overseas Military Forces to the
    Churches of Canada
  The War and the Christian Church
  The War and Divine Providence

Anglican Diocese of Toronto Archives

Organizations/Department Records:
  Journal of the Incorporated Synod of the Diocese of Toronto of the
    Church of England in Canada
  Synod Records

Archives of the Roman Catholic Archdiocese of Toronto

Personal Papers:
  McNeil, Neil

Organizations/Department Records:
  File of the War Effort
  War Box

Canadian Baptist Archives

Organizations/Department Records:
  Baptist Yearbook, 1915–19
  Deacon's Minutes

Minute Book of the Dorcas Society of Walmer Road, Baptist Church, Toronto
Minutes Toronto Association
Toronto Immanuel Mission Circle Minutes

Presbyterian Archives

Organizations/Department Records:
  Presbyterian Yearbook – Annual Reports

Other Primary Sources

Directorate of History

Recruiting in Canada, August 1914 to May 1917

Mount Pleasant Cemetery

Internment Register Number 3

SECONDARY SOURCES

Acton, Janice, Penny Goldsmith, and Bonnie Shephard, eds. *Women at Work: Ontario, 1850–1930*. Toronto: Canadian Women's Educational Press, 1974.
Addison, Paul, and Angus Calder, eds. *Time to Kill: The Soldier's Experience of War in the West*. London: Pimlico, 1997.
Airhart, Phyllis. *Serving the Present Age: Revivalism, Progressivism, and the Methodist Tradition in Canada*. Montreal: McGill-Queen's University Press, 1992.
Aitken, Max. *Canada in Flanders: The Official Story of the Canadian Expeditionary Force*. London: Hodder and Stoughton, 1916.
Allen, Richard. *The Social Passion: Religion and Social Reform in Canada, 1914–1928*. Toronto: University of Toronto Press, 1971.
Allinson, Sidney. *The Bantams: The Untold Story of World War I*. London: Howard Baker Press, 1981.
Armstrong, Elizabeth. *The Crisis of Quebec, 1914–18*. New York: AMS Press, 1967.
Arthur, Eric. *Toronto, No Mean City*, 3rd ed. Toronto: University of Toronto Press, 1964.
Bacchi, Carol Lee. *Liberation Deferred? The Ideas of English-Canadian Suffragists, 1877–1918*. Toronto: University of Toronto Press, 1983.
Barker, Pat. *Regeneration*. New York: William Abrahams, 1991.

Barnard, W.T. *The Queen's Own Rifles of Canada, 1860–1960: One Hundred Years of Canada.* Don Mills: Ontario Publishing Company, 1960.

Baynes, John Christopher Malcolm. *Morale: A Study of Men and Courage; The Second Scottish Rifles at the Battle of Neuve Chapelle, 1915.* New York: Praeger, 1967.

Beattie, Ken. *48th Highlanders of Canada, 1891–1928.* Toronto: 48th Highlanders of Canada, 1932.

Beaven, Brian P.N. 'Partisanship, Patronage, and the Press in Ontario, 1880–1914: Myths and Realities.' *CHR* 64, no. 3 (1983): 317–51.

Becker, Jean Jacques. *The Great War and the French People.* Trans. Arnold Pomerans. New York: St Martin's Press, 1986.

Benn, Carl. 'The Military Context of the Founding of Toronto.' *OH* 81, no. 4, (1989): 303–22.

Berger, Carl. *The Sense of Power: Studies in the Ideas of Canadian Imperialism, 1867–1914.* Toronto: University of Toronto Press, 1970.

Bliss, Michael. *A Canadian Millionaire: The Life and Times of Sir Joseph Flavelle, Bart, 1858–1939.* Toronto: Macmillan, 1978.

– 'The Methodist Church and World War I.' *CHR* 64, no. 3 (1968): 212–33.

Borden, Henry, ed. *Robert Laird Borden: His Memoirs.* Toronto: Macmillan, 1938.

Bothwell, Robert, Ian Drummond, and John English. *Canada, 1900–1945.* Toronto: University of Toronto Press, 1987.

Boudreau, Joseph Amedée. 'The Enemy Alien Problem in Canada, 1914–1921.' PhD thesis, University of California, 1965.

Bray, Robert Matthew. 'The Canadian Patriotic Response to the Great War.' PhD thesis, York University, 1976.

– '"Fighting as an Ally": The English-Canadian Patriotic Response to the Great War.' *CHR* 61, no. 2 (1980): 141–68.

– 'A Conflict of Nationalisms: The Win the War and National Unity Convention, 1917.' *JCS* 15, no. 4 (1980–1): 18–31.

Briggs, Catherine. 'Women, Men and the Minimum Wage in Ontario, 1916–1940.' MA thesis, University of Guelph, 1992.

Brown, Robert Craig. *Robert Laird Borden: A Biography.* Volume 1. *1854–1914.* Toronto: Macmillan, 1975.

– *Robert Laird Borden: A Biography.* Volume 2. *1914–1937.* Toronto: Macmillan, 1975.

Brown, Robert Craig, and Ramsay Cook. *Canada, 1896–1921: A Nation Transformed.* Toronto: McClelland and Stewart, 1974.

Brown, Robert Craig, and Donald Loveridge. '"Unrequited Faith": Recruiting and the CEF, 1914–1918.' *Revue internationale d'histoire militaire* 51 (1982): 53–78.

Bruce, Jean. 'The Toronto *Globe* and the Manpower Problem: 1914–1917.' MA thesis, Queen's University, 1967.

Butler, Janine. 'St. Andrew's Presbyterian Church, Toronto's "Cathedral of Presbyterianism."' *OH* 83, no. 3 (1991): 169–92.

Butlin, Susan. 'Woman Making Shells: Marking Women's Presence in Munitions Work, 1914–1918 – The Art of Frances Loring, Florence Wyle, Mabel May, Dorothy Stevens.' *CMH* 5, no. 1 (1996): 41–8.

Byers, Daniel T. 'The Conscription Election of 1917 and Its Aftermath in Orillia, Ontario.' *OH* 83, no. 4 (1991): 275–96.

Careless, J.M.S. *Toronto to 1918: An Illustrated History.* Toronto: James Lorimer, 1984.

Carrington, Phillip. *The Anglican Church in Canada: A History.* Toronto: Collins, 1963.

Carter, D.J. *Behind Canadian Barbed Wire: Alien Refugee and Prisoner of War Camps in Canada, 1914–1946.* Calgary: Tumbleweed Press, 1980.

Chalmers, Floyd S. *A Gentleman of the Press.* Toronto: Doubleday, 1969.

Chambers, Ernest J., ed. *The Canadian Parliamentary Guide, 1918.* Ottawa: Mortimer Company, 1918.

Chief Electoral Officer. *A History of the Vote in Canada.* Ottawa: Minister of Public Works and Government Services, 1997.

Christie, Edward A. 'The Presbyterian Church in Canada and Its Official Attitude toward Public Affairs and Social Problems, 1875–1925.' MA thesis, University of Toronto, 1955.

Cleverdon, Catherine L. *The Woman Suffrage Movement in Canada.* 2nd ed. Toronto: University of Toronto Press, 1974.

Coetzee, Frans, and Marilyn Shevin-Coetzee, eds. *Authority, Identity and the Social History of the Great War.* Providence: Berghahn Books, 1995.

Colquhoun, A.H.U. *Press, Politics and People: The Life and Letters of Sir John Willison, Journalist and Correspondent of the Times.* Toronto: Macmillan, 1935.

Conrad, Margaret 'The Re-Birth of Canada's Past: A Decade of Women's History.' *Acadiensis* 12, no. 2 (1983): 140–62.

Cook, Ramsay, Robert Craig Brown, and Carl Berger, eds. *Conscription 1917.* Toronto: University of Toronto Press, 1969.

Cook, Ramsay, and Wendy Mitchinson, eds. *The Proper Sphere: Woman's Place in Canadian Society.* Toronto: Oxford University Press, 1976.

Cooke, William G. 'The Diocese of Toronto and Its Two Cathedrals.' *JCCHS* 27, no. 2 (1985): 98–115.

Corelli, Rae. *The Toronto That Used to Be.* Toronto: Toronto Star Limited, 1964.

Craick, W.A. *A History of Canadian Journalism: Last Years of the Canadian Press Association, 1908–1919.* Toronto: Ontario Publishing Company, 1959.

Crerar, Duff. 'Bellicose Priests: The Wars of the Canadian Catholic Chaplin, 1914–1919.' *Canadian Society of Church History Papers* (1991): 13–32.

– 'The Church in the Furnace: Canadian Anglican Chaplains Respond to the Great War.' *JCCHS* 35, no. 2 (1993): 75–103.

– *Padres in No Man's Land.* Montreal: McGill-Queen's University Press, 1995.

Crutwell, C.R.M.F. *A History of the Great War, 1914–1918.* 2nd ed. London: Granada, 1936.

Currie, Phillip. 'Reluctant Britons: The Toronto Irish, Home Rule, and the Great War.' *OH* 87, no. 1 (1995): 65–76.

– 'Toronto Orangeism and the Irish Question, 1911–16.' *OH* 87, no. 4 (1995): 397–409.

Delhi, Kari. 'Love and Knowledge: Adult Education in the Toronto Home and School Council, 1916–1940.' *OH* 88, no. 3 (1996): 207–28.

Dubinsky, Karen. *Improper Advances: Rape and Heterosexual Conflict in Ontario, 1880–1929.* Chicago: University of Chicago Press, 1993.

Eksteins, Modris. *Rites of Spring: The Great War and the Birth of the Modern Age.* New York: Doubleday, 1989.

– '*All Quiet on the Western Front* and the Fate of a War.' *JConH.* 15, no. 2 (1980): 345–66.

English, John. *The Decline of Politics: The Conservatives and the Party System, 1901–1920.* Toronto: University of Toronto Press, 1977.

– *Shadow of Heaven: The Life of Lester Pearson.* Volume 1. *1897–1948.* Toronto: Lester and Orpen Dennys, 1989.

Errington, E. Jane. '"And What about the Women?": Changing Ontario's History.' *OH* 90, no. 2 (1998): 135–55.

Ferns, H.S., and Bernard Ostry. 'Mackenzie King and the First World War.' *CHR* 36, no. 2 (1955): 93–112.

Ferraro, Patrick. 'English Canada and the Election of 1917.' MA thesis, McGill University, 1971.

Fischer, Fritz. *War of Illusions: German Policies from 1911 to 1914.* New York: W.W. Norton, 1975.

Foot, Rosemary. 'Where Are the Women? The Gender Dimension in the Study of International Relations.' *DH* 14, no. 4 (1990): 615–22.

Ford, Arthur R. 'Some Notes on the Formation of the Union Government in 1917.' *CHR* 19, no. 4 (1938): 357–64.

Frager, Ruth A. *Sweatshop Strife: Class, Ethnicity, and Gender in the Jewish Labour Movement of Toronto, 1900–1939.* Toronto: University of Toronto Press, 1992.

Fussell, Paul. *The Great War and Modern Memory.* London: Oxford University Press, 1975.

Gaffield, Chad. *Language, Schooling, and Cultural Conflict: The Origins of the French-Language Controversy in Ontario.* Montreal: McGill-Queen's University Press, 1987.

Gardner, Nick. 'Crazy to Get Overseas: The Short and Tumultuous History of the 118th Battalion, C.E.F.' MA cognate, Wilfrid Laurier University, 1994.

Gauvreau, Michael. *The Evangelical Century: College and Creed in English Canada from the Great Revival to the Great Depression*. Montreal: McGill-Queen's University Press, 1991.

– 'War, Culture and the Problem of Religious Certainty: Methodist and Presbyterian Church Colleges, 1914–1930.' *JCCHS* 29, no. 1 (1987): 12–31.

Geiss, Imanuel. 'The Outbreak of the First World War and German War Aims.' *JConH* 1, no. 3 (1966): 75–92.

Glazebrook, G.P. de T. *The Story of Toronto*. Toronto: University of Toronto Press, 1971.

Gordon, Alan. 'Patronage, Etiquette, and the Science of Connection: Edmund Bristol and Political Management, 1911–21.' *CHR* 80, no. 1 (1999): 1–31.

– 'Taking Root in the Patronage Garden: Jewish Businessmen in Toronto's Conservative Party, 1911–1921.' *OH* 88, no. 1 (1996): 31–46.

Gordon, Donald C. 'The Admiralty and Dominion Navies, 1902–1914.' *Journal of Modern History* 33, no. 4 (1961): 407–22.

– *The Dominion Partnership in Imperial Defense, 1870–1914*. Baltimore, Md.: Johns Hopkins University Press, 1965.

Gorham, Deborah. 'Vera Brittain, Flora Macdonald Denison and the Great War: The Failure of Non-Violence.' In *Women and Peace: Theoretical, Historical and Practical Perspectives*, ed. Ruth Roach Pierson, 192–221. London: Croom Helm, 1987.

Granatstein, J.L., and J.M. Hitsman. *Broken Promises: A History of Conscription in Canada*. Toronto: Oxford University Press, 1977.

Grant, John Webster, ed. *The Churches and the Canadian Experience: A Faith and Order Study of The Christian Tradition*. Toronto: Ryerson Press, 1963.

Graves, Robert. *Goodbye to All That: An Autobiography*. London: Jonathan Cape, 1931.

Greene, B.M., ed. *Who's Who and Why, 1921*. Toronto: International Press Limited, 1921.

Griffith, Paddy. *Battle Tactics of the Western Front: The British Army's Art of Attack, 1916–1918*. New Haven: Yale University Press, 1994.

Groves, Hubert. *Toronto Does Her 'Bit'*. Toronto: Municipal Intelligence Bureau, 1918.

Guillet, Edwin C. *Toronto: From Great Trading Post to Great City*. Toronto: Ontario Publishing Company, 1934.

Gwyn, Sandra. *Tapestry of War: A Private View of Canadians in the Great War*. Toronto: HarperCollins, 1992.

Hand, Christopher M. 'John Terraine: A Study of a First World War Revisionist.' *CMH* 6, no. 2 (1997): 54–61.

Harkness, Ross. *J.E. Atkinson of the Star.* Toronto: University of Toronto Press, 1963.

Harney, Robert F., ed. *Gathering Place: Peoples and Neighbourhoods of Toronto, 1834–1945.* Toronto: Multicultural History Society of Ontario, 1985.

Harney, Robert F., and Harold Troper. *Immigrants: A Portrait of the Urban Experience, 1890–1930.* Toronto: Van Nostrand Reinhold, 1975.

Harris, Stephen J. *Canadian Brass: The Making of a Professional Army, 1860–1939.* Toronto: University of Toronto Press, 1988.

Harrison, Charles Yale. *Generals Die in Bed.* Hamilton: Potlatch Publications, 1928.

Haycock, Ronald G. 'The 1917 Federal Election in Victoria-Haliburton: A Case Study.' *OH* 67 (1975): 105–18.

– *Sam Hughes: The Public Career of a Controversial Canadian, 1885–1916.* Waterloo: Wilfrid Laurier University Press, 1986.

Heick, W.H. '"If We Lose the War, Nothing Else Matters": The 1917 Federal Election in North Waterloo.' *OH* 72, no. 2 (1980): 67–92.

Heron, Craig. *The Canadian Labour Movement: A Short History.* Toronto: James Lorimer, 1989.

Heron, Craig, ed. *The Workers' Revolt in Canada, 1917–1925.* Toronto: University of Toronto Press, 1998.

Heron, Craig, and Bryan D. Palmer. 'Through the Prism of the Strike: Industrial Conflict in Southern Ontario, 1901–1914.' *CHR* 8, no. 4 (1977): 423–58.

Holton, Margaret Lindsay, ed. *Spirit of Toronto, 1834–1984.* Toronto: Image Publishing, 1983.

Hynes, Samuel. *A War Imagined: The First World War and English Culture.* New York: Atheneum, 1991.

Institute for Behavioural Research. *Canadian Women of Note.* Volumes 1–4. Downsview: York University Press, 1981.

Jarvis, Eric, and Melvin Baker. 'Clio in Hogtown: A Brief Bibliography.' *OH* 76, no. 3 (1984): 287–94.

Joll, James. *The Origins of the First World War.* 2nd ed. London: Longman, 1992.

Kealey, Gregory. *Toronto Workers Respond to Industrial Capitalism, 1867–1892.* 2nd ed. Toronto: University of Toronto Press, 1980.

– 'State Repression of Labour and the Left in Canada, 1914–1920: The Impact of the First World War.' *CHR* 72, no. 3 (1992): 281–314.

Kealey, Linda. 'Canadian Socialism and the Woman Question, 1900–1914.' *LLT* 13 (1984): 77–100.

– *Enlisting Women for the Cause: Women, Labour and the Left in Canada, 1890–1920.* Toronto: University of Toronto Press, 1998.

Kealey, Linda, ed. *A Not Unreasonable Claim: Women and Reform in Canada, 1880s–1920s.* Toronto: Women's Educational Press, 1979.

Kealey, Linda, and Joan Sangster, eds. *Beyond the Vote: Canadian Women and Politics.* Toronto: University of Toronto Press, 1989.

Keegan, John. *The Face of Battle: A Study of Agincourt, Waterloo and the Somme.* London: Penguin Books, 1976.

Kerr, Donald, and Jacob Spelt. *The Changing Face of Toronto: A Study in Urban Geography.* Ottawa: Information Canada, 1971.

Keshen, Jeffrey. 'All the News That Was Fit to Print: Ernest J. Chambers and Information Control in Canada, 1914–1919.' *CHR* 73, no. 3 (1992): 315–43.

– *Propaganda and Censorship during Canada's Great War.* Edmonton: University of Alberta Press, 1996.

Kluckner, Michael. *Toronto the Way It Was.* Altona, Man.: Friesen Printers, 1988.

Leed, Eric J. *No Man's Land: Combat and Identity in World War I.* Cambridge, Mass.: Cambridge University Press, 1979.

Lower, A.R.M. *Colony to Nation: A History of Canada.* 4th ed. Toronto: Longmans, 1964.

Luciuk, Lubomyr. *A Time for Atonement: Canada's First Internment Operations and the Ukranian Canadians, 1914–1920.* Kingston: Limestone Press, 1988.

MacKinnon, Mary. 'Canadian Railway Workers and World War I Military Service.' *LLT* 40 (1997): 213–34.

Maroney, Paul. '"The Great Adventure": The Context and Ideology of Recruiting in Ontario, 1914–17.' *CHR* 77, no. 1 (1996): 62–98.

– 'Recruiting the Canadian Expeditionary Force in Ontario, 1914–1917.' MA thesis, Queen's University, 1995.

Marquis, Greg. 'Police Unionism in Early Twentieth-Century Toronto.' *OH* 71, no. 2 (1989): 109–28.

Marshall, David B. 'Methodism Embattled: A Reconsideration of the Methodist Church and World War I.' *CHR* 66, no. 1 (1985): 48–64.

– *Secularizing the Faith: Canadian Protestant Clergy and the Crisis of Belief, 1850–1940.* Toronto: University of Toronto Press, 1992.

Martin, Chester, ed. *Canada in Peace and War: Eight Studies in National Trends since 1914.* London: Oxford University Press, 1941.

Marwick, Arthur. 'The Impact of the First World War on British Society.' *JConH* 3, no. 1 (1968): 51–64.

– *Woman at War, 1914–1918.* London: Fontana Paperbacks, 1977.

McEwen, John M. 'The National Press during the First World War: Ownership and Circulation.' *JConH* 17, no. 3 (1982): 459–86.

McGowan, Mark G. 'Sharing the Burden of Empire: Toronto's Catholics and the Great War, 1914–1918.' In *Catholics at the "Gathering Place": Historical Essays on the Archdiocese of Toronto 1841–1991,* ed. Mark G. McGowan and Brian P. Clarke, 177–207. Toronto: Dundurn Press, 1993.

– '"We Are All Canadians": A Social, Religious and Cultural Portrait of Toronto's English-Speaking Roman Catholics, 1890–1920.' PhD thesis, University of Toronto, 1988.

McGowan, Mark G., and David B. Marshall, eds. *Prophets, Priests, and Prodigals: Readings in Canadian Religious History, 1608 to Present.* Toronto: McGraw-Hill Ryerson, 1992.

Middleton, Jesse Edgar. *Toronto's 100 Years.* Toronto: The Centennial Committee, 1934.

Millar, Carmen. 'English-Canadian Opposition to the South African War as Seen through the Press.' *CHR* 55, no. 4 (1974): 422–38.

Miller, Ian. '"Until the End": Brantford's Response to the First World War.' MA cognate, Wilfrid Laurier University, 1995.

Moir, John S. *Church and Society: Documents on the Religious and Social History of the Roman Catholic Archdiocese of Toronto.* Toronto: Archdiocese of Toronto, 1993.

– *Enduring Witness: A History of the Presbyterian Church in Canada.* Canada: Bryand Press, 1975.

Moorhouse, Geoffrey. *Hell's Foundations: A Town, Its Myths and Gallipoli.* London: Hodder and Stoughton, 1992.

Morgan, Henry James, ed. *The Canadian Men and Women of the Time: A Handbook of Canadian Biography of Living Characters.* 2nd ed. Toronto: William Briggs, 1912.

Morton, Desmond. 'A Canadian Soldier in the Great War: The Experiences of Frank Maheux.' *CMH* 1, nos. 1 & 2 (1992): 79–89.

– 'Polling the Soldier Vote: The Overseas Campaign in the Canadian General Election of 1917.' *JCS* 31, no. 4 (1975): 39–58.

– 'Sir William Otter and Internment Operations in Canada during the First World War.' *CHR* 55 (1974): 32–58.

– *When Your Number's Up: The Canadian Soldier in the First World War.* Toronto: Random House, 1993.

Morton, Desmond, and J.L. Granatstein. *Marching to Armageddon: Canadians and the Great War, 1914–1919.* Toronto: Lester and Orpen Dennys, 1989.

Morton, Desmond, and Glenn Wright. *Winning the Second Battle: Canadian Veterans and the Return to Civilian Life, 1915–1930.* Toronto: University of Toronto Press, 1987.

Mosse, George L. 'Two World Wars and the Myth of the War Experience.' *JConH* 21, no. 4 (1986): 491–514.

Naylor, James. 'The Canadian State, the Accumulation of Capital, and the Great War.' *JCS* 16 (Fall–Winter 1981): 26–55.

Nicholson G.W.L. *Canadian Expeditionary Force 1914–1919: Official History of the Canadian Army in the First World War.* Ottawa: Queen's Printer and Controller of Stationary, 1962.

Palmer, Bryan D. *Descent into Discourse: The Reification of Language and the Writing of Social History.* Philadelphia: Temple University Press, 1990.

– *Working Class Experience: Rethinking the History of Canadian Labour, 1800–1991.* Toronto: McClelland and Stewart, 1992.

Parker, Pat. *The Old Lie: The Great War and the Public-School Ethos.* London: Constable, 1987.

Parr, Joy. *The Gender of Breadwinners: Women, Men, and Change in Two Industrial Towns, 1880–1950.* Toronto: University of Toronto Press, 1990.

Pateman, Andrew. 'Keep the Home Fires Burning: Fuel Regulation in Toronto during the Great War.' MA thesis, University of Western Ontario, 1988.

Paterson, David W. 'Loyalty, Ontario and the First World War.' MA thesis, McGill University, 1986.

Pederson, Diane. *Changing Women, Changing History: A Bibliography of the History of Women in Canada.* 2nd ed. Ottawa: Carleton University Press, 1996.

Petroff, Lillian. *Sojourners and Settlers: The Macedonian Community in Toronto to 1940.* Toronto: University of Toronto Press, 1995.

Pettigrew, E. *The Silent Enemy: Canada and the Deadly Flu of 1918.* Saskatoon: Western Producer Prairie Books, 1983.

Pierce, John 'Constructing Memory: The Vimy Memorial.' *CMH* 1, nos. 1 & 2 (1992): 5–8.

Pierson, Ruth Roach, ed. *Women and Peace: Theoretical, Historical and Practical Perspectives.* London: Croom Helm, 1987.

Piva, Michael J. *The Condition of the Working Class in Toronto, 1900–1921.* Ottawa: University of Ottawa Press, 1979.

Porter, John. *The Vertical Mosaic: An Analysis of Social Class and Power in Canada.* Toronto: University of Toronto Press, 1965.

Poulton, Ron. *The Paper Tyrant: John Ross Robertson and the Toronto Telegram.* Toronto: Clarke, Irwin, 1971.

Prang, Margaret 'Clerics, Politicians, and the Bilingual Schools Issue in Ontario, 1910–1917.' *CHR* 41, no. 4 (1960): 281–307.

– '"The Girl God Would Have Me Be": The Canadian Girls in Training, 1915–1939.' *CHR* 66, no. 2 (1985): 154–84.

– *N.W. Rowell: Ontario Nationalist.* Toronto: University of Toronto Press, 1975.

Preston, Richard A. *Canada and 'Imperial Defense': A Study of the Origins of the British Commonwealth's Defense Organization, 1867–1919.* Durham: Duke University Commonwealth-Studies Center, 1967.

Prince, Robert S. 'The Mythology of War: How the Canadian Daily Newspaper Depicted the Great War.' PhD thesis, University of Toronto, 1998.

Profit, Beth. '"The Making of a Nation": Nationalism and World War One in the Social Gospel Literature of Ralph Connor.' *Historical Papers 1992: Canadian Society of Church History* (1992): 127–38.

Pulker, Edward. *We Stand on Their Shoulders: The Growth of Social Concern in Canadian Anglicanism.* Toronto: Anglican Book Centre, 1986.

Ramkhalawansingh, Ceta. 'Women during the Great War.' In *Women at Work, Ontario, 1850–1930,* ed. J. Acton, P. Goldsmith, and B. Shephard, 261–308. Toronto: Canadian Women's Educational Press, 1974.

Rawling, Bill. *Surviving Trench Warfare: Technology and the Canadian Corps, 1914–1918.* Toronto: University of Toronto Press, 1992.

Read, Daphne. *The Great War and Canadian Society: An Oral History.* Toronto: New Hogtown Press, 1978.

Remarque, Erich Maria. *All Quiet on the Western Front.* New York: Grosset and Dunlop, 1929.

Rider, Peter. 'The Imperial Munitions Board and Its Relationship to Government, Business and Labour, 1914–1920.' PhD thesis, University of Toronto, 1974.

Roberts, Barbara. *'Why Do Women Do Nothing to End the War?' Canadian Feminist Pacifists and the Great War.* Ottawa: CRIAW, 1985.

Robin, Martin. *Radical Politics and Canadian Labour, 1880–1930.* Kingston: Industrial Relations Centre, 1968.

Ruggle, Richard I. 'Canadian Attitudes Towards Peace 1890–1920.' *JCCHS* 35, no. 2 (1993): 133–42.

– 'Canadian Chaplains: A Special Issue.' *JCCHS* 35, no. 2 (1993): 65–74.

Russell, Victor L., ed. *Forging a Consensus: Historical Essays on Toronto.* Toronto: University of Toronto Press, 1984.

Rutherdale, Robert A. 'The Home Front and Consensus and Conflict in Lethbridge, Guelph and Trois-Rivières during the Great War.' PhD thesis, York University, 1993.

Rutherford, Paul. *The Making of the Canadian Media.* Toronto: McGraw-Hill Ryerson, 1978.

– *A Victorian Authority: The Daily Press in Late Nineteenth Century Canada.* Toronto: University of Toronto Press, 1982.

Rutherford, Paul, ed. *Saving the Canadian City: The First Phase, 1880–1920.* Toronto: University of Toronto Press, 1974.

Sanders, M.L., and Philip M. Taylor. *British Propaganda during the First World War, 1914–18.* London: Macmillan, 1982.

Sassoon, Siegfried. *Memoirs of an Infantry Officer.* London: Faber and Faber, 1930.

Schurman, Donald. 'Writing about War.' In *Writing about Canada: A Handbook for Modern Canadian History,* ed. John Schultz, 231–50. Scarborough: Prentice-Hall, 1990.

Sharpe, C.A. 'Enlistment in the Canadian Expeditionary Force 1914–1918: A Regional Analysis.' *JCS* 18, no. 4 (1983–84): 15–29.

Sheehan, Nancy M. 'The IODE, the Schools and World War I.' *History of Education Review* 3, no. 1 (1984): 29–44.

Skelton, O.D. *Life and Letters of Sir Wilfrid Laurier.* Volume 2, *1896–1919.* Toronto: McClelland and Stewart, 1965.

Smith, Leonard V. *Between Mutiny and Obedience: The Case of the French Fifth Infantry Division during World War I.* Princeton: Princeton University Press, 1994.

Socknat, Thomas P. 'Canada's Liberal Pacifists and the Great War.' *JCS* 18, no. 4 (1983–84): 30–44.

– *Witness against War: Pacifism in Canada, 1900–1945.* Toronto: University of Toronto Press, 1987.

Sotiron, Minko. *From Politics to Profit: The Commercialization of Canadian Daily Newspapers, 1890–1920.* Montreal: McGill-Queen's University Press, 1997.

Speisman, Stephen A. *The Jews of Toronto.* Toronto: McClelland and Stewart, 1979.

Spelt, Jacob. *Toronto.* Toronto: Collier Macmillan, 1973.

Stacey, Charles P. *Canada and the Age of Conflict: A History of Canadian External Policies.* Volume 1. *1867–1921.* Toronto: Macmillan, 1977.

– '"A Dream of My Youth:" Mackenzie King in North York.' *OH* 76, no. 3 (1984): 273–86.

Statistics Canada. *Toronto 150: Portrait of a Changing City.* Ottawa: Statistics Canada, 1984.

Steinhart, Allan L. *Civil Censorship in Canada during World War I.* Toronto: Unitrade Press, 1986.

Stephen, Martin. *The Price of Pity: Poetry, History and Myth in the Great War.* London: Leo Cooper, 1996.

Stevenson, David. *French War Aims against Germany, 1914–1919.* Oxford: Clarendon Press, 1982.

Stewart, Ian, and Susan L. Carruthers, eds. *War, Culture and the Media: Representations of the Military in 20th Century Britain.* Madison: Fairleigh Dickinson University Press, 1996.

Strange, Carolyn. *Toronto's Girl Problem: The Perils and Pleasures of the City, 1880–1930.* Toronto: University of Toronto Press, 1995.

Strong-Boag, Veronica, and Anita Clair Fellman, eds. *Rethinking Canada: The Promise of Women's History.* Toronto: Copp Clark Pitman, 1986.

Swettanham, John. *To Seize the Victory: The Canadian Corps in World War I.* Toronto: Ryerson Press, 1965.

Terraine, John. *The Smoke and the Fire: Myths and Anti-Myths of War, 1861–1945.* London: Sidgwick and Jackson, 1980.

Terryson, Brian D. 'Premier Hearst, the War, and Votes for Women.' *OH* 57, no. 3 (1965): 115–21.

Thompson, John. *The Harvests of War: The Prairies West, 1914–1918.* Toronto: McClelland and Stewart, 1978.

Tomlinson, H.M. *All Our Yesterdays.* Toronto: Musson Book Company, 1930.

Travers, Timothy. *The Killing Ground: The British Army, the Western Front, and the Emergence of Modern Warfare, 1900–1918.* London: Allen and Unwin, 1987.

Underhill, Frank H. 'Canada and the Last War.' In *Canada in Peace and War: Eight Studies in National Trends Since 1914,* ed. Chester Martin, 120–49. London: Oxford University Press, 1941.

Van Die, Marguerite. *An Evangelical Mind: Nathanael Burwash and the Methodist Tradition in Canada, 1839–1918.* Montreal: McGill-Queen's University Press, 1989.

Vance, Jonathan F. *Death So Noble: Memory, Meaning, and the First World War.* Vancouver: UBC Press, 1997.

Vetch, Colin. '"Play Up! Play Up! and Win the War!" Football, the Nation and the First World War, 1914–1915.' *JConH* 20, no. 3 (1985): 363–78.

Vipond, Mary. *The Mass Media in Canada.* Toronto: James Lorimer, 1989.

Voeltz, Richard. 'The Antidote to "Khaki Fever"? The Expansion of the British Girl Guides during the First World War.' *JConH* 27, no. 4 (1992): 627–38.

Waites, B.A. 'The Effect of the First World War on Class and Status in England, 1910–1920.' *JConH* 11, no. 1 (1976): 27–48.

Walden, Keith. *Becoming Modern in Toronto: The Industrial Exhibition and the Shaping of a Late Victorian Culture.* Toronto: University of Toronto Press, 1997.

Walker, James W. St. G. 'Race and Recruitment in World War I: Enlistment of Visible Minorities in the Canadian Expeditionary Force.' *CHR* 70, no. 1 (1989): 1–26.

Wallace, W. Stewart. *A History of the University of Toronto, 1827–1927.* Toronto: University of Toronto Press, 1927.

West, Bruce. *Toronto.* Toronto: Doubleday, 1979.

White, William C. *Canon Cody of St. Paul's Church.* Toronto: Ryerson Press, 1953.

Wilkinson, Glenn R. '"The Blessings of War:" The Depiction of Military Force in Edwardian Newspapers.' *JConH* 33, no. 1 (1998): 97–115.

Williams, David Richards. *Duff: A Life in the Law.* Vancouver: University of British Columbia Press, 1984.

Williams, John. *The Other Battleground: The Home Fronts Britain, France and Germany, 1914–18.* Chicago: Henry Regnery Company, 1972.

Williamson, Janice, and Deborah Gorham, eds. *Up and Doing: Canadian Women and Peace.* Toronto: Women's Press, 1989.

Wilson, Barbara M. *Ontario and the First World War.* Toronto: University of Toronto Press, 1984.

Wilson, Keith, ed. *Decisions for War: 1914.* London: UCL Press, 1995.

Winter, Charles F. *Lieutenant-General the Hon. Sir Sam Hughes: Canada's War Minister, 1911–1916.* Toronto: Macmillan, 1931.

Winter, J.M. *The Great War and the British People*. Cambridge, Mass.: Harvard University Press, 1986.

Wolfe, Morris, ed. *A Saturday Night Scrapbook*. Toronto: New Press, 1973.

Woodlacott, Angela. '"Khaki Fever" and Its Control: Gender, Class, Age and Sexual Morality on the British Homefront in the First World War.' *JConH* 29, no. 2 (1994): 325–47.

Wright, Robert A. 'The Canadian Protestant Tradition 1914–1945.' In *The Canadian Protestant Experience, 1760–1990*, ed. G.A. Rawlyk, 139–97. Burlington, Ont.: Welch Publishing, 1990.

Young, W.R. 'Conscription, Rural Depopulation and the Farmers of Ontario, 1917–1919.' *CHR* 53, no. 3 (1972): 289–320.

Zeman, Jarold K., ed. *Baptists in Canada: Search for Identity amidst Diversity*. Burlington, Ont.: G.R. Welch, 1980.

Zimmerman, David. *The Great Naval Battle of Ottawa*. Toronto: University of Toronto Press, 1989.

Zucchi, John E. *Italians in Toronto: Development of a National Identity, 1875–1935*. Montreal: McGill-Queen's University Press, 1988.

Illustration Credits

National Archives of Canada

Department of National Defence Collection: Royal Grenadiers, PA-005122; 48th High-landers, PA-004910; Recruiting meeting at City Hall, C-019200; Overland Float, PA-024685

John Boyd Collection: Recruiting scene at the Armouries, PA-071676; Recruiting soldiers, A-072627; Recruits up for conscription, PA-071239

Index